NO1

GRANDPARENTHOOD

SOME PAST VOLUMES IN THE
SAGE FOCUS EDITIONS

6. **Natural Order**
   Barry Barnes and Steven Shapin

8. **Controversy (Second Edition)**
   Dorothy Nelkin

14. **Churches and Politics in Latin America**
   Daniel H. Levine

21. **The Black Woman**
   La Frances Rodgers-Rose

24. **Dual-Career Couples**
   Fran Pepitone-Rockwell

31. **Black Men**
   Lawrence E. Gary

32. **Major Criminal Justice Systems**
   George F. Cole, Stanislaw J. Frankowski,
   and Marc G. Gertz

34. **Assessing Marriage**
   Erik E. Filsinger and Robert A. Lewis

36. **Impacts of Racism on White Americans**
   Benjamin P. Bowser and
   Raymond G. Hunt

41. **Black Families**
   Harriette Pipes McAdoo

43. **Aging and Retirement**
   Neil G. McCluskey and Edgar F. Borgatta

47. **Mexico's Political Economy**
   Jorge I. Dominguez

50. **Cuba**
   Jorge I. Dominguez

51. **Social Control**
   Jack P. Gibbs

52. **Energy and Transport**
   George H. Daniels, Jr., and Mark H. Rose

54. **Job Stress and Burnout**
   Whiton Stewart Paine

56. **Two Paychecks**
   Joan Aldous

57. **Social Structure and Network Analysis**
   Peter V. Marsden and Nan Lin

58. **Socialist States in the World-System**
   Christopher K. Chase-Dunn

59. **Age or Need?**
   Bernice L. Neugarten

60. **The Costs of Evaluation**
   Marvin C. Alkin and Lewis C. Solmon

61. **Aging in Minority Groups**
   R. L. McNeely and John N. Colen

62. **Contending Approaches to World System
   Analysis**
   William R. Thompson

63. **Organization Theory and Public Policy**
   Richard H. Hall and Robert E. Quinn

64. **Family Relationships in Later Life**
   Timothy H. Brubaker

65. **Communication and Organizations**
   Linda L. Putnam and
   Michael E. Pacanowsky

66. **Competence in Communication**
   Robert N. Bostrom

67. **Avoiding Communication**
   John A. Daly and James C. McCroskey

68. **Ethnography in Educational Evaluation**
   David M. Fetterman

69. **Group Decision Making**
   Walter C. Swap and Associates

70. **Children and Microcomputers
   Research on the Newest Medium**
   Milton Chen and William Paisley

71. **The Language of Risk**
   Dorothy Nelkin

72. **Black Children**
   Harriette Pipes McAdoo and
   John Lewis McAdoo

73. **Industrial Democracy**
   Warner Woodworth, Christopher Meek,
   and William Foote Whyte

74. **Grandparenthood**
   Vern L. Bengtson and Joan F. Robertson

75. **Organizational Theory and Inquiry**
   Yvonna S. Lincoln

GRANDPARENTHOOD

Edited by
Vern L. Bengtson
and
Joan F. Robertson

Published in cooperation with
The National Institute for the Family
and The National Jewish Family Center

SAGE PUBLICATIONS
Beverly Hills / London / New Delhi

For information address:

SAGE Publications, Inc.
275 South Beverly Drive
Beverly Hills, California 90212

SAGE Publications India Pvt. Ltd.
M-32 Market
Greater Kailash I
New Delhi 110 048 India

SAGE Publications Ltd
28 Banner Street
London EC1Y 8QE
England

Printed in the United States of America

Library of Congress Cataloging in Publication Data

Main entry under title:

Grandparenthood.

   (Sage focus editions ; v. 74)
   Based on papers presented at the National Conference on Grandparenting and Family Connections, held at the Wingspread Conference Center in Racine, Wis., Oct. 9-11, 1983.
   Bibliography: p.
   1. Grandparents—United States—Congresses.
2. Grandparents—United States—Family Relationships—Congresses. I. Bengtson, Vern L. II. Robertson, Joan F. III. National Conference on Grandparenting and Family Connections (1983 : Racine, Wis.)
HQ759.9.G72 1985   306.8'7   85-8337
ISBN 0-8039-2483-6
ISBN 0-8039-2384-4 (pbk.)

FIRST PRINTING

CONTENTS

Foreword
      YEHUDA ROSENMAN
      DONALD B. CONROY   7

1. Diversity and Symbolism in Grandparental Roles
      VERN L. BENGTSON   11

**PART I   GRANDPARENTS, DIVERSITY,
         AND SOCIALIZATION**   **27**

2. Continuity and Connectedness
      GUNHILD O. HAGESTAD   31

3. Styles of Grandparenting Among White Ethnics
      WILLIAM C. McCREADY   49

4. Black Grandmothers: Issues of Timing and Continuity
   of Roles
      LINDA M. BURTON
      VERN L. BENGTSON   61

**PART II   CHANGING STRUCTURES, EXPECTATIONS,
         AND FUNCTIONS**   **79**

5. Grandparenting Options in Divorcing Families:
   An Anthropological Perspective
      COLLEEN L. JOHNSON   81

6. Styles and Strategies of Grandparenting
      ANDREW CHERLIN
      FRANK F. FURSTENBERG   97

7. Parent-Adult Child Relations as Affected by
   the Grandparent Status
      JOAN ALDOUS   117

**PART III   GRANDPARENTHOOD, PERSONHOOD,
AND THE LIFE COURSE**   **133**

8. The Contingencies of Grandparenting
LILLIAN E. TROLL   135

9. Grandparenthood and Mental Health: Meaning,
Behavior, and Satisfaction
HELEN Q. KIVNICK   151

10. Grandparenthood and the "New Social Contract"
ARTHUR KORNHABER   159

11. Deculturation and the American Grandparent
DAVID L. GUTMANN   173

**PART IV   GRANDPARENTS, RELIGION, AND THE
CONTEXT OF VALUES**   **183**

12. Judaic Perspectives on Grandparenthood
HARLAN J. WECHSLER   185

13. Christian Perspective on the Role of Grandparents
DONALD B. CONROY
CHARLES J. FAHEY   195

**PART V   TURNING KNOWLEDGE INTO
POLICY AND PROGRAMS**   **209**

14. Grandparenthood: From Knowledge to Programs and Policy
JOAN F. ROBERTSON
CAROL H. TICE
LEONARD L. LOEB   211

References   225

About the Contributors   235

FOREWORD

With the rise in the numbers of grandparents and concern about passing on familial values to succeeding generations, the present volume has a certain relevance that would have escaped most people only a few years ago. The chapters in this work explore the nature and importance of the grandparent role, and offer to both scholars and practitioners in various fields insights into this often neglected, but increasingly important, function within the contemporary family.

The history of this particular effort goes back to a meeting in 1981 in Washington, DC, where representatives from the National Institute for the Family (Washington, DC) and the William Petschek National Jewish Family Center of the American Jewish Committee (New York City) agreed that the role of grandparents was of mutual concern. In October of 1982 with a grant from the American Council of Life Insurance a planning and evaluation meeting was held in the Offices of the American Jewish Committee in Washington, DC. Eleven experts in the field of gerontology were present for the discussion; they concluded with a recommendation that a scholarly conference should be convened to examine the topic of grandparenthood in contemporary society with a special eye to the transmission of religious values and attitudes.

This recommendation resulted in the development of a proposal for a special research conference of behavioral scientists and religious experts dealing with family life. The Johnson Foundation responded to this intiative with an offer of their facilities at the Wingspread Conference Center in Racine, Wisconsin, along with other logistical assistance. Thus on October 9-11, 1983, this conference was convened with scholars from fourteen major universities in the United States participating. The interdisciplinary nature of this endeavor, involving sociologists, psychologists, anthropologists, theologians, and other experts in the field of family studies, has resulted in a deeper insight into the importance and complexity of the grandparenting role in the 1980s.

This National Conference on Grandparenting and Family Connections required immense preparation and a great deal of cooperation from all the participants. We owe a note of thanks for the expertise of Dr. Ann Bloom, who coordinated the authors and respondents, and to Carolyn Gutowski, who did logistical coordination for the conference. The value of the three days of interaction and scholarly sharing cannot be overestimated given what has resulted in these papers.

The chapters in the volume represent a significant effort to pull together much of the available research and thinking about grandparenting. The authors themselves modestly point out the limitations of their studies. Each author recommends further study in order to obtain more generalizable and reliable data so that we may understand more fully the dynamic subtleties and nuances of grandparenting in our changing society.

Although such additional research is needed—and governmental and private agencies should promote it—this work provides us with much information about and insight into intergenerational relations and needs. The essays also present a rich agenda of thought and discussion for students and communal agencies such as churches. Moreover, for the latter, there are significant implications for new communal and pastoral programs to enhance the well-being of all members of intergenerational families. Interaction between scholars and researchers, on the one hand, and practitioners, community planners and programmers on the other—a relationship that occurs too infrequently— has been the primary purpose of the sponsors of the conference on grandparenting and of this volume. Too often the work of scholars lies neglected on the shelves, while practitioners muddle through their work on a trial and error basis. The two groups too seldom get together to share ideas, information, and needs that would enable them to benefit from each other's knowledge and experience. It is therefore the aim of the two sponsoring organizations to facilitate such interaction.

"Why do grandparents get along well with their grandchildren? Because they have common enemies." This old saying expresses the view that because grandparents are more patient with and more indulgent of grandchildren than parents are, grandchildren could find refuge and support with grandparents from the frequent ordeal of parental discipline and punishment. Was this ever the case and is it so now? American grandparents today live considerably longer and are better educated than their counterparts of a generation ago. Many of them work and have different personal needs than grandparents in the past. In fact, a large number of America's grandchildren have great-grandparents, thus creating a new constellation of relationships. Such fluid and changing relationships and roles need to be negotiated with the parents and other members of the family network. In the past these roles tended to be natural and taken for granted. Whose function is it in the community to assess the dynamics of the new relationship and to decide if and when to intervene for the benefit of the family?

It is in the case of divorce—which in recent decades has accelerated in geometric proportions—that the issues and conflicts of intergenerational relations arise in sharp focus. We learn from this volume that in many divorce cases grandparents come to the rescue and assume active, supportive roles. In cases of noncustodial parents, however, the grandparents are often denied contact with their grandchildren. Then, when remarriage occurs, further confusion may set in with an additional set of grandparents. It is not uncommon these days for grandchildren to accumulate several sets of grandparents. How diffused, confusing, and frustrating must such phenomena be for the grandchildren? And what possibilities do the noncustodial grandparents and their grandchildren have for a meaningful relationship?

As some families become isolated and weakened, often becoming islands in large urban centers, are we weakening or merely changing the nature and content of our communities and culture? Does the trend toward individualism, self-fulfillment and pleasure-seeking fundamentally weaken the family's ability to mold societal values and teach social responsibility? Can individuals within such a culture find real happiness and meaning without a sense of intergenerational connection and continuity? Do children really need grandparents, and if so what are these needs?

One is struck by recent movies, such as *Kramer vs. Kramer* and more recently *Old Enough*, depicting isolated nuclear families suspended in the air, without roots, without transcending social values and visions. In the travail of *Kramer vs. Kramer*, no grandparents, other relatives, or religious figures are visible. The movie portrays our lives and culture as an aimless pursuit of personal-professional success in a cruel, plastic, and impersonal world. Do these and similar movies accurately portray the reality of much of contemporary life? Could the frightening recent rise in the rate of teenage suicides be related to the emptiness of life without family love, celebration, joy, and social purpose transcending immediate individualistic ambitions and drives?

We raise these issues to provoke hard thinking and analysis. The chapters in this volume will stimulate profound discussion of these and many other issues. They also should serve as models for the study of other aspects of our family life and of American society as a whole.

We are hopeful that this volume will be helpful to researchers in various fields. We also hope that religious educators, social workers dealing with families and the aging, pastors and rabbis ministering to the needs of today's families, lawyers in the practice of family law dealing with divorce and its consequences, and community leaders planning for future programs that truly serve the generations will be assisted in addressing the needs of both grandchildren and grandparents. In this way the intergenerational process so vital to handing on the cultural and the religious heritage will be truly advanced in our time.

A word of thanks is due to Vern L. Bengtson, Director of the Gerontology Research Institute, University of Southern California, and Joan Robertson, Associate Professor of Social Work, University of Wisconsin—Madison, for their remarkable job of co-editing this volume so that it is not merely a record of past findings but a challenging probe into the future, useful for researchers, students, and practitioners of various kinds. We also wish to thank the Johnson Foundation and Sage Publications for their contribution to and involvement in this worthy project. Finally, the preparation and processing of this manuscript was supported by funds from a National Institute on Aging grant (AG-04092) to the University of Southern California (Vern L. Bengtson, Principal Investigator).

Yehuda Rosenman, M.A. S.W.
*Director, William Petschek National
Jewish Family Center of
The American Jewish Committee*

Donald B. Conroy, Ph.D.
*Director, The National
Institute for the Family*

1

DIVERSITY AND SYMBOLISM IN GRANDPARENTAL ROLES

Vern L. Bengtson

Grandparenthood, though certainly one of the oldest social roles in human experience, has suddenly become the object of scholarly attention and popular concern. Never before in our history have so many humans lived long enough to become grandparents. Never before, perhaps, have their activities and feelings been so varied in enacting grandparental roles.

In this volume we have attempted to bring together multiple perspectives on both traditional and emergent aspects of grandparenthood. The systematic study of grandparenthood—although of surprisingly recent origin—represents a complex and varied intellectual agenda. This is clear from the chapters included in this volume, which reflect a developing body of knowledge and opinion about grandparenthood from a wide variety of scholarly and professional perspectives—sociology, psychology and psychiatry, anthropology, and the law. These perspectives, and the empirical or practical experience reflected by them, suggest the development of cumulative knowledge-building concerning grandparenthood, a social role and phase of life too long neglected by scholarly research.

From these chapters, and from other studies of grandparenthood, I see two principal themes emerging as reflective of the developing state of the art: *diversity* and *symbolism* in the grandparent role. The growing body of empirical research points to the heterogeneity among grandparents, to the dangers in stereotyping and overgeneralizing, and to the likelihood of increasing differentiation in grandparents' roles in the

Author's Note: *Support for the preparation of this chapter came from the National Institute on Aging (grant AG 04092) and the National Institute of Mental Health (grant MH 38244).*

future. Similarly, these studies emphasize the symbolic functions of grandparenthood, in addition to functions in directly observable behavior. Such studies show that the effects of grandparents can be felt simply from their presence and what they mean for a family.

In commenting on these two themes, I will draw on data from three empirical sources, as well as on chapters by others in this volume. The first is a study of 2044 individuals (described elsewhere; Bengtson, 1975) who are members of 3-generation families—grandparents, middle-aged children, and young adult grandchildren—who first completed questionnaires in 1972. We are currently in the process of contacting these families again, in order to obtain a 14- and a 16-year picture of changes and continuities over time in intergenerational behavior.

The second data source is a study of 1428 middle-aged and elderly individuals in three ethnic groupings: Blacks, Mexican-Americans, and non-Hispanic Caucasians, hereafter referred to as Whites. Our interviews, conducted in 1975, explored variations in perceived problems, needs, and resources on the basis of four social structural variables: age groups (45-54, 55-64, 65-74); ethnicity; social class; and gender (see Bengtson, Grigsby, Corry, & Hruby, 1977 for descriptions of the unusual process of this study, which involved the collaboration of advocates from each minority community).

My third source of data arises from participant observation in one family—my own. The use of anecdotal information from nonrandom samples must of course be viewed with caution, perhaps even apology, in the social and behavioral sciences. However, the insights they provide can be illuminating and their fascination is irresistible. My most personal introduction to gerontology came from Grandpa Engstrom, who died in 1974 at the age of 106. Born in northern Sweden in 1869, his life spanned a remarkable period of social and technological innovation, the equal to which perhaps has never before been experienced by humanity; and the nature and timing of events in his own family life cycle were equally dramatic. He became a grandfather very late in life—at the age of 72—and was a great-grandfather at the age of 95, a few years after he signed up to receive his first Social Security check (an independent and highly-principled man, he felt that if he had paid nothing into the Social Security system, he should take nothing from it). His comments about the diversity and symbolism in intergenerational relationships have affected, in ways of which I may be unaware, my own approach to research on this topic.

DIVERSITY AND HETEROGENEITY
IN THE GRANDPARENT ROLE

Too often, professionals unwittingly ignore the rich diversity and heterogeneity among the contemporary population of grandparents. Unless we are aware of the manifest and latent differentiations that exist between individuals and groups in the enactment of grandparental roles, we run the risk of stereotyping, ignoring important variations, and oversimplification. From existing research, it appears that five major dimensions of social differentiation among grandparents can be seen, reflecting contemporary differences in grandparenting: (1) across historical time; (2) between men and women; (3) between older and younger individuals in the role; (4) among ethnic and subcultural groups; and (5) among individuals who may be in similar social locations.

CONTRASTS (AND SIMILARITIES) ACROSS HISTORICAL TIME

Differences across historical periods in grandparenting are perhaps more significant than we realize. The analysis in Hagestad's chapter of *Good Housekeeping* with its contrasting portrayals of grandmothers in 1880 and 1970 can be generalized. It reflects some dramatic changes in grandmotherly style: a shift from the pedestal to the peripatetic. The kindly, aged, passive grandmother who rocks and knits with quiet resignation has been replaced, in the recent pages of *Good Housekeeping* at least, by the active midlife juggler, arranging matrices of roles and schedules. The research of Johnson and Troll reported in this volume similarly reflects this trend. The contemporary grandmother's difficulty stems in part from uncertainty as to what one should *do* in the grand-parental role, and in part from the fear of doing *too much*.

Perhaps this dilemma is not new. Although the Scriptures contain both prescriptions and proscriptions concerning the parent-child relation-ship, they give few if any admonitions concerning grandparent-grand-child roles, as indicated in the chapters by Wechsler as well as Conroy and Fahey. What is new, as Hagestad and others in this volume point out, is the increase in numbers and proportions of the population who survive to attain grandparenthood and even great-grandparenthood.

Many contemporary grandparents can be said to be demographic pioneers. So it was with Johan Petrus Engstrom: He was the first male of his family line in three centuries, according to parish records, to witness the birth of a great-grandchild—he was 95 at the time. Indeed, the historical changes that contemporary grandparents may have experienced is astonishing to consider. I once asked Grandpa Engstrom what was the technological innovation he thought had had the greatest impact on his family, from his grandparents to his great-grandchildren (a span of 150 years). I expected him to mention the radio, airplane, automobiles, or telecommunications. His reply: "The bicycle." He told me that his father, to his knowledge, had never traveled more than six miles from the Swedish farm on which he was born. The mass-produced bicycle was a revolutionary innovation for people of his father's generation, people who did not have the capital to purchase or maintain a horse, but who did have the relatively little investment required to purchase a bicycle. The result was a signficant transition in world view and in personal contact, a development that might in fact be tied to the decrease in age of marriage and the rise in birth rate in Northern Europe at about the same period of time.

Certainly, across historical periods there are changes in the grandparent role simply because of the remarkably different events that those who achieve the grandparent status have experienced within their own lifetimes.

However, it is important to remember the continuities that also are evident through historical time, and that historical contrasts may be mitigated by family connections. It is interesting to recall that the "generation gap" became a popular preoccupation only within the past two decades (evidence cited in Bengtson, 1970). Perhaps historical trends in demography created this concern: The bulge of the "baby boom" cohort, and an unprecedented number of those over 50, coincided with social and political events to create what appeared to be a unique and unanticipated cleavage based on age in technologically advanced societies (see Mead, 1970). This "gap" between contemporary cohorts is certainly experienced by today's elderly (see Bengtson, 1971). What is significant from the Southern California three-generation families data is that these were seen more as a "cohort gap" (differences between the young, middle-aged, and elderly in the broader society) than as a "lineage gap" (contrasts between generations within the respondent's family). In this study of three generations, launched following a period of age-group conflict, it appeared that our respondents—in each generation, but particularly the grandparents—were asserting: "Yes, there *is* a generation gap today—but not in *my* family" (data presented in Bengtson, 1971).

Also of interest is the way in which generational differences may not be linear—that the grandchildren and grandparents may be "generational allies." In one part of the USC study focusing on values (Bengtson, 1975) it was clear that the young and their grandparents displayed astonishingly similar values reflecting "humanism-materialism," whereas the perspectives of the middle-aged generation were quite different (the parents being higher on the materialism pole). At the same time, on another dimension ("individualism-collectivism") there was a linear trend by generation, with the grandparents valuing collectivism most highly and the grandchildren placing higher emphasis on individualism. (Here, the middle-aged parents were more similar to their young adult children than to their aging parents.) On values, at least, generational trends are complex and must not be stereotyped.

Thus, although there may be obvious differences across historical periods in stereotypic attributes of grandparenthood and in demographic probabilities of achieving the role (as noted by Hagestad), it would be unwise to assert that the younger and older generations within families are far apart—at least in values—as a consequence of these trends. This is illustrated in some unexpected similarities in values and opinions that were evident between Grandpa Engstrom and his new grandson-in-law in 1964, when I first became acquainted with him. I found Grandpa unexpectedly sympathetic to young men of my cohort who burned their draft cards and resisted induction into the Viet Nam conflict. In private, he confided that he himself left Sweden in 1888, in part to avoid national conscription into the army.

CONTRASTS BETWEEN MEN AND WOMEN AS GRANDPARENTS

A second aspect of diversity in the grandparent role concerns contrasts between men and women. Hagestad's data suggests less sharp contrasts between G2 (middle generation) males and females than between G1 (grandparent generation) males and females. This is similar to findings of the Southern California study of generations, which I conducted in collaboration with other researchers (Bengtson, Mangen, & Landry, 1984), in which closeness for the G1s was significantly differentiated by sex as well as by age, whereas for the G2s it was not. We asked our grandparental respondents about ten different dimensions of the relationship: How much do you do with your grandchild? How well do you get along with your grandchild? Do you feel your grandchild understands you? How much do you understand your grandchild? We also asked these questions to the middle-generation parents about their young adult offspring—the grandchildren of the G1s.

These different dimensions of affect, factored together, are differentiated by sex for G1-G3 relations, with grandmothers having higher affect scores than grandfathers, as well as by sex linkage (grandfathers and grandsons had higher closeness than grandfathers and granddaughters). However, the differences were not great, and these data suggest that what the respondents were suggesting is that relations between grandchildren and grandparents are closer than we had originally expected. These data may be an example of attribution, of selective perception, of an ideology of relationship that goes far beyond the primitive, empirical data usually collected in survey research.

Hagestad (in this volume) and Troll (1983) suggest role differentiations between grandfathers ("minister of state") and grandmothers ("secretary of the interior"). Rosenthal and Marshall (1983) point to the gender differences in allocation of informal roles such as "head of the family" (75 percent males); Rosenthal (in press) notes similar sex contrasts in the family roles of "kinkeeper" (65 percent females). Grandpa Engstrom was clearly "head of the family"; he acted as minister of state and chief executive officer in his relations with his grandchildren and great-grandchildren. He was interested in the way his granddaughters could get adequate training, find good jobs, and deal successfully with money. His granddaughter once noted, "He never asked me what I felt, if I was happy—he asked what I did. But he cared about me; he just didn't ask about it."

CONTRASTS BETWEEN BIRTH COHORTS
AND MATURATIONAL AGE

The third contrast that reflects diversity in the grandparent role is between older and younger grandparents. Hagestad's Chicago data, and the earlier Neugarten and Weinstein (1964) study, suggest that older grandparents tend to be the more formal, whereas the younger grandparents represent more the "fun-seeker" enactment of the role. A similar pattern is reported by Cherlin and Furstenberg. Does differentiation represent aging or the effect of history? Does this difference reflect maturational effects of aging—of tenure in the grandparent role—or some historical events that influenced the cohorts into which they were formed? Hagestad points to the conceptual problems in our field, especially in the term "generation" with its strain between cohort and lineage meanings (see Bengtson, Cutler, Mangen, & Marshall, 1985), which hinder our research conceptualizations—and especially our communication of research findings.

Whether the cause is aging or cohort effects, in the USC data the younger members of each generation within the family reported more family strain and conflict than did the older members of the generation. The older grandparents tended to minimize the strain or contrast between themselves and their children or grandchildren, more than younger grandparents did.

The chapter by Burton and Bengtson (this volume) indicates another side of differentiation by age within the grandparent status. Burton's study collected data from two samples of Black first-time mothers, their parents, and their grandparents. In one sample the pregnancy was normatively "on time"; that is, birth occurred among mothers over the age of 21. In the second sample the birth occurred among teenage mothers, ages 11-18. The focus of this study was on intergenerational relationships in which norms of timing may be violated. Specifically, it examined the reaction of the "off-time" (very young) grandmothers, in their 20s and 30s, compared to the older, "on-time" grandmothers, in their 40s and 50s.

What this study suggests is that the support and degree of satisfaction of the older generation during this transition to parenthood may be a function of the age of the new grandmother. Although many of the youngest grandmothers appeared reluctant to accept the role—in fact, denying it in some cases—the "on-time" grandmothers tended to welcome the birth and greatly facilitated the mother's transition.

But it is equally plausible that quite different aspects of the grandparent's social network may be determinative of grandparenting behavior and investments. In my best social survey style, I asked Grandpa Engstrom about his social network. I said, "Who are your friends now, Grandpa?" He replied after a pause, "No one. My last friend died—let's see—it was twenty-six years ago." Imagine living 26 years without someone who is regarded as a friend. But then he said,

"There is this 70-year-old man who I see at the bakery frequently and we talk—we talk about the old days; he came from Norway. But you know he complains so much about his family that I can hardly stand to talk to him." Perhaps this one case example suggests that older individuals—at least in the "omega" generation, to use Hagestad's (1981) term—distance themselves from some of the relationships, and thereby the conflicts, by minimizing them in their own eyes; perhaps more than younger members of their families, or even younger cohorts who are in the same grandparent role.

CONTRASTS BY ETHNICITY OR SUBCULTURE

A fourth example of diversity pointed out in the chapters by McCready and Cherlin and Furstenberg is the diversity among ethnic groups in the grandparental role. In our 1975 survey of Mexican-Americans, Blacks, and Whites, we saw some decided contrasts in older respondents' reports of family activities and attitudes—but the ethnic contrasts were not always in the direction that we anticipated. We were testing the hypothesis that age was a leveler of prior social and economic distinctions, as against the multiple jeopardy hypothesis (Dowd & Bengtson, 1978). That is to say, we expected that there would be less ethnic contrast, less indication of variability by ethnic group, in the oldest birth cohort (64-75-year-olds) than in the younger cohort (45-54-year-olds) in our sample. This was not the case. Ethnic contrasts were pronounced in family life indicators at each cohort level.

However, we also learned that the "minorities" in our sample were quite heterogeneous, and there was no "minority versus White" pattern in our data. In fact, the Blacks and the Whites were extremely similar to each other in most analyses we made of family activity and satisfaction patterns. It was the Mexican-Americans who clearly had a distinctive pattern, a pattern that we saw manifest in four ways; (a) in the structure of intergenerational connections, with the Mexican-Americans having many more children, grandchildren, and great-grandchildren who might serve as a potential source of social support; (b) in the patterns of intergenerational affect, with the Mexican-American family members reporting higher satisfaction in present contact with grandchildren than the Blacks and the Whites; (c) in the amount of contact between generations, with the Mexican-Americans reporting higher contact than the other two groups; and (d) in the expectations each group had of intergenerational assistance. The research reported by McCready (this volume) indicates even more finely drawn contrasts among White ethnics in styles of grandparental endorsement concerning desirable characteristics of potential grandchildren.

Parenthetically, there was one empirical issue that would not have occurred to the research team (predominantly White) and that was pointed out by the minority advocates who assisted in planning the research endeavors. They suggested that we had missed, in the construction of our interview schedule, the importance of "fictive kin": of nonbiologically related "children" and "grandchildren" that the older respondents raised. This turned out to be one of the most striking ethnic group contrasts in our examination of family relations: Of the Blacks in our sample above the age of 60, 47 percent reported having raised children other than their own, and an equal percentage indicated "fictive" grandchildren. This high frequency suggests ethnic differences in potential support systems among the older individuals—among the Anglos only 8 percent reported having raised children other than their own; many fewer indicated nonrelated grandchildren with whom they were in contact.

Particularly in the area of family norms, ethnic differences are indicative of the diversity in intergenerational roles. We asked our respondents the normative question, "would you like to live in the same neighborhood as your children?" We also asked the question, "Would you like to live in the same household with one of your children if something happens that you cannot live alone?" The majority of the Mexican-Americans (66 percent) responded that they would like to live in the same neighborhood with their children. Only one-third of the Blacks and one-fifth of the Whites responded that they would like to live in the same neighborhood. In terms of possible intergenerational household structure, slightly over 50 percent of the Mexican-Americans reported they would like to live with a child, whereas only 10 percent of the Blacks and 4 percent of the Whites reported that as a preference. There are clear differences among ethnic groups in intergenerational relations, especially in terms of norms.

CONTRASTS BETWEEN INDIVIDUALS

A fifth difference in grandparenting, reflected in data presented by several authors in this volume, concerns diversity among individuals who are grandparents—heterogeneity within what Hagestad (1982) calls the "omega generation." A plausible hypothesis of the life-course perspective on aging is that if we follow aging individuals over time we will observe a fanning out, an increasing variability in styles and patterns of behaviors with the passage of time. Moreover, inter-generational relationships, such as the grandparent-grandchild dyad, develop and change over time.

Indeed, as any relationship matures, what Turner (1970) terms "crescive bonds" develop on the basis of accumulated and shared experiences. Grandparent and grandchild, with time, become con-sociates. The result is that this dyad, composed of two highly complex and changing individuals moving through time, becomes highly dif-ferentiated over the years. As suggested elsewhere (Kuypers & Bengtson, 1983) historical agendas of past unresolved conflicts and past satis-factions or triumphs in the consocation are worked out within these crescive intergenerational relationships. These crescive bonds may become especially prominent at a time of social or physical stress involving a role transition, such as widowhood, retirement, an acute illness, or residential relocation. In each event, alteration and negoti-ation of the relationship can be seen between indiviuals as they move through time within a family.

I am reminded of Grandpa Engstrom and his attempts to negotiate some sense of autonomy and control about his position in the family of his daughter, with whom he lived for 43 years. Although he had cataracts, he continued to try to make the family breakfast and do the dishes, one means of negotiating the fact that he had neither a pension nor other financial resources. He was attempting to exchange services for the care he was receiving from his daughter. His family attempted to retire him from his role. His cataracts made the source of ingredients for the daily breakfast an increasing source of surprise.

Individuals attempt to build in an incremental or crescive fashion on previous relationships. This is very clear in the grandparent-grandchild dyad. As the grandparent generation becomes older, as more and more individuals become great-grandparents, and as more and more five-generation families are part of the demographic structure of our communities, so too will there be longer durations of the "career" of grandparent and of these crescive relationships between grandparent and grandchild. Perhaps in consequence, there will be increasing importance of that relationship, increasing salience of the grandparent role for both members of the generational dyad.

SYMBOLISM AND THE MULTIPLE
MEANINGS OF GRANDPARENTING

The symbolism expressions of the grandparent role is perhaps as important—and is certainly as varied—as are the behaviors grandparents can be observed to perform. Though even more difficult for social scientists to measure, these symbolic functions, and the multiple meanings they reflect, are crucial to our understanding of grandparenthood. I want to emphasize four of these symbolic dimensions: (1) simply "being there"; (2) as the "national guard" or "family watchdog"; (3) as arbitrators; and (4) as active participants in the family's social construction of its history.

THE "BEING THERE" SYMBOL

Hagestad (this volume) quotes a grandfather, aged 84, who pointed to his "being there" as the most important function he fulfills for his grandson. Certainly this is true of other grandparents, who may shield their families in time of trouble more by affirming their availability than by any specific act of intervention.

I think there are two ways in which "being there" is experienced as helpful, often unexpectedly, by younger generation members. The first is as potential deterrents to familial disruption. The presence of grandparents mitigates against the obtrusive events of the outside world and disruptive events of role transitions. Their presence serves to maintain the identity of the family and to provide a buffer against its mortality. In another of her works, Hagestad (1984) points out ways in which family continuity may be seen most directly in its loss. For example, there is the buffer against the next generation's mortality, and the loss that creates a sense of vulnerability and aloneness, as is reflected in her 39-year-old colleague's comment on the death of his parent: "I'm an orphan now!"

A second function is seen in the simple presence of the older generation during such transitions as divorce, or the transition to parenthood. Simply by their presence, the grandparents of children undergoing divorce in Johnson's study appeared to exert a calming influence in often catastrophic transitions. The same is reflected in

Hagestad's (1982) study of middle-aged divorcees. The presence of grandparents—whether or not called upon or volunteering any active assistance in role transitions such as divorce—appears to reflect an anchor of stability, an expression of family continuity, perhaps more for the children than for the divorcing parents.

In the research on grandparental "timing" reported by Burton and Bengtson, the same anchoring function is reflected among some of the grandmothers of early teenage mothers—in the celebration of babies, new members of the generational chain. The 91-year-old great-great-great-grandmother, who herself gave birth to her first child at the age of 14, articulated this theme: "My ma say women are 'pose to have babies. . . . I say have 'um when you young. Then you have mo' people to look out behind you when you old like me."

THE "FAMILY NATIONAL GUARD"

A second function that is perhaps more symbolic than enacted, and thus hard to measure, is reflected in what Hagestad calls the "national guard" and what Troll calls the "family watchdog." Grandparents may be the family's militia, pursuing a policy of active alert, being there to protect and give care if needed.

We have no direct data as yet concerning how many grandparents see themselves in this symbolic function, nor of how many families enact this aspect of grandparenthood. But we do know, as Hagestad's (1982), Johnson's (1983), and Cherlin and Furstenberg's research on divorce suggests, that grandparents are often called upon to go beyond the passive or ready-reserve situation into the active frontline management of supporting children, forming active intergenerational relationships.

GRANDPARENTS AS ARBITRATORS:
FROM TRANSMISSION TO NEGOTIATION

A third symbolic attribute may be called the arbitrator function, reflecting a change in focus from transmission to negotiation in intergenerational relationships. Hagestad rightly notes that the socialization literature has undergone a significant shift in the last two decades, from an assumption of intergenerational replication to an active awareness of the bilateral influence of children on parents.

Certainly it is important to look at the active, creative side of enhancing and effecting intergenerational negotiation, as opposed to a passive, cookie-cutter image of intergenerational continuity. It is true that intergenerational continuity can no longer adequately be researched as the extent to which people in different generations replicate each other's opinions and lifestyles. Continuity between generations can no longer be regarded as a simple process of unidirectional transmission from old to young—if indeed it ever was.

Rather, intergenerational continuity is a reflection between generations of the "interactional confrontation between developing individuals, in which those factors leading to continuity, and those leading to change are negotiated" (Bengtson & Black, 1973). Grandparents may play a crucial role in this process. They may be active arbitrators, negotiating carefully between parents and children concerning values and behaviors that may be more central, in the long run, to family continuity and individual enhancement than those that the parents' authority status allow to be expressed.

Some of the issues that the older generation may otherwise choose to transmit do not come into negotiation because they are considered too risky. Others may have simply lost their relevance because of secular cohort changes that affect the younger generation. In either event, grandparents frequently are unofficial arbitrators—the interaction management function that Hagestad (1981) calls attention to in her discussion of "conversational demilitarized zones." Differences between parent and youth that may be volatile or disruptive may be downplayed by the interaction management shown by the older generation. Also, "cohort gaps" related to historical styles are prevented from becoming "generation gaps" within the family, because of protections in the conversational demilitarized zone worked out by grandparents as negotiators. After all, grandparents have encountered similar issues before.

There is, of course, also a more direct mediational function. Grandparents are important, but it's often hard to document how. One of the ways that they may think of themselves as being important is in the area of protection, for example, protecting the younger generation from a variety of imagined or perceived insults.

THE SOCIAL CONSTRUCTION OF BIOGRAPHY

A final symbolic function of grandparenthood, suggested in the chapters by McCready, Gutman, Kornhaber, Conroy and Fahey, Troll, and Hagestad, has to do with the interpretive function—the auto-biographical function—that many families find important. We rewrite our autobiographies so that "a given present has enough connections with the past so that we can face the future" (Berger & Luckman, 1960). Grandparents may play an enormously important role in this building of reasonable connections among our past, present, and future.

The oldest generation has the greatest "stake" in the grandchild's continuity with the past—a stake that may distort perceptions (Bengtson & Kuypers, 1971), but which is interpretative and identity-molding. This provision of meaning is personal and immediate. The generational stake idea suggests the interpretive function grandparents have provided for us since time immemorial.

CONCLUSION

Grandparenthood—though a traditional social role reflected in historical record and moral philosophy down through the centuries—has rather suddenly become an emergent social phenomenon. In part, demographic changes (increased longevity, higher divorce rates) have occasioned such attention; in part, the awareness that grandparenthood is a complex social role, understudied and perhaps misunderstood, has been the catalyst for increased analysis. Whatever the cause, social and behavioral scientists in the past few years have begun studying grandparenthood. The chapters in this volume, representing scholarly disciplines ranging from sociology to theology, reflect the first wave of this effort.

In research on grandparenthood to date, two themes stand out: the *diversity* of grandparents and their actions in the role, and the *symbolism* of grandparenthood reflected in their presence as well as their behaviors. The growing body of research on this role points to the heterogeneity among grandparents, the dangers of overgeneralizing and stereotyping, and the likelihood of even greater differentiation in grandparental roles in the future. Similarly, these studies emphasize the symbolic functions of grandparenthood, in addition and perhaps in contrast to directly observable behavior: Grandparents are important simply because of their presence and what they mean for a family.

This chapter has reviewed diversity among grandparents and the symbolism reflected by their presence or actions from a growing body of research studies (many of which are reflected in this volume). It was suggested that five major dimensions of social differentiation in grandparenthood can be seen. The first reflects contrasts (and some surprising similarities) across historical time; a second is between men and women as grandparents. A third contrast is between young and old grandparents, in either chronological or subjective time; and a fourth is seen in ethnic or cultural differences among grandparents in behaviors, satisfactions, or values regarding childrearing. Finally, there are differences between individuals as grandparents, aging men and women with unique histories and resources who attempt to build in crescive fashion on their relationships with younger generation members.

Symbolic functions of grandparenthood, which can be seen despite the diversity of grandparental styles and the social differentiation reflected by contemporary cohorts, are a second important theme in the literature to date. This chapter has suggested four of these as being particularly evident. First is the symbol of "being there" as an indicator of intergenerational continuity or as a buffer against the family's potential mortality. A second symbol is reflected in images of the "family national guard" or the "family watchdog" that grandparents often portray. A third symbolic function is as an arbitrator, spanning the psychosocial distance "from transmission to negotiation" in issues of intergeneration continuity within the family. Fourth, grandparents, whether active or passive, are figures in the "social construction of biography" for younger family members, interpreting and giving meaning to the personal past.

The study of grandparenthood involves a highly complex psychosocial agenda. In their diversity and their symbolism, contemporary grandparents represent important links between the past and the future. It is the fortune of today's children and youth that their birth cohort has more grandparents and great-grandparents available to them than any conceivable cohort in the past. We can only hope they appreciate this advantage, and exploit the resource of grandparents in developing their own diversity and symbolism throughout life.

PART I

GRANDPARENTS, DIVERSITY, AND SOCIALIZATION

In the first chapter, Bengtson suggested that there are two principal themes that characterize the scholarly research to date on grandparental roles: *diversity* in the styles, characteristics, behaviors, and satisfactions of grandparents; and the *symbolism* that grandparenthood represents in quickly changing societies. Whether in their simply "being there," as "family watchdogs," as arbitrators, or as the catalyst of personal history for younger family members, the symbolic importance of grandparents is felt by younger generations.

The chapters in this section present specific examples of diversity and symbolism in the grandparental role, seen in both traditional and emergent manifestations. One of the traditional functions of grandparents involves input to the socialization process of grandchildren, specifically the transmission of what is most highly valued from generation to generation within the family. It is important to note, as Bengtson suggested, the diverse ways in which such transmission is effected, and the differences between social categories within the current grandparental cohort in the manifestations of socialization.

Hagestad focuses on grandparenthood as an intergenerational phenomena essential to family continuity and connectedness. Her chapter provides a comprehensive review of the research literature to date, and suggests an important theoretical perspective for identifying the dimensions and concepts that are essential for examining intergenerational processes. She focuses on the roles, functions, meanings, and contexts that form the "scripts" for grandparental socialization processes ensuring continuity and connectedness over time. In particular, she describes specific interactional components between and within generational chains.

One of the more salient contributions of Hagestad's chapter is her attempt to identify concepts that would more precisely describe and examine grandparent phenomena. She emphasizes the need to differentiate processes of socialization from the products and contexts of socialization. The contexts of socialization, according to Hagestad, involve the range of personality and social-structural variables that reflect antecedent or consequent influences on socialization processes. Socialization, seen as intergenerational continuity and connectedness, can be examined by focusing on the *developing* of relationships that reflect role functions, meaning, and behaviors (symbolic and real). The chapter demonstrates formidable challenges facing researchers in defining socialization and processes, in the context of "in-process life events." Hagestad conveys the elusive and ephemeral nature of socialization processes. The patterning and developing of intergenerational relationships may defy precise description or measurement owing to the complementary blend of subjective and objective factors that give rise to their development, change, and maintenance over time.

McCready uses national survey data on six ethnic groups (Irish, English, Poles, Scandinavians, Italians, and Germans) to discuss three issues relevant to grandparent socialization and transmission. He stresses that cultural diversity in grandparental functions is a socialization force in American society. He suggests that the influence of grandparents as perpetuators of the cultural legacy of the family should be emphasized. Grandparents provide family members with opportunities to relate and represent the generative chain that links the family. Further, McCready indicates that White ethnics of the grandparental cohort reflect somewhat different values of what is desirable in the socialization of children than other ethnics. The presence of grandparents, real or symbolic, is a significant issue in the transmission of subcultural patterns.

The chapter by Burton and Bengtson provides another indication of diversity among contemporary grandparents. They link the symbolism involved in enactment of that role to two important variables in such diversity: age of becoming a grandparent and the consequences of social clocks that measure "on-time" and "off-time" grandparenthood. Their focus is on two groups of new grandmothers, some very young (ages 25-38) and some normatively "on-time" (42 to 58 years). They describe the reactions of these two groups in entering a role over which they had no direct control in time of entry—grandparenthood.

It is a sociological postulate that the existence of social norms can most clearly be seen in their violation. The reactions of the young ("off-time") grandmothers in this study provides a good example. These respondents symbolically experienced a conflict between their chronological age and their family lineage position, expressed most directly in their being "too young" for entry to a role that they perceive as associated with aging.

Burton and Bengtson comment on two other themes associated with transmission and change over time. The first concerns the context of grandmotherhood in traditional (perhaps stereotypic) portrayals of Black subculture, and the contrast between these views of the heroic matriarch and what their respondents report about adopting the role. Second, they examine the hypothesis of continuity between generations in the timing and "legitimacy" of first birthing. They find considerable support for such intergenerational patterns of similarity—but only in the most recent cohorts, again suggesting the necessity for awareness of historical contexts in describing grandparenthood.

2

CONTINUITY AND CONNECTEDNESS

Gunhild O. Hagestad

GENERATIONS: FAMILY AND HISTORY

The term "generation" refers to two quite different concepts, on two levels of social reality. (For a detailed overview, see Bengtson, Cultler, Mangen, & Marshall, 1985.) Both are necessary to consider when discussing grandparents. On the one hand, "generation" refers to a location in a system of ranked descent in family lineages. Grandparents, of course, are found in families with at least three generations, and they have at least two generations below them. A family's generational structure changes over time. As new family members are born and old members die, processes of generational turnover alter the generational composition of the family line. At one point in time, a family may have only two "tiers" of lives; decades later it may have five. A woman may become a grandmother at the age of 40, when she is a member of a middle generation in a four-generational structure. She may be the oldest member of a three-generational structure 25 years later.

So far, we have used the term generation for a position in a set of vertical family ties. Often, when we say that Grandpa represents "a different generation," we mean something else. We recognize that the historical times when people are born, mature, and age shape their experiences, opportunities, and outlooks. In the rest of this chapter, the term *cohort* is used for generations of people born in the same period, whereas the term *generation* is reserved for location in a family lineage. Throughout this discussion, we need to keep in mind both of these generational phenomena—one reflecting the pulse of family life, such as the timing of births and deaths, and the other showing the "footprints" of history.

In their generational structures, families constitute meeting places for members of different cohorts. Through intergenerational contacts, family members provide one another with bridges to historical times they themselves never knew or have trouble understanding. What we often tend to forget, however, is that generational position does not tell us much about age/cohort and vice versa. Family members do not file into generation by cohort (Hagestad, 1981). An 18-year-old can have maternal and paternal grandfathers who not only are strikingly different in age and vigor, but who also represent sharp contrasts in life experiences because of their respective cohort memberships. For example, the paternal grandfather may have been born before the turn of the century. He witnessed World War I, watched automobiles become common, and was established in his adult life when the Great Depression hit. In contrast, his mother's father may have been born in 1920. This grandfather did not experience World War I and grew up thinking of cars as a normal part of life. As a young boy, he took odd jobs to help his family after his father became one of the many unemployed during the 1930s, and as a young adult he was active in World War II.

HISTORICAL CONTEXT

It is difficult to find neatly assembled source material on grandparenthood in the past. An active and pioneering group of family historians have given us much needed discussions of family life in earlier times, gathered from a variety of sources: diaries, municipal papers, letters, and records from mills and factories. However, little or no systematic work has been done on centuries of grandparenthood. I am not qualified to attempt such a task, but can offer some general comments and a few speculations about recent historical changes affecting grandparenthood. This discussion will build on two sets of materials: a small-scale content analysis of popular magazines, and the work of family demographers.

EMERGING GRANDPARENTHOOD:
REFLECTIONS IN THE POPULAR PRESS

In a content analysis, Hagestad and Cogley (n.d.) explored changing images of grandparenthood as reflected in popular magazines. Four volumes of *Good Housekeeping* were read, two from the 1880s and two from the 1970s. In both centuries, when items referring to grandparents were found, they typically pertained to grandmothers.

In the 1880s, it was taken for granted that the reader knew grandparents were old. No specific age was mentioned in the majority of items, but physical descriptions provided indications that grandma had lived a long and hard life: "Silvered head, eyes grown dim with the mist of age." The grandmother from the late nineteenth century had toiled for decades and now had her "hands stilled from loving service" as a reward. She was frequently described as sitting in a chair by a fire or a lamp.

When grandchildren were mentioned, they tended to be very young. In nearly half the poems, however, there was no mention of grandchildren. Seldom, if ever, was the 1880s grandmother described as dealing with the nitty-gritty aspects of everyday family life. The frail figure by the fire was not *withdrawn* from everyday living, but was *above* it. She had a place on a pedestal, and she had earned it.

The 1970s provided quite a different set of images. Two aspects of the modern grandparents struck us. First, it was difficult to find any themes in these descriptions. There was no ready replacement for the weary, quiet figure by the 1880s fire. The 1970s presented no uniform, consistent picture of grandma. Indeed, there appeared to be as many styles as there were grandmothers and grandchildren. The grandparents ranged in age from the fifties to past one hundred; the grandchildren ranged from toddlers to adults. Ages of grandparents were typically indicated and they were described or discussed in relation to particular grandchildren.

A second, related aspect of recent items was one not at all encountered in the old magazines. There was a new uncertainty about what it means to be a grandparent. Members of several generations revealed puzzlement over what grandparents are supposed to do. What are their rights and obligations? We found descriptions of grandparents who were manipulated by grandchildren. On the other hand, we read accounts of the intrusive grandparent, who trespassed on parents' turf. In question and answer columns, grandparents and their relatives asked: "What are grandparental rights?" "How *should* they behave?"

Magazine items from the 1880s and the 1970s are probably good mirrors of changes in grandparenthood over the last century. Grandma definitely is not what she used to be, and simple categories and expectations cannot capture the current spectrum of grandparenting styles and grandparenting experiences.

Over the last fifty years or so, demographic change has been the most powerful force in reshaping the social and personal realities of grandparenthood.

THE CHANGING DEMOGRAPHY
OF INTERGENERATIONAL RELATIONS

Two key demographic changes have altered the nature of grand-parenthood in our society: increased life expectancy and new rhythms in the family cycle (Treas & Bengtson, 1982). As is well known, general life expectancy has increased dramatically in this century. American women can currently look forward to eight decades of life. Although we have seen a steady increase in the average number of life years, a smaller proportion of adult life is spent actively involved in parenting. The overall trend during the last century has been toward smaller families and children who are more closely spaced. These changes in mortality and fertility have led to some important shifts in grandparenthood:

(1) More people become grandparents than ever before.
(2) The entry into grandparental status typically occurs at midlife, and many people spend four or more decades as grandparents.
(3) Multigenerational families are common, and many grandparents also become great- and great-great-grandparents.
(4) Parenthood and grandparenthood have become more distinct, both as individual life experiences and as two kinds of family status.

It is estimated that three-fourths of Americans over the age of 65 are grandparents (Shanas, 1979, 1980). Shanas suggests that nearly half of all grandparents will also become great-grandparents. Indeed, a growing number of women may spend a few years when they are both grandmothers and granddaughters. Of course, throughout human history, societies have had some very old members and individuals with several family generations below them. However, today's society is experiencing a situation that is historically unique. We now view long life as the rule, not the exception, and we *count on* intergenerational ties to be durable. Until very recently, it was only a lucky few young adults who had living grandparents, and many adults did not live to see their grandchildren (Uhlenberg, 1980). As historian Hareven (1977) states: "The opportunity for a meaningful period of overlap in the lives of grandparents and grandchildren is a 20th century phenomenon" (p. 62).

The reduction in the age at which women have finished childbearing has made it rare to find overlaps between active parenting and grandparental status. The two have become more clearly sequenced in the life course than was the case when women bore children throughout their fertile years. The emphasis on old grandmothers observed in the 1880s magazine may in part be a result of the fact that at that time, middle-aged women were still occupied with child rearing, even if their oldest children had made them grandmothers.

MEN AND WOMEN

It is necessary to make a brief comment about men and women in today's demographic picture. American women currently outlive men by nearly eight years. In addition, they tend to marry men who are older than themselves. As a result, the oldest member of a given family lineage is most often a woman, and more women than men live to see their great- and great-great-grandchildren. Furthermore, most older men are married; most older women are widowed. For example, in 1979 67 percent of all men over the age of 75 were living with a wife. Only 21 percent of women in this age bracket were living with a husband (Uhlenberg & Meyers, 1981). This means that most men have a significant horizontal, *intragenerational* relationship until the end of their lives; women do not.

There is a sizable literature arguing that women's lives are to a greater extent shaped by the parent role than are men's lives. There is no corresponding literature on grandmothers and grandfathers. Indeed, much of past research on grandparents has only studied grandmothers. One often finds an unstated "unisex" view of grandparenting not unlike trends in past decades of research that assumed that if fathers "parent," they "mother." Much work is needed before we can map how grandmothers and grandfathers are alike, and how they are different.

THE LACK OF GRANDPARENT ROLES

The rapidity and scope of recent demographic changes have caught us off guard, We still tend to associate grandparenthood with old age only; we still have trouble thinking of 40-year-old grandchildren. The image of grandma commonly found in TV commercials is not in step with current demographic realities. Often, the grandmother presented on the screen should be a great-grandmother. The woman who has small, golden-haired grandchildren is not likely to have silver hair in a bun, serve lemonade on the porch, or worry about slipping dentures and "irregularity." She would more realistically be portrayed dressed in a jogging suit on her way to aerobic dancing, or in a suit coming home from work.

Many authors have recently discussed the lack of a grandparent role. Fischer and Silverman (1982) use Rosow's (1976) term "tenuous role," a social status without clear normative expectations attached to it; Wood (1982) calls it ambiguous. These authors are conveying the message we found reflected in current popular magazines: It is not at all clear what the rights and obligations of grandparents are. Part of this uncertainty may simply reflect the fact that current grandparents are demographic pioneers (Shanas, 1980). In a society where grandparents range in age from 30 to 110, and grandchildren range from newborns to retirees, we should not be surprised to find a wide variety of grandparenting styles (Neugarten & Weinstein, 1964) and few behavioral expectations regarding grandparenting (Robertson, 1977).

GRANDPARENTHOOD AND FAMILY CONTINUITY

As families find themselves with three or more generations of people, they are increasingly faced with the challenge of finding and maintaining a core of "sameness," transcending time and change. Much of my own thinking on the creation of family continuity has been shaped by a study in which we interviewed three generations of adults from modern urban families.

THE CHICAGO STUDY

In the late 1970s B. Cohler, B. Neugarten, and I headed a team studying members of three generations in 148 families living in the

Chicago area. In each family, we conducted separate interviews with one young adult grandchild, both the middle-aged mother and father, and one aging grandparent. Approximately equal numbers of grandsons and granddaughters were interviewed. Median age for the grandchildren was about 21.5. As would be expected, many more grandmothers (N = 108) than grandfathers (N = 40) were interviewed. The median age for grandfathers was 80; for grandmothers it was 76. There were 83 maternal and 65 paternal grandparents.

The interview focused on relationships. Both members of intergenerational pairs were asked to discuss each other and their relationship. We therefore had reciprocal data, reflecting two individuals' views of their relationship. A major section of the interview dealt with what family members talked about. A set of eleven "topic cards," each with a list of subtopics, was shown to the respondents. They were then asked, "Do you and _____ talk about any of these?" If the answer was positive, the interviewers asked follow-up questions and recorded whether there had been attempts to influence the other member of the pair. The interview also included a number of open-ended questions about the relationships under discussion.

Based on work with this material, I make four points about intergenerational continuity:

(1) It is problematic in a heterogeneous, changing society.
(2) It is an ongoing process of negotiation and careful interaction management.
(3) It shows great interfamily variability.
(4) Grandmothers and grandfathers approach it quite differently.

Family continuity in a changing society. In a homogeneous, stable society, where people live adult lives very similar to those of their parents, the creation of family continuity is not likely to be problematic. The main task is to ensure that a family line is maintained through the birth of new generations. Young members have their lives fairly well charted for them, and "like father, like son" is an axiom of life. In preparing the young for adult living, family and community are mutually supportive because they are part of the same social and moral fabric (Laslett, 1965). In a complex, heterogeneous society, families need to build their own bridges between the old and the young. A "common ground" is not provided by the surrounding community, but has to be developed through family interaction. Such common ground has to accommodate different stages of life, generational positions, and strikingly different historical experiences represented by family members.

From transmission to negotiation. No doubt, the creation of family continuity involves influence from old to young, because it is a question of "what is passed on" along generational lines. However, intergenerational continuity can no longer be seen as a matter of a simple, unidirectional process of transmission from old to young or "the extent to which people in different generations replicate each other" (Troll & Bengtson, 1979). The creation of family continuity is a process of socialization, but an ongoing reciprocal one: "an interactional confrontation between developing individuals, in which those factors leading to continuity and those leading to change are negotiated" (Bengtson & Black, 1973).

In reading interview protocols from grandparents and grandchildren in the Chicago study, we were often struck by the amount of effort to which family members go in seeking to maintain their ties (Hagestad & Kranichfeld, 1982). When asked for a general description of their relationship with the grandchild, the grandparent often declared: "We never have disagreements!" That seemed to be important. Throughout the interviews, particularly with the grandchild, we often found that the lack of open conflict reflected some careful maneuvering—what E. Goffman would call "interaction management." A common mechanism for avoiding intergenerational friction is the establishment of conversational "demilitarized zones": silent pacts about what not to talk about. One grandson commented: "We are careful what we talk about. . . . We don't want to rock the boat." Such avoidance of topics was more common in the families where we talked to a grandfather. The intergenerational pair in which it was the most common was that between grandfather and granddaughter (Hagestad & McDonald, 1979). Typically, topics treated as DMZs represented areas of life in which sociocultural change had occurred. To paraphrase Bengtson (1971), they represented instances where cohort gaps might turn into generation gaps. One grandfather said about his relationship with his grandson: "We talk about most anything . . . except sex. I am not comfortable talking to young people about sex." His grandson said: "He thinks too many young people are sleeping together today. . . . It's the general complaint of older people."

Interfamily variability. What did these grandparents and grandchildren talk about? The Chicago data point to the wide variability in the issues that families deem worthy of attention, time, and energy. When family members from different generations struggle to find "common ground," they may not concentrate on *how* to think on certain issues, but rather *what* issues to think about. There is a great deal of variability in what families deem worthy of attention. In the Chicago study, some families talked a lot about money. The issue was not necessarily that there was a "right" way to deal with finances, but that money as an issue deserved time and attention. Other families seemed to have very little interest in money and its management, but spent a great deal of time discussing politics and current social policy. As a researcher, I have become skeptical about using standardized opinion and attitude measures to assess intergenerational continuity. In some families, observed differences among family members on such measures may not *make a difference,* because the issues at hand hold no salience for family interaction. Furthermore, standardized instruments may easily miss the core areas of concern for some families—the domains on which they concentrate most of their efforts to build some basic similarity.

In spite of the great interfamily variability, one trend stands out from the Chicago data: Men and women showed systematic differences in what they emphasized in their interactions with younger generations. These contrasts were particularly sharp among the grandparents.

Grandmothers and grandfathers. The contrast between grandmothers and grandfathers fits Parson's and Bales's (1955) distinction between "instrumental" and "emotional-expressive" leadership. The older men emphasized task-oriented involvements in spheres outside the family; the women were more likely to emphasize interpersonal dynamics and the quality of ties in the family. Although the men spoke as "ambassadors" or "foreign ministers"; the women appeared to be "ministers of the interior." Overall, grandmothers covered a wider spectrum of influence in their conversations with grandchildren. They, like grandfathers, talked with grandchildren about practical issues of adult life in society, but added concerns about friendships and family relations. The grandmothers also distinguished less between grandsons and granddaughters than did grandfathers. It appeared that, in these cohorts of grandparents, the grandmothers had assimilated more of the cultural changes in the roles of men and women than had grandfathers.

The grandfathers, many of them born before 1900, appeared to see themselves as advisers to young men. They thought it appropriate to seek influence over their grandchildren with regard to instrumental matters: getting an education, finding a job, dealing with money, managing life's responsibilities and challenges. They appeared, for the most part, to consider interpersonal issues outside their domain. These grandfathers appeared to have quite clear notions of what constitutes "men talk." As a consequence of distinctions between men's and women's matters, they concentrated most of their influence on grandsons. However, for both grandmothers and grandfathers, links to same-sex children and grandchildren stood out. That is, from grandfathers, the widest spectrum of influence was reported in families where the grandchild was the son of a son. Among grandmothers, the most involvement appeared to be with daughters of daughters.

As several authors have pointed out (e.g., Gilford & Black, 1972; Hill, Foote, Aldous, Carlson, & MacDonald, 1970; Robertson, 1975), the middle generation seems to perform a mediating function. In the case of paternal grandfathers and grandsons, there is the additional factor of "carrying on the family name." I know of no research that has addressed this issue.

The Chicago study also found contrasts between grandmothers and grandfathers when we asked about strain and conflict across generational lines. It has been commonly found that younger generations are more ready to report family strain and conflict than are members of the older generations (e.g., Bengtson & Kuypers, 1971; Troll & Bengtson, 1979). The same trend emerged from the Chicago families. When other family members discussed grandfathers, views on social issues were by far the most commonly mentioned "sore spots." Race relations, social policy, and sex roles were commonly identified as "touchy subjects" around Grandpa. In discussions of grandmothers, reported troublespots were topics related to interpersonal issues, particularly in the family realm. These findings are remarkably similar to a recent study of German families (Lehr, 1982). The German study found that intergenerational disagreements among men focused on nonfamily spheres. Among women, conflict typically occurred over how to relate in the family.

At this point, my hunch is that because of their strong emphasis on nonfamily spheres, grandfathers may be more likely than grandmothers to experience cohort changes in the wider society as potential threats to the search for a "common base" across generations in the family. When it comes to negotiating styles of relating and "family ways," women are the main negotiators. Furthermore, both because of their strong family focus and their previous long-term, day-to-day involvement with the young, women seem more ready to accept influence "up" generational lines from the young. It was exactly in relations to the outside world, in such areas as views on social issues, involvement in work and education, and changing styles in dress and grooming that Chicago grandmothers and mothers recognized such "reversed socialization" from the young (Hagestad & Snow, 1977). However, they were not ready to heed such efforts when the young focused on "how to run a family," even though we saw from interviews with the grandchildren that such influence had been attempted.

The "matrifocal tilt." The contrasts between grandmothers and grandfathers discussed above fit some patterns that have been reported in a wide range of studies of modern families. It has been argued repeatedly that contact and exchanges between generations to a large extent are facilitated and carried out by women. They are the kin-keepers (Adams, 1968; Bahr, 1976; Cohler & Grunebaum, 1981; Townsend, 1957). In the Chicago study the same pattern was found: Women bring families together. They organize get-togethers, remember birthdays, write Christmas cards. Women are also "family monitors," who more than men observe the course of relationships and register changes in them (Hagestad & Smyer, 1982; Wilen, 1979).

Research on grandparenthood has tended to find the same kind of martrifocal tilt. Kahana and Kahana (1970) found the closest grand-parent-grandchild relationship to be that between maternal grand-mothers and granddaughters. Hoffman (1979-1980) studied young adults and found them to be closer to maternal than to paternal grandparents. Fischer (1982-1983) found more hesitance and uncertainty about expectations among paternal than among maternal grand-mothers. In the Chicago families, warm and emotionally complex relationships were more common among maternal grandparents and grandchildren. Thus, there are strong suggestions that the quality of bonds between grandparents and grandchildren reflects the work of a kin-keeper in the middle generation—a mother.

It has been suggested that aspects of modern social structure make it easier for women to find intergenerational continuity than is the case for men. With the nature of modern work and the high rates of occupational mobility, men seldom have similar work experiences to those of their fathers and grandfathers. This also holds for women, but family roles are more salient in their lives. Thus, it is argued, women in different generations can more easily see a core of continuity in key life roles than men can (Chodorow, 1978).

Changing sex roles. With an ideological emphasis on equality, and with most women working outside the home, will the patterns discussed above prevail? Will women still be kin-keepers? Will grandmothers still be different from grandfathers in their family roles? Recent research on young men and women still shows that girls grow up with a stronger orientation toward interconnectedness in the interpersonal realm (Block, von der Lippe, & Block, 1973; Chodorow, 1978; Gilligan, 1982). The Chicago study found fewer sharp contrasts between fathers and mothers in the middle generations than those observed between grandfathers and grandmothers, suggesting cohort trends of less differentiation between men's and women's involvement in family relationships. Yet, the middle-generation women clearly emerged as family monitors and kin-keepers. Based on available evidence, it appears that even though more and more women are active in nonfamily spheres, they are not relinquishing their position as minister of the interior, focusing strongly on the inner familial world and its workings.

Impact of divorce and family reconstitution. Most research on family effects of divorce has looked "down" generational lines and concentrated on children. Parents and grandparents of divorce have for the most part been ignored. Yet, when nearly half of recent marriage cohorts experience marital break-up, two sets of parents, and often some grandparents, feel ripple effects of this transition (Hagestad, 1982). Because of congressional hearings and a push for legislation, the legal protection of grandparents' rights has received a good deal of attention (Wilson & DeShare, 1982). Custody still goes to the mother in nine cases out of ten, which means that paternal grandparents are more likely to have problems with access to their grandchildren. Research on kin interaction following divorce (e.g., Anspach, 1976; Cherlin, Furstenberg, Lee & Miller, in press; Hagestad, Smyer, & Stierman, 1984) has found lower rates of contact on the "noncustodial" side. This weakening of ties to paternal kin is not likely to be simply a matter of custody arrangements and sporadic contact between divorced fathers and their children. In our study of midlife divorce (Hagestad, Smyer, & Stierman, 1984), most of the children were young adults, and 75 percent of the respondents were in the empty nest phase of family development. Thus, custody was not an issue in most cases, and one would expect less need for parental mediation of contact between grandparents and grandchildren than in younger families. Nevertheless, when we asked the divorced members of the middle generation about their parents' reaction to the divorce, more than half of the men said the parents were worried about losing touch with their grandchildren. The corresponding figure for women was under 10 percent. In several parts of the interview, the men expressed a sense of "not having a family anymore." What some of them seemed to be struggling with was the loss of their kin-keeper, the wife.

Patterns of remarriage and family reconstitution added challenges to individuals and families. The majority of divorced people remarry within three years (Spanier & Glick, 1980). Many remarriages result in some form of "blended family." A growing number of children spend part of their childhood living with a stepparent and stepsiblings or half-siblings. For grandparents, there are the ambiguities of relating to "grandchildren" with whom they have no blood ties. Furstenberg (1981), one of the first researchers to examine grandparenthood within the context of a divorcing society, suggests that many of today's children will have opportunities for enriched intergenerational ties, with multiple sets of grandparents. I must confess that I remain skeptical while we are waiting for data because, as was discussed above, the creation and maintenance of viable intergenerational ties require considerable care and effort. Furthermore, a growing number of children and grandparents will experience the break-up of the middle generation's second marriage. Demographer Bumpass (1981) has presented some thought-provoking data from a longitudinal study of children's divorce experiences. He estimates that among children whose divorced mothers remarried in the 1970s, close to 50 percent will experience the mother's second divorce. There has been very little discussion of the fact that there is no legal protection of step-parents and step-grandparents. A growing number of individuals in our society will have the experience of spending a great deal of effort on making step-relationships work, only to find them dissolved.

As is well known, men and women have quite different patterns of remarriage. The contrasts are particularly stark after the age of 40, when the majority of divorced women do not remarry whereas the majority of men do. The men are also quite likely to remarry someone considerably younger than they, and a fair number of them start "second families." Because of these trends, a growing number of paternal lineages will have children and grandchildren who are the same age. We will also see a number of children who grow up without a parental grandfather. Thus, more men's lineages will have the traits of families from the early parts of this century than is the case for women's family lines.

Based on some of the factors discussed above—women's roles as kin-keepers, trends in custody arrangements, and sex differences in remarriage patterns—one might venture two conclusions about grandparent-grandchild relations in years to come:

(1) The most vulnerable intergenerational bond is that between paternal grandfather and grandson.
(2) Our society may become increasingly matrilineal in its patterns of intergenerational continuity.

GRANDPARENTS AND INTERCONNECTED LIVES

Studies of divorce and remarriage illustrate how lives in the family are intimately interconnected. Our knowledge of such webs of connectedness has been limited by two trends in past research:

(1) We have looked at grandparent-grandchild relations in isolation, overlooking the fact that intergenerational ties are interlocked and interrelated.
(2) We have taken an overly behavioral view, focusing on what grandparents do or should do.

TOWARD A FAMILY SYSTEMS VIEW

When we study grandparents and grandchildren, we cannot limit our attention to this pair only (Fischer & Silverman, 1982). We really need to consider three sets of relationships: grandparent-parent, parent-grandchild, and grandparent-grandchild. It may not be until the grandchild is an adult that most interactions and exchanges occur *directly,* without mediation through the middle generation. Although the grandchildren are young, so many of their connections with grandparents go through the parents. I would like to explore a few indirect ways in which grandparents and grandchildren are interdependent. Furthermore, I suggest that, in some cases, effects of grandparents can be felt simply from their *presence,* not their *actions.*

What do I do for my grandson? I guess just being here . . . in case he needs me. (Chicago grandfather, age 84)

GRANDPARENTS AS FAMILY STABILIZERS

Several of us who have studied grandparents and grandchildren have been puzzled by some seeming paradoxes in our data. On one hand, interviews and questionnaires present an overall impression of grandparents as important forces in the lives of the grandchildren. On the other hand, it is hard to pinpoint what it is that grandparents *do*. Robertson (1976) discusses such questions in her article on young adults and their grandparents. We have faced similar issues in attempts to make sense of data from the young adults in the Chicago study. Our problem might be that we have concentrated too narrowly on concrete behavior and actions, and have not considered the wider family context.

One way in which grandparents may affect grandchildren is by serving as a stabilizing force on the middle generation—the parents. It is difficult to get adults to speak of what it means to have living parents, but there is general agreement that it is a major life transition to lose them (Marshall & Rosenthal, 1982). Grandparents provide a buffer against the next generation's mortality, and the loss of this buffer is likely to bring a new feeling of vulnerability and aloneness. Wood and Robertson (1976) urged us to compare families with active grandparents and families without grandparents. My hunch would be that if we found differences between members of the young generation in such families it would mostly be accounted for indirectly—mediated through the parents, who themselves were without parents.

There may be a wide range of second-order effects of grandparents, through parents—especially mothers. Tinsley and Parke (1984) present a current discussion of research that points to such effects. Cross-cultural work has pointed to the importance of grandmothers as "stabilizers" of mothers, resulting in greater maternal warmth and competence (Minturn & Lambert, 1964; Rohrer, 1975). In an American sample, Abernathy (1973) found that frequency of contact between women and their own mothers was the best predictor of the women's sense of competence in the role of parent. Other authors have pointed to the importance of support from the older generation during the transition to parenthood (e.g., Belsky & Tolan, 1981; Wandersman, Wandersman, & Kahn, 1980).

The presence of grandparents, especially older grandmothers, may also serve as a catalyst for wider family cohesion. Even if they are not the persons who handle the logistics of "bringing the family together," they are the focus of family contact—the "excuse" for get-togethers. Young and Willmott (1962) say of working-class families in London: "They all see a good deal of each other because they all see a good deal of *mum.*" In the study of midlife divorce (Hagestad, Smyer, & Stierman, 1984), we found indications that the presence of an older generation increased middle-aged individuals' use of kin support, particularly from the third generation—their children. Individuals without living parents were more likely to report that they turned to no family members during the divorce crisis, even though they all had mature children.

Grandparents have also been discussed as a moderating force, whose presence softens the intensity of modern family life (Baranowski, 1982; Hader, 1965; Kornhaber & Woodward, 1981). It has commonly been argued that because of reduced family size, altered expectations, and a weakening of community ties, nuclear families have become increasingly intense socioemotional environments. A clear and provocative statement of such a view can be found in Skolnick's (1978) text, *The Intimate Environment.* Grandparents can deflate some of the intensity by allowing the other two generations "a place to go." They may also serve as mediators and "interpreters" between the two generations. Grandparents can help make parents more understandable for the children (Mead, 1974; Streltzer, 1979), or serve as arbitrators in conflicts between parents and children (Smith, 1965; Troll, 1981). Konopka's (1976) study of adolescent girls found that grandmothers frequently served as confidantes in times of conflict with parents. *How often* such mediation and arbitration occurs is probably not the right question to ask. Rather, the important question is to what extent families perceive grandparents as a potential "safety valve."

THE FAMILY NATIONAL GUARD

Ramian (see Rasmussen, 1983) has studied the elderly and their families in Denmark and argues that we have underestimated the importance of this safety valve function of the older generation. He suggests that often when families make plans, for example regarding major purchases, they count on the grandparent generation as a potential back-up if something should go wrong. He reminds us that most older people own property, whereas it is becoming increasingly difficult for the young to do so. In the majority of cases, the young may not end up actually turning to their elders, but their decision making and behavior would have been different if the older generation were not there as potential back-up. I believe Ramian is pointing to an extremely important and much neglected aspect of modern grandparenthood. In a current work, Troll (1983) calls grandparents "family watchdogs." They are there if needed, and when they are needed they are ready for a diversity of functions.

When the family system or an individual member faces a crisis, grandparents are "stress-buffers" (Pearlin & Schooler, 1978). Von Hentig (1946) wrote of this aspect of grandparenthood nearly four decades ago, at a time when history had brought it to light: "They stand ready to intervene as first and last aid as soon as the framework of the group is flagging or breaking up" (p. 389). Von Hentig's observation was based on a decade when a world war had put stress on family units. Recently, authors have pointed to current social trends that are likely to activate grandparents as stress-buffers, such as divorce (Hetherington, Cox, & Cox, 1978) and the growing number of single adolescent parents (Kellam, Ensminger, & Turner, 1977). In such cases of "structurally incomplete" families, grandparents often move beyond the role as supportive boosters for parents and become adjunct parents or co-parents. How often divorce leads to three-generational living, and how often grandparents provide substantial financial support to grandchildren following divorce is not known (see chapters by Johnson and Cherlin and Furstenberg, this volume).

THE CHALLENGE OF MODERN GRANDPARENTHOOD

In 1980, at the age of 75, Robert Penn Warren published a collection of poems. It was dedicated to his grandfather. After the dedication came a brief dialogue:

Old Man: "You get old and you can't do anybody any good any more."
Boy: "You do me some good, Grandpa. You tell me things."

As was discussed above, grandfathers do tell things to the young, not all of them equally appreciated! But I believe the *title* of Penn Warren's book gets closer to the essence of Grandpa: *Being Here*.

Today's grandparents are demographic pioneers. They may also find themselves in another vanguard position, created by the emergence of postindustrial society. They, and the rest of us, will need to find ways of being in a world so focused on *doing*. One of their key functions is an elusive "being here," a comforting presence not easily captured with the language and tools of social science.

We will need the help of poets, photographers, and painters to help us capture this presence:

- as symbols of connectedness within and across lives,
- as people who can listen and have the time to do so,
- as reserves of time, help, and attention,
- as links to known and unknown pasts, and
- as people who are sufficiently varied, flexible, and complex to defy easy categories and clear-cut roles.

3

STYLES OF GRANDPARENTING AMONG WHITE ETHNICS

William C. McCready

Recent research examining the lives of older people has focused on more positive aspects of life than some previous studies, which were primarily oriented toward social problems. For example, the 1974 publication by Maas and Kuypers from the Berkeley longitudinal studies concludes with the following passage:

> Most clearly, however, the majority of lives in this study run contrary to the popular and literary myth of inescapable decline in old age. Whether one considers the women or the men, and whether one examines their psychological capacities and orientation or their styles of living, most of these aging parents give no evidence of traveling a downhill course. By far most of these parents in their old age are involved in rewarding and diversely patterned lives. (Maas & Kuypers, 1974, p. 215)

It is possible that one of the reasons we have not seen much emphasis on grandparenting in the sociological and psychological literature is that old age is commonly defined as being a negative time of life. Grandparenting is a positive aspect of aging in many ways, and it is possible that social scientists have been ignoring this dimension for murky and ineffable reasons.

There is some evidence that grandparenting was considered a mutually beneficial activity between the grandparents and the grandchildren even back as far as old New England (Demos, 1978). Examinations of probate records at that time indicate that grandparents often provided the role of surrogate parent, taking care of young children, and that children often provided a companionship role and a caretaking role for grandparents. A minister of the time, Reverend John Robinson, even warned that grandparents could ruin children by being overindulgent, a fear that some parents apparently still carry with them even to this day. However Robinson had another—I believe more salient—observation when he said:

> Grandfathers are more affectionate towards their children's children than to their immediates, as seeing themselves as further propogated in them, and by their means proceeding on to a further degree of eternity, which all desire naturally, if not in themselves, yet in their posterity. (Robinson, 1851, p. 246)

The reason this is a salient quotation today is that it identifies a phenomenon that may well be a very important part of contemporary grandparenting: the fact that the relationship between grandparents and grandchildren represents the generative chain that bonds the family longitudinally. Among the more important elements of culture are such factors as continuity and a sense of belonging, both of which can be symbolized by the grandparent-grandchild relationship. It may not be as important for grandchildren and grandparents actually to be in communication with each other, as to have been in communication with each other at one time, so that memories and experiences can be recalled and relived and reused symbolically during the course of the life cycle.

For most people, there are only two opportunities within their own life cycle to interact with their actual grandparents—when they are children and again when they are adolescents. Children tend to interpret the grandparent as a strong, foundational element in the family experience. In a wonderful paragraph, Kornhaber and Woodward (1981) summarize what children thought of grandparents:

> These children portrayed their grandparents in a variety of roles. They functioned as mentors, caretakers, mediators between child and parents, same sex role models and family historians. From them grandchildren learned about how it was in "the good old days," and what mother or father was like as a child, their own roots, and an inkling of "how to be" in the future. These vital connections were real to them because they were transmitted through close personal experience and embodied in living, Great Parents. (p. 81)

These grandchildren clearly indicated that their perception of their grandparents was connected to what the anthropologist Clifford Gertz (1973) calls "models of" reality. He distinguishes the use from "models for" reality by noting that models for reality are blueprints, whereas models of reality are the way things really are. In other words, when a grandchild says that the grandparent provides a hint of "how to be" in the future, the grandchild is really articulating that the grandparent is a "model of" the child's own reality.

This is a profoundly cultural activity and one would expect that it would be affected by the cultural background of the people who are doing the experiencing. There are data to indicate that family styles, even in an assimilated population, are still responsive to cultural differences. These data are not specifically about grandparents but they are related because they establish the familial context of cultural differentiation about which we will be speaking.

The family is particularly important in studying the persistence of ethnicity because of its dual function as the repository of the cultural legacy and as the situs of the process by which that legacy is transmitted from one generation to the next. The center of social interaction for most of the immigrants in their countries of origin was the family. It played an essential organizing role in the life of the villages they left behind. Families were where the young were trained by the old, a process that ensured generational continuity.

Migration to a new land changed the context for the family. The city replaced the village. The cultural values transmitted within the family no longer reflected the outside society and were not necessarily operative within it. The family was no longer ensured of its traditional preeminent position in the lives of its members. Children now had to move away from their parents in order to survive and prosper. The new land encouraged independence and "striking out on one's own." Oscar Handlin (1951, p. 258) describes the dilemma of the immigrant parents most poignantly:

Perhaps they never took the time to make a balance sheet of their lives, those two old ones left alone, never stopped to reckon up how much they had gained and how much lost by coming. But certainly they must occasionally have faced the wry irony of their relationships with their offspring. What hope the early seasons of their years had held was hope of efforts for their children's sake. What dreams they had had were dreams of the family transplanted, that generation after generation would bear witness to the achievement of migration. In the end, all was tinged with vanity, with success as cruel as failure. Whatever lot their sons had drawn in this new contentious world, the family's oneness would not survive it. It was a sad satisfaction to watch the young advance, knowing that every step forward was a step away from home.

A "step forward" was indeed a step away from home in many ways, but the immigrant could never really leave that home behind. Roots planted there would remain to influence the future growth of his or her children as they made their own ways.

Migration was only the beginning point of the life of an ethnic group. Such a group had no function in the country of origin; it was a product of the migration experience. An ethnic group begins with a cultural legacy from the native land that helps the individual interpret and understand the world around him. This legacy is most useful to the first generation; it provides instructions about how to carry life forward in the new surroundings. As time and generations go by, mutations in the instructions occur. We can see the results of these mutations in successive generations. It is important to note that we are not observing a phenomenon that is disappearing at a linear rate; rather we are seeing one that is changing from point to point and adapting to various contexts. Ethnicity appears in different forms from one generation to the next (McCready, 1978; McCready & McCready, 1973; McCready & Greeley, 1975).

Our most primal needs and emotions declare themselves first within the family. We learn our greatest fears, loves, hatreds, and hopes within this social unit. Berger and Luckmann (1967) have described socialization as possibly the greatest "confidence trick" that society plays on the individual. It makes what in fact is a bundle of contingencies appear as a necessity, and thus makes meaningful the accident of birth. When grandchildren tell us that they learn "how to be in the future" from the memories and recollections about their grandparents, they are in effect telling us that their images of their grandparents are an important part of their "model of" reality.

We have seen that there is evidence of cultural differentiation in the ways in which supposedly assimilated young people envision and describe their own parents and that these differences can be at least linked to differences between cultures in the countries of origin.

DISCUSSION OF THE DATA

Previous research has shown that there is considerable ethnic diversity in the way in which adults view their own parents (McCready, 1974).

Using data from several large national surveys, we will now explore whether or not ethnicity is also an important factor in the ways in which older people view which characteristics are appropriate for children and which are not. Although not every respondent in these surveys is an actual grandparent, they represent a "grandparent cohort" of people of like age and experience. It is likely, given the fertility rates in our country, that most of these respondents are in fact grandparents. The central question we shall explore with these data is whether older people from different ethnic backgrounds think differently about the qualities they desire in children and if so, what those differences might mean for their well-being and that of the generations to follow them.

The data for this chapter are from the General Social Survey (GSS), gathered between 1972 and 1984, funded by the National Science Foundation as an ongoing social indicator survey. The data are collected by NORC (National Opinion Research Center) of the University of Chicago. The pertinent sets of items for this chapter are those asking the respondents for their ethnic heritage, expectations for the qualities to be desired in children, sources of satisfaction, age, and whether or not they were ever married and ever had children of their own. The method of attempting to look at the attitudes of grandparents was to look at those respondents who were over 60 years old and who had at least one child. This is, at the very least, a population that is quite likely to be grandparents, and many of them undoubtedly are.

There is evidence of ethnic differentiation in the sources of satisfaction in the lives of these respondents. Table 3.1 presents the satisfaction scores of the sample for various aspects of life according to ethnic group. Overall, the respondents were most likely to say that where they lived was a great source of satisfaction, perhaps reflecting the independent living status of many older people and their attachment to their community. The Poles and Italians tended more toward the mean than did the other groups with regard to this variable, and if we look at the scores for the importance of friendships we can see that the Poles and Italians are more likely to emphasize these factors as important sources of their overall satisfaction. None of the groups is above the mean with regard to saying that their families are a source of satisfaction.

These differences in satisfaction with residence and family become a bit clearer when we examine these data controlling for the sex of the respondent. Italian and Polish women are more likely than the men in those respective groups to say that where they live is a source of their satisfaction. The English and Scandinavian women and Polish men are

TABLE 3.1

Degree of Satisfaction Derived from Various Areas of Life
by Grandparents from Different Ethnic Groups

	Family Life	Place Where You Live	Friendships[a]	Leisure Activities[a]
English grandmothers (426)[b]	−21[c]	27	7	−2
English grandfathers (324)	−5	33		
Scandinavian grandmothers (136)	−20	43	2	11
Scandinavian grandfathers (88)	2	49		
German grandmothers (280)	−10	35	11	4
German grandfathers (270)	4	34		
Irish grandmothers (201)	−5	41	10	−3
Irish grandfathers (154)	0	35		
Italian grandmothers (72)	−3	18	18	−26
Italian grandfathers (62)	−8	7		
Polish grandmothers (83)	−5	19	15	−30
Polish grandfathers (83)	−27	6		

a. Numbers in the last two columns are for grandmothers and grandfathers combined.
b. Numbers in parentheses indicate total respondents.
c. Numbers are standard points with a mean of zero and a standard deviation of 100.

the ones most likely to be below the mean in citing their families as sources of satisfaction. Given the ethnographic literature for the Poles, this is a consistent finding. The Polish father was likely to be in an ambiguous role in the traditional family and such ambiguity may not lend itself to a perception of satisfaction with the family system.

An additional speculation from these data concerns the matter of the relative importance of the role of the neighborhood in the lives of the older ethnic. Although the item does not use the term "neighborhood," it is likely that many of the respondents' frame of reference for answering the question was in fact a smaller geographic area than a city; for many it was probably their neighborhood. The high scores would indicate that neighborhood was a much more important factor in the lives of the older person than for the general population and that, as a source of satisfaction, it was much more unevenly distributed than was family.

Table 3.2 consists of standard scores for characteristics that represent in an approximate fashion the five types of grandparenting described in an empirical research project with actual grandparents (Neugarten & Weinstein, 1964). These are descriptions of the grandparenting styles:

TABLE 3.2
Degree of Difference in Styles of Grandparenting
for Members of Different Ethnic Groups

	Formal/ Distant	Fun seeker	Surrogate	Wisdom
English grandmothers (426)[a]	6	−7	−3	7
English grandfathers (324)	15	−10	9	−9
Scandinavian grandmothers (136)	10	−5	17	−17
Scandinavian grandfathers (88)	18	−21	18	−11
German grandmothers (280)	−4	−1	14	−8
German grandfathers (270)	13	−17	22	−17
Irish grandmothers (201)	18	−23	16	−3
Irish grandfathers (154)	18	−6	9	−8
Italian grandmothers (72)	13	−15	12	2
Italian grandfathers (62)	23	−21	18	−8
Polish grandmothers (83)	−11	−11	16	−14
Polish grandfathers (83)	21	−19	24	−28

NOTE: The numbers are standard points with a mean of zero and a standard deviation of 100.
a. Numbers in parentheses indicate total respondents.

(1) The "Formal" are those who follow what they regard as the proper and prescribed role for grandparents. Although they like to provide special treats and indulgences for the grandchild, and may occasionally take on a minor service such as baby-sitting, they maintain clearly demarcated lines between parenting and grandparenting, and they leave parenting strictly to the parent. They maintain a constant interest in the grandchild but are careful not to offer advice on childrearing.

(2) The "Fun Seeker" is the grandparent whose relation to the grandchild is characterized by informality and playfulness. He or she joins the child in specific activities for the specific purpose of having fun, somewhat as if he or she were the child's playmate. Grandchildren are viewed as a source of leisure activity, as an item of "consumption" rather than "production," or as a source of self-indulgence. The relationship is one in which authority lines—either with the grandchild or with the parent—are irrelevant. The emphasis here is on mutuality of satisfaction rather than on providing treats for the grandchild. Mutuality imposes a latent demand that both parties derive fun from the relationship.

(3) The "Distant Figure" is the grandparent who emerges from the shadows on holidays and on special ritual occasions such as Christmas and birthdays. Contact with the grandchild is fleeting and infrequent, a fact

that distinguishes this style from the "Formal." This grandparent is benevolent in stance but essentially distant and remote from the child's life, a somewhat intermittent St. Nicholas.

(4) The "Surrogate Parent" occurs only, as might have been anticipated, for grandmothers in this group. It comes about by initiation on the part of the younger generation, that is, when the young mother works and the grandmother assumes the actual caretaking responsibility for the child.

(5) The "Reservoir of Family Wisdom" represents a distinctly authoritarian patricentered relationship in which the grandparent—in rare occasions on which it occurs in this sample, it is the grandfather—is the dispenser of special skills or resources. Lines of authority are distinct, and the young parents maintain and emphasize their subordinate positions—sometimes without resentment. (Neugarten & Weinstein, 1964, pp. 200-201)

We have attempted to draw some comparisions with these types using items from the General Social Survey. There is obviously not a perfect fit and there will undoubtedly be considerable disagreement as to the appropriateness of these items, but they can be defended as approximations that have the benefit of allowing us to examine these images and perceptions of children's behavior according to an empirically generated typology. Although this procedure is rough and preliminary it does allow for the use of some interesting data from large national samples.

The comparisons between the 1964 empirical typology and the current perceptual data are as follows:

The Formal and Distant typologies have been combined because there was no measure of "contact frequency" upon which to base distance. The characteristics that would best seem to accompany the description of these types are that they wish children to have *good manners*, be *neat and clean*, and have *self-control*. These were selected because they would seem to relate to concerns about "proper" behavior.

The Fun Seeker typology is represented by three characteristics that would seem to indicate an interest in the qualitative aspect of the child's life. These are that the children *get along well with other children*, be *considerate of other people*, and be *interested in how and why things happen*. Fun Seeking grandparents would seem to be more interested in the child's potential for having pleasant relationships and pleasant interactions with people, hence these selections.

The Surrogate Parent style of grandparenting was limited in the original study to grandmothers who actually cared for the day-to-day needs of children, but for our purposes we have connected four characteristics to this type because they seem to represent the kinds of expectations one would expect actual caretaking parents of children to have. They are that the children *try hard, obey their parents,* be *good students,* and *act in sex-appropriate ways.*

Finally, the Reservior of Family Wisdom style of grandparenting, which was found rarely in the original study, is linked in this analysis to three characteristics: that the children be *honest, have good sense,* and be *responsible.* (These may also be though of as "civic virtues," which may be the post-immigrant version of familial wisdom.)

As can be seen in Table 3.2, males are more likely to exhibit those attitudes and responses that might be linked to a more 'formal' style of relating to grandchildren, whereas the women, in general, emphasize the more informal and affect-oriented styles of behavior. (The Irish appear to be a rather singular exception to this rule.) The English, Irish, and Italian women are likely to emphasize self-control, as are the Irish and Polish men. All the men were at least a quarter standard deviation above the mean when it came to stressing manners for the child, which appears to be an important theme in ethnic grandparenting.

The scores for those characteristics having a more qualitative aspect to them are at or well below the mean in most cases. (Here, the Polish women prove the exception.) Does this indicate that the affectionate and informal aspect of grandparenting as evidenced by Fun Seeking is on the decline? Certainly not in any conclusive way; but it does indicate that the qualitative descriptions of children are not as important to these respondents as are other, more behaviorally linked, characteristics. It may well be that they feel the qualities will follow the behaviors. This does appear to present some evidence, however, that the affective dimensions of the grandparent-grandchild relationship are not as prized by these respondents as the more behavioral and "correct" dimensions of childrens' behaviors.

The surrogate scores are more closely connected to the kinds of things parents like to see their children doing and being. Here some interesting differences between these ethnic groups begin to emerge. The English are just near the mean and the Scandinavian women are high on obedience and sex-role appropriate behavior for their grandchildren. German men and women are both high on obedience and the men are high on studiousness. The Irish men and women are both high on obedience and the women are high on studiousness. (Recall the strong role of the Irish mother in the ethnographic literature.) The Italians of both sexes are high on studiousness but only the males are high on sex-role appropriate behavior. This is the greatest difference on this characteristic and it is certainly what we would expect given the strong distinctions that are made in the Italian culture between the appropriate behaviors for boys and girls. The Polish men and women are both high on obedience and the women are high on studiousness, although the men fall just below the quarter-standard deviation mark.

Overall, it would seem that there is a willingness on the part of the grandparents to express "parentlike" attitudes concerning the expectations for children. Undoubtedly, most of these are not surrogate in the sense that they are responsible for actual child care; however the surrogate role is certainly one with which many of these ethnic respondents feel confortable.

Finally, it appears that the older people do not particularly see themselves as "reservoirs" of wisdom. Only the English and Italian women are even positive on this indicator.

If grandparents' perceptions of the desirable characteristics for children are all sorted out, the behavioral and parentlike ones seem to be the attractive qualities that are mentioned most frequently. There does seem to be considerable diversity in how these qualities are arrayed among ethnic groups, however. At least one question, among many possible others, is this: Does the ethnic diversity have any implications for the lives of grandparents and grandchildren?

CONCLUSION

The first topic we explored was the differences in sources of satisfaction for older people from different ethnic backgrounds. Some, for example the Polish and Italian women, are more likely to say that their residence is a source of satisfaction than are others. Some are less likely than most to refer to their families as sources of satisfaction—Polish men and English and Scandinavian women, for example. Although some of the findings concerning relative differences in the salience of the family are like those findings we see in the ethnographic literature, the more important fact may be the importance that so many of the older people attach to the place where they live, their home, or perhaps their neighborhood. Although the GSS does not use the exact word, "neighborhood" in these items, it is likely that that is the frame of reference for many of the elderly. The role of the neighborhood should take a much more prominent place in the research literature on the elderly—both as a social context for their lives and perhaps as an important source of satisfaction and support.

The second and principal topic for this chapter has been to consider the relative differences in attitudes toward children within this elderly, multiethnic, grandparentlike population. The major findings for each of the groups in our sample are described and the intergroup differences noted:

(1) The English are significantly above the mean for only two characteristics: The men express a desire that children have good manners; the women desire that they be honest.

(2) The Scandinavians are above the mean on four items: The men express a desire that children have good manners and be studious; the women desire that they have good manners, be neat and clean, be studious, and act in sex-role appropriate ways.

(3) The Germans are also above the mean on four items but the proportion between the sexes is different: The women express a desire only that the children be obedient, whereas the men want them to have good manners, be neat and clean, obey, and be good students.

(4) The Irish are above the mean of four items as well, and they are more nearly divided according to the sex of the respondent: The women want children to be neat and clean, obedient, and good students, whereas the men focus on them having good manners and being obedient.

(5) The Italians also chose four characteristics prominently, but their division between the sexes was quite skewed: The women chose only that children should be good students; the men were above the mean by 25 points or more in terms of the children having good manners, being neat and clean, being good students, and especially behaving in sex appropriate ways.

(6) The Poles were significantly above the mean for five characteristics and they were quite evenly divided by sex: The men supported having good manners, being neat and clean, and being obedient; the women focused on obedience, being a good student, and getting along well with people. (The latter was a score of 22 but has been included because it was the only high positive score in that table.)

It may be that grandparents can be encouraged to examine their own attitudes and expectations for their grandchildren to see how much consonance or dissonance there is. These data seem to indicate a diversity of attitudes that may reveal a diversity of grandparenting styles. People from different heritages ought to be encouraged to reflect upon their heritage and its particular style of grandparenting, but even more, we who are in the middle of the generations ought to reflect upon the richness of the resources that the grandparent generation contains. The middle generation is, to some extent, the gatekeeper and can act to enable and permit more exchange of imagery, symbol, and perception between the generation of grandparents and grandchildren, to the benefit of both.

But perhaps most important is the necessity of calling attention to the cultural diversity that exists within the grandparent population of our nation of immigrants. The various groups know their own culture but frequently are not supported in their efforts to achieve real respectability for their cultural differences. All too often they are given the message that their differences are socially deviant or old-fashioned and embarrassing. As is pointed out by Kornhaber and Woodward (1981), the grandparents are perceived as the foundation of the family by many children. They are the "model of" reality for the growing person. If one's model is part of a rich divergent tapestry that is prized by others, then growing up and growing old can be positive, hopeful, and satisfying. If one's "model of" is uniform and unattainable, or if it is socially disapproved of or criticized, then the obstacles to maturing into a hopeful, satisfied, accomplished older person are many, and frequently insurmountable.

4

BLACK GRANDMOTHERS
Issues of Timing and
Continuity of Roles

Linda M. Burton
Vern L. Bengtson

I am too young to be a grandmother. You made this baby, you take care of it. (27-year-old grandmother)

My daughter and granddaughter keep making these babies and expect me to take care of them. I ain't no nursemaid; I ain't old; and I ain't dead yet. (56-year-old great-grandmother)

I could break my daughter's neck for having this baby. I just got a new boyfriend. Now he will think I'm too old. It was bad enough being a mother so young—now a grandmother too! (28-year-old grandmother)

These statements were made by women who share a common social role—that of grandmotherhood—and who were propelled into the role at an early age. They were participants in an informal, two-year pilot study among Black families that explored the effects of early child-bearing on familial relationships. The study was inspired by an observed 40 percent rate of pregnancy among very young teenage girls who were members of a Black youth activity group for which the senior author was co-moderator.

The intent at the beginning of the pilot interviews was to observe the nature of relationships between both mothers and daughters, and

Authors' Note: *This study is based on the senior author's dissertation at the University of Southern California (Burton, 1985). Support for the preparation of this chapter came from the National Institute on Aging (grant AG 04092) and the National Institutes of Mental Health (grant MH 38244). Acknowledgment should also be made to the American Sociological Association's minority fellowship program and the John Randoff Haynes and Dora Haynes Foundation. We are grateful to Gunhild Hagestad and Victor Marshall for their helpful criticism of an earlier draft.*

grandmothers and granddaughters, when a nonnormative (teen and unwed) pregnancy occurred in the family. A serendipitous finding, however, upstaged the original focus. The new grandmothers in these families were reacting quite negatively to their new roles, but not for the reasons initially assumed. The fact that their daughters were early, unwed mothers did not seem to concern them as much as the fact that they themselves were young grandmothers. These young women (ages 27 to 39) voiced discomfort with becoming grandmothers because of the problems that acquiring an "old age" role caused in their lives. For example, one 27-year-old felt that her transition to grandmotherhood was in direct conflict with her young adult roles:

> Here I am, 27-year-old mother of a 12-month-old baby and a grandmother of a 2-month-old baby. When I got out in the street and I have my daughter, her baby, and my baby with me people always look at me. . . . I know what they're thinking. . . . They're thinking this lady sure puts them [babies] out fast. . . . None of my friends are grandmothers. As a matter of fact, most of them right now are having babies for the first time.

She further comments about familial cohesion among herself, her daughter, and her mother (the great-grandmother) as a product of their early transitions:

> Everyone is pissed off at each other. No one wants to take responsibility for raising this baby. Not even my mother; she's too busy doing her own thing. . . . I'm so mad. . . . But, who do I have to talk to about the way *I* feel?

The realization that the experience of grandmotherhood may be most strongly related to timing and family intergenerational dynamics led to the study reported in this chapter. Black grandmothers represent an important tradition within Afro-American culture, perhaps to the point of stereotype; Frazier (1939) called them "guardians of generations," and the image of matriarch pervades their description even today. But what are the realistic dimensions of this role among contemporary, urban Black women of varying ages? And what variations occur between "early" and "on-time" grandmothers? What are the implications of being a dramatically "early" grandmother? Are there patterns of intergenerational similarity in the timing of becoming a grandmother, within or without marriage, as is commonly assumed?

STUDY DESIGN

This study involves a sample of four-, five-, and six-generation Black female lineages living in the south central Los Angeles area. We interviewed 41 such family lineage units (n = 120 respondents), including the new mother (G3), the grandmother (G2), and great-grandmother (G1). In addition, one great-great-great-grandmother and seven great-great-grandmothers, were available to be interviewed. Families were contacted from lists supplied by physicians asked to identify teenage and young-adult first-time mothers in their practice. Of 63 families originally identified and contacted, 22 did not participate in the study, primarily due to lack of familial consensus for participation.

The mothers (designated G3 in this study) were divided into two subsamples: the "early" or teenage mothers, ages 11-18, and the "on-time" or young adult mothers, ages 21-26. The early grandmothers (G2) were between the age of 25 and 38 years old; the on-time grandmothers ranged from 42 to 57 years of age. The great-grandmothers between 42-57 years old were categorized as early and those 60-70 years old were considered on-time (see Table 4.1).

The median ages for generations represented in the early grand-mothers subsample is as follows: for the young mothers (G3), 16 years; for the grandmothers (G2), 32 years; and for the great-grandmothers (G1), 56 years. In the on-time sample the median ages are as follow: 21 (G3); 46 (G2); and 67 (G1).

The "early" and "on-time" categories were established in accordance with current demographic data concerning age at which a woman becomes a grandmother for the first time, as inferred from the available literature. Establishing these categories with some degree of *ethnic* precision was a formidable task as no information existed on the normative age ranges of Black grandmothers. Therefore, the estimate of normative age for role entry was based on general population patterns. Sprey and Matthews (1982) note that the median age of contemporary grandmothers at role entry is in the range of 42-45. Troll (1983) suggests that the maximum normative age for grandparental role entry is 60 years. To be under or over these ages when entering the transition to grandparenthood may be perceived as off-time. To obtain the effect of role entry, G3 had to be a first-time mother and G2 had to be a first-time grandmother. Their transitions to these roles had to have occurred within a maximum of one year prior to the date of the interview.

TABLE 4.1
Early and On-Time Age Ranges for the
Three-Generation Respondents

	G3 Mothers		G2 Grandmothers		G1 Great-Grandmothers	
	Early	*On-Time*	*Early*	*On-Time*	*Early*	*On-Time*
Criteria age range based on norms	< 18	21-26	< 38	42-57	< 58	> 60
Birth cohort	after 1965	1956-1963	after 1946	1927-1942	after 1926	before 1924
Actual age ranges in the sample	11-18	21-26	25-38	42-57	46-57	60-73
N	21	20	18	23	12	26

Socioeconomic data indicate that in general these multigenerational families were upwardly mobile. Less than 15 percent of the 120 respondents were receiving Aid to Families with Dependent Children. In terms of G2 grandmothers, it was determined that the median years of education completed for both the on-time and early grandmothers was 12. The monthly median income for early grandmothers was $1850, and for on-time grandmothers, $1575. A slightly higher proportion of on-time grandmothers (66 percent) were in the work force compared to the early grandmothers (44 percent). Of the early G2s, 45 percent were currently married, as were 39 percent of the on-time grandmothers.

Data on timing of respective role entries, intergenerational cohesion, and grandparental role satisfaction were collected from the lineage members in a lengthy interview administered by indigenous interviewers. Both quantitative data (responses to prestructured scales reflecting family solidarity) and qualitative data (responses to open-ended questions) were collected from the family lineage units to illuminate the possible impact of the respondents' ethnic social world on timing, cohesion, and grandparental role satisfaction.

BLACK GRANDMOTHERS: STATUS AND ROLE

STATUS AND ROLE IN GRANDPARENTHOOD

Rosow (1976) has presented an analysis of role and status in the study of adulthood that has useful implications for the analysis of grandmotherhood. He suggests that *roles* are enactments of normatively governed behavior, and that *status* occurs as a result of delineation of rank within position. He notes that both role and status are social phenomena that can occur either simultaneously or independently of each other. His schema suggests four role types in microsocial organization: the institutional, the tenuous, the informal, and the non-role. It is the first two role types that are particularly applicable to the study of contemporary grandmotherhood.

The *institutional role*, according to Rosow, exists when a social status is accompanied by a specified identifiable role. Institutional roles are manifest when normative, active, and reactive behavior is linked to a particular status position. A grandmother who acts as a surrogate parent for her grandchild may represent the institutional dimension of the role. The grandparent/surrogate parent role has distinct status within the family system accompanied by normatively expected behavior befitting that status (e.g., as primary socializing agent). However, this type of grandmother role represents the exception rather than the rule. It is only under conditions of family crisis or need that this role behavior is assumed (Neugarten & Weinstein, 1964; Johnson, this volume). Grandparents' rights groups who are lobbying for the legislated right to visit the offspring of their divorced children are "mapping a role territory" for grandparents (Manuel, 1983). They are identifying grandparenthood as not only a significant status position in the family and society but as one with specific functions. Through legislation, they are attempting to implement rights to engage in the behavior corresponding to this status.

According to Rosow the *tenuous role* consists of "definite social positions without roles or only vague, insubstantial ones" (Rosow, 1976, p. 463). The grandparent role, as it is frequently represented in the literature, approximates this definition (Fischer & Silverman, 1982; Hagestad & Speicher, 1981; Wood, 1982). Grandparenthood presumably has an ascribed status within the family system. However, this status is not always accompanied by normative expected role behavior. George (1980, p. 88) concludes that normative guidelines for grandparents are so few and so vague that individuals pursue the style of relationship they find most comfortable. Karp and Yoels (1982) note that grandmotherhood is not a fixed status that elicits a consistent standard of role behavior from role entry to role exit. Perlam (1968, p. 153), in a characterization of an aging grandmother, provides an example of grandmotherhood as a tenuous role, a function of the progression of time and shifting family priorities:

She may be a grandmother and draw from her young grandchildren that spontaneous, uncalculated, carelessly spilled-out loving and attention that refueled her sense of worth and source. But as the grandchildren grow older, and as she does too, the pleasure of her company grows less and her use narrow for they compete with the hundred other things and people that fill up young people's lives today. So her role grows thin as the blood in her fine blue veins.

The grandparent role as tenuous derives its form from two sources: society and the family. From a societal perspective, grandparenthood is not generally considered a functional role within the macrosocial structure. Its presence or absence has no definitive effect on whether or not "society is possible." There are no universal behavioral expectations governed by the "collective conscience" (Durkheim, 1969). Thus, within a societal context, there is no expectation-sanction system to guide grandparental role behavior (Riley, Foner, Hess, & Toby, 1969).

Within the microstructure, the family, grandparenthood assumes an idiosyncratic character (Troll, 1980; Sprey & Matthews, 1982). Whether the grandparent status is accompanied by specific behavior is a matter of individual circumstance. A grandparent may elect not to engage in any role behavior regardless of familial expectations. Grandparental behavior may be restricted by the grandchild's parent (Apple, 1956; Wood & Robertson, 1976; Hagestad & Speicher, 1981; Hagestad, Smyer, & Stierman, 1982). Lopata (1973), in a study of older widows, reports that a few of her respondents bluntly stated that their own children would not let them get close to the grandchildren. Distance, physical decrements, and economics are just a few other factors that have also impeded grandparental role performance (Neugarten & Weinstein, 1964; Cherlin & Furstenburg, 1983).

BLACK GRANDMOTHERHOOD AS A TENUOUS ROLE: HISTORICAL AND CONTEMPORARY EVIDENCE

Any examination of contemporary Black grandmothers must acknowledge historical portrayals of the role. Jones (1973) depicts Black grandmothers from the early ninetieth century to the mid-1960s as the "lofty" occupants of a traditional rather than tenuous role. As "guardians of generations" (Frazier, 1939) within their family system, these grandmothers held a status that reflected wisdom, strength, and leadership. They were also actively engaged in role behavior befitting that status. Jones (1973, p. 20) describes the "rights and duties" associated with the role:

> [The Black grandmother] was an authority on the mysteries of life—having babies and caring for them, curing common illnesses, preparing tasty meals from meager food. If there was not enough food for the Black family, the grandmother often pretended not be hungry so that that other family members could eat her share. Younger people listened to her, and valued her advice. As she grew older, she was even more respected and esteemed for her knowledge and for her contributions to people, for she willingly helped neighbors, as well as her own kin. In fact, it was not uncommon for the Black grandmother to accept and rear, in addition to her own grandchildren, a niece, a nephew, a cousin, or even an orphan who had nowhere to turn for societal aid.

The nature of the grandmother role in this era as described by Jones appears to be a function of culture, family dependency, and socio-historical context.

Although this description of an institutional grandmother role appears to have been part of the socialization of many of the present study's respondents, the role may have changed as they themselves became grandmothers. Jones's evaluation of this contemporary Black grandmother suggests that the grandmother role has changed and has even became diminished. Is it possible, then, that the modal role type among contemporary Black grandmothers has become tenuous in nature, with a more frequent occurrence of a grandparental status in the family structure unaccompanied by normatively expected, active role behavior? With the exception of a few notable studies (Jackson, 1976; Yelder, 1976), the relatively sparse empirical research that exists on the Black grandmother focuses exclusively on the role in the traditional sense (e.g., grandmothers as surrogate parents, or as family matriarchs).

The absence of empirical, multiperspective role assessments of contemporary Black grandmothers suggests the need to speculate about the pervasiveness of the tenuous role type as described by Rosow (1976). Intuitively, the social context of today's Black women implies that the dominant grandparental role type may well be tenuous. Unlike her grandparental predecessors whose assumption of the role may have been influenced by a sense of commitment to or pressures toward family survival, the role of contemporary Black grandmothers may reflect the effects of quite different factors (George, 1982; Sprey & Matthews, 1982; Troll, 1980). Two cases from the pilot study illustrate this point. The first is a 39-year-old grandmother whose decision to assume a tenuous role was reflected in her desire to "relinquish" traditional maternal roles:

> I'm 39, footloose, and fancy-free. I love my grandbaby, but I don't have time for knitting booties and babysitting. I've done my part. Now it's my turn and I could care less who doesn't like it.

The second case is a grandmother, age 31, who assumes a tenuous role because of pressures of "role overload." She describes her circumstance as follows:

> I'm really a grandmother in name only. I don't have time to do what I would like to do as a grandmother. I work everyday. I have young children. Right now I'm just too busy.

In a later interview it became apparent that other forces were active in this woman's assessment of her situation. She admitted that one of the main reasons she was not more involved with her grandchild was because she felt that the grandmother role was for "old ladies":

> You may think I'm a terrible person for feeling this way but I can't help it. I am just too young to be a grandmother. That's something for old folks, not for me.

This woman's circumstance highlights a variable that has been mentioned with increasing frequency as important for its effects on the character of the grandparent role—the *timing of entrance* into the role (Fallo-Mitchell & Ryff, 1982, Hagestad, 1984; Sprey & Matthews, 1982; Woods & Robertson, 1976). Her responses also indicate that *generational structure* affects responses to the grandmother role.

GRANDPARENTAL ROLE BEHAVIOR:
EFFECTS OF TIMING
AND GENERATIONAL STRUCTURE

Hagestad (1984) has formulated a framework for evaluating transitions to specific generational role stations within a family lineage. She uses the term "alpha-omega chain" to designate a vertical system of parent-child linkages in multigeneration families. Her model illustrates the possible consequences of occupying a specific position along the chain. For example, in three-generation families, members of the middle generation are simultaneously parents and adult children. They have linkages in both directions. However, members of the end generations are linked only at the one end, downward to children or upward to parents, respectively.

Generational role stations imply more than just a system of parent-child linkages. In the context of this research, which focuses only on the adult component of the lineage, each generational station can be considered as representing a specific set of roles within a multi-generational family system. For example, at the omega end of the chain the generational role station reflects the familial role set of great-grandmother, grandmother, mother, and grandchild; the middle station--the grandmother, mother, daughter and grandchild; and the alpha station—mother, daughter, and granddaughter and great-grandchild.

The new maternal grandmother occupies center stage in vertical linkage of multigeneration families studied in this research. The generational role station (Hagestad, 1984) she occupies in relation to her mother and daughter has salient implications on grandparental role behavior. This position has been termed by some the "sandwich generation" (Brody, 1981). Individuals who occupy this role are often confronted by demands both from above and below them.

Kruse (1984) notes that in studies of three-generation families the "accumulation of task" (familial and occupational) is evident in the middle generation. One task, characterized by Treas (1977) and Rosenthal (in press) as "kin-keeping" and by Hill, Foote, Aldous, Carlson, and MacDonald et al. (1970) as being the lineage bridge, involves the promotion of contact between the upper and lower generation (Brody, 1981; Shanas, 1979). Another task of the "woman in the middle" is her function as a source of emotional and instrumental support to her daughter and mother. This task is augmented during her transition to grandmotherhood, particularly on behalf of her daughter, who is adjusting to a new role as mother. The grandmother may be called upon to serve as a babysitter, medical advisor, infant care specialist, hand holder, and even as a source of emotional support for the new father. If this grandmother is in the work force—which is highly likely as half the women aged 45-54 years now work (Treas, 1977)—she also has to integrate the demands of both her family and occupation. If family demands include those of a husband and a host of other dependent relatives— possibly including her mother-in-law, an elderly aunt or uncle, or, particularly in the case of a Black female, a cousin, niece, or nephew that she is raising—the burden she carries can be overwhelming.

OFF-TIME GRANDMOTHERHOOD
AND ITS CONSEQUENCES

When a woman assumes the grandmother role off time, given her generational position, she may experience what Lehr (1982) terms "crisis accumulation." Consider, for example, the case of one 27-year-old mother of a teenage mother in our study. Her task potentially includes the assumption of a grandparent/surrogate parent role if her daughter is unable to care for the new baby. But she also has a small child of her own. Parenting and grandparenting demands, coupled with those of work and from other generational family members, place her in a vulnerable position to experience "role overload."

The effects of role overload are potentially catastrophic. Ann, a 56-year-old great-grandmother, represents a case of such overload. She occupies the lineage position of "women in the middle." She is flanked upwardly by the 76-year-old great-great-grandmother (her mother) in the lineage and downwardly by a 29-year-old grandmother (her daughter) and a 15-year-old mother (her granddaughter).

Ann functioned as caregiver to her elderly mother, and as surrogate parent to her granddaughter and grandson, while working full-time. Ann commented, "My granddaughter and daughter keep making these babies and expect me to take care of them. I ain't no nursemaid; I ain't old; and I ain't dead yet."

> When her great-grandson was about seven months old, Ann began a relationship with a 34-year-old white man. She let him move in with her, but one day while she was at work, he disappeared with her car and money. Shattered, Ann said, "I don't feel like no mother, no grandmother, no woman, no nothing. I'm too old for this. Lord knows I don't get it from my family. Why me, Lord? Why me?"

Ann's circumstance illustrates not only the effects of role overload on "women in the middle," but also the effects of off-time lineage transitions on individual well-being. Her granddaughter's early child-bearing initiated a chain reaction of timing-based problems. Ann's granddaughter had difficulty responding as mother to her child because she still wanted to do "teenage things." Ann's daughter did not engage in any grandparental behavior because she felt that it made her look "old" to her boyfriend. Ann, saddled with the responsibilities of those below and above her in the lineage chain, began to feel older than her 56 years and sought rejuvenation and relief in a youthful romance.

The "off-timeness" of the *lineage* role transitions also created tensions and conflict in this particular family system. Bonds that were already weak between mother and daughter and between grandmother and granddaughter were further jeopardized. Consequently, there was no intergenerational support system for these women in adjusting to their new roles.

Entry to the grandmother role has been labeled a counter-transition—a life change that is dependent on the role transitions of other family members (Riley & Waring, 1976). A mother becomes a grandmother when her daughter becomes a mother. In what Hagestad (1981) terms the "ripple effect" and Riley and Waring (1976) speak of as "countertransitions," the interconnectedness of family role transitions is acknowledged. In effect, transitions by one family member spark role transitions for another. For example, "marriage in one generation creates in-laws in another; parenthood creates grandparenthood and great grandparenthood; voluntary childlessness may creat involuntary grandchildlessness" (Hagestad, 1981).

An example of the effects of such countertransitions is seen in the case of Sarah, a 32-year-old grandmother from the present study:

> Sarah is the mother of three children and grandmother of one. Her eldest daughter who is 16 (G3) is the mother of her grandson. Sarah expressed

much regret in becoming a grandmother at such a young age. "I just ain't ready," she delcared, "too much responsibility."

Sarah's daughter, Debra, offers some insights as to why her mother is not ready for the role. "The bitch makes me sick. She's so hungry for some young meat (a young man). . . . She don't want her men to know she's a grandma. . . . She even makes me tell her niggas that I'm her sister. . . . How can my momma be any kind of a grandma, her own momma and grandma ain't shit. What makes you think she could be any better? . . . All my momma's friends do is party. They live for the weekend and there my momma is right along with them."

The reactions of Sarah were indicative of the majority of early grandmothers in the sample. These 25-37-year-old grandmothers elected not to engage in grandparental role behavior because they associated the role with old age and the role came at the time when they were overcommitted.

However, there were some chronologically early grandmothers who felt that their transition was on time, and who, although immersed in several life roles found time to be grandma. The case of Mrs Hill illustrates this:

Mrs Hill, the 38-year-old mother of nine and grandmother of one, considers herself very much on-time in her roles. Her daughter is a teenage mother, unwed, and still in high school.

Mrs. Hill is a very "traditional" grandmother. She takes care of her grandchild while her daughter goes to school. Every morning she feeds, bathes, and puts the baby to sleep. She takes the baby to the doctor for appointments, to visit with relatives, to take baby pictures, and so on. Mrs. Hill performs these duties even though she has seven children still at home.

She comments: "I have never thought of myself as doing anything less than I do for my grandchild. This baby has only added joy to my life . . . I take pride in being a grandmother . . . I have never thought of myself as being too young to be a grandmother. . . . Many of my friends are also grandmothers. We talk about our grandbabies all the time . . . I learned about being a grandmother from my father's mother. I knew what kind of a grandmother I was going to be ever since I was a little girl."

These attitudes about the grandmother role were shared by many of the on-time grandmothers in the study. The majority of on-time grandmothers, because of generational structure (or sequencing of related transitions), did not have the role strain of the early grandmothers. These grandmothers also felt very good about *when* they became grandmothers (whether their daughters were married or not) and as such pursued more active grandparental behavior. Mrs. Smith, a 46-year-old grandmother, says:

> This is best time for me to become a grandma. I'm not too young to regret it and I'm not so old that I can't enjoy it. . . . I have the time, the money, and the knowledge to deal with my grandchild. I have no commitments to anyone except Anthony (her grandchild). . . . My daughter's grown, she can take care of herself. . . . My mother takes care of herself . . . I spend quite a bit of time with Anthony. . . . On the weekends I take him so that my daughter and her husband can have respite time.

The temporal context on the grandparental role entry is a function of what might be called a "domino effect." The timing of entry to grandparenthood hinges not only upon the ages at which the grandparents themselves becomes parents, but also upon the ages at which their children reproduce for the first time (Hagestad & Neugarten, 1985; Riley & Waring, 1976; Sprey & Matthews, 1982). It is often believed, perhaps stereotypically, that teenage pregancy (and thus "early" grandmotherhood) runs in families. This may be a stereotype particularly attributed to Black families. Thus, examining timing of entry to the grandmother role warrants a discussion of intergenerational family patterns of procreation.

GENERATIONAL TRENDS IN EARLY CHILDBEARING

The strategy for sample selection in this study dictated that half of the G3 mothers in the study be teenagers. A logical set of questions concerns the continuity over generations of early and on-time childbearing families. Is there evidence of intergenerational patterns of teenage pregancy among the respondents? How do family patterns of age at birth of first child differ for early grandmothers compared to on-time grandmothers?

Contrary to what might have been expected, only *one* family in this study had a pattern of teenage pregnancy across three or more subsequent generations. Age at first birth in this family of seven generations (all living) were 17, 14, 18, and 14. Interviews with the seven generations in this family suggested that their values on teenage pregnancy exemplify a stereotype not found in other lineages interviewed. For this family early childbearing was considered a valued family tradition—a way of ensuring posterity. The 91-year-old senior member in this maternal line, a great-great-great grandmother who gave birth to her first child at the age of 14, articulated this "family theme":

> My ma say women are'pose to have babies. That why God put us here. I say have'um while you young. Then you have mo' people to look out behind you when you old like me.

The 34-year-old new grandmother (G2) in this family stated:

> Children are God's blessing. It doesn't matter when they come, only that they are loved.

Such an ideology concerning age and motherhood is one that has been associated with Black women since slavery. Staples (1973) suggests the notion that a woman's duty to bear children is a conditioned response to the slave mentality of viewing Black women as baby factories. Ladner (1971, p. 78), in a discussion of a Black girl's transition to adulthood in the rural community she studied, suggests that some Black women define their womanhood in terms of their ability to reproduce:

> If there was one common standard for becoming a woman that was accepted by the majority of the (Black) people in the community, it was the time when girls gave birth to their first child. This line of demarcation was extremely clear and separated the girls from the women. This sharp change in status occurs for a variety of reasons. Perhaps the most important value it has is that of demonstrating the procreative powers that the girls possess. Children are highly valued and a strong emphasis is placed on one's being able to give birth. The ultimate test of womanhood, then, is one's ability to bring forth life.

This view does not appear to characterize the respondents in our study, either in attitudes or behaviors.

Further examination of our data, however, does indicate a two-generation pattern of teenage pregnancy in the families of the early G2 grandmothers. Of the G2 early grandmothers, 83 percent had been teenage mothers themselves (median age at first birth = 16.8). However, in most cases the G2 early grandmother's attitude about their own teenage pregnancies and those of their daughters was not necessarily one of acceptance. The notion of "do as I say not as I do" was pervasive, as this 28-year-old grandmother illustrates:

> I was pregnant for the first time when I was 13 ... then one year later I was pregnant again. . . . Shit . . . my asshole daughter did the same thing.

A 31-year-old grandmother comments:

> I had Karen when I was 16 and then Lynn when I was 17. I promised that my daughters would never be like me. I even sent them to Catholic school. Now look . . . Karen just had her baby and her sister is due in 3 months. I hope I can just get my last girl (aged 13) through high school.

The perceptions of those respondents who had given birth on time or, as one respondent defines it, "at a respectable age," were measurably different from those who were and had been teenage mothers. Only 13 percent of the G2 on-time grandmothers had been teenage mothers. In those families where G3 was a teenage mother, none of the G2s had been a teen parent. The majority of the respondents in this "on-time" sample gave birth in their late teens (19) and early 20s. The median age at birth of first child for G1 was 19.6; for G2, 21.1; for G3, 21.3. A 24-year-old G3 talked about the timing of her childbearing:

> I got pregnant with Anthony at just the right time. I was ready, my husband was ready, my mother was ready, my father was ready, my grandmother couldn't wait.

One G2 grandmother explains the rationale for her on-time pregnancy:

> All my friends were messing up getting pregnant when they were teenagers. . . . I held off; got the boogie (fun) out my system and had my

first baby when I was old enough to know what, when, how, and why I was doing what I was doing.

Although these data point to some support for a notion of intergenerational continuity in the timing of motherhood, and thus grandmotherhood, the comments of respondents do not indicate affirmation of a Black cultural ethic that is markedly deviant to traditional American majority values, as some observers have suggested. Rather, they suggest that "off-time" transitions to the role of grandmother (and mother) represent deviance from normatively-governed rules for role accession that have many negative sanctions experienced by respondents.

CONCLUSION

This study has focused on issues of timing and generational structure as they affect grandparental role behavior between two samples of contemporary Black grandmothers. The early grandmothers (median age 32 years) and the on-time grandmothers (median age 46) indicated quite different reactions to the role of grandparent, many of which related to an asynchrony between chronological age and family lineage position expressed by the early grandmothers. The off-time accession to the lineage role created, for many of these young grandmothers, tensions and conflict, not only in their view of themselves, but also in the family system of cohesion and social support.

The data also allow an examination of intergenerational transmission in the timing of procreation between early versus on-time childbirth. Although there was only one family with a pattern of teenage pregnancy across three or more generations, there was a two-generation pattern in most (83 percent) of the early grandmothers' families. By contrast, only 13 percent of the on-time grandmothers had themselves been teenaged mothers. Thus there are indications of intergenerational similarity in the timing of first birth in this sample—but only across two generations.

The central finding of this study is that both *timing of entry* and *generational structure* affects grandparental role behavior in ways not usually acknowledged. The discomfort expressed by many early grand-

mothers can be traced in part to the association between grandparenthood and being an "elder," and in part to the competing demands they
feel in the multigenerational family structure. Such tensions are not
reported in portrayals of the "traditional" Black grandmother's role,
which themselves may be stereotypic or romanticized; or it may be that
the social context has changed in ways that have made social time clocks
more important. In any event, these results suggest grandmotherhood is
experienced as a tenuous role by many of these respondents and is
exacerbated by off-time accession to the role. In short, timing of
accession to the grandparental role appears to be a crucial factor—not
mitigated by previous generations' similar experience—in indications of
satisfaction with grandparenthood.

PART II

CHANGING STRUCTURES, EXPECTATIONS, AND FUNCTIONS

The recent "discovery" of grandparenthood as a topic for scholarly investigation reflects in part the changing structures of population distributions (by age) and family composition (by divorce). As a consequence of the first change, there are many more grandparents than ever before, and the expected course of life involves many more years in the role. A consequence of the second change is that grandparents are more than ever before the symbols of family continuity, and many of them carry out different functions than did their own elders in the same lineage role.

This section addresses a number of structural issues that reflect such change, and examines the ways these shape the expectations, meaning, and functions of grandparenthood. Structural issues germane to the grandparent status (examined in other sections as well) include divorce, socioeconomic status, race and ethnicity, health, employment, marital status, living situation, and proximity to grandchildren. The chapters in this section examine some consequences of these structural differences.

Johnson's chapter presents an anthropologist's perspective on a number of situational and cultural factors affecting the voluntaristic nature of grandparental involvements with grandchildren, as well as with the middle generation. In particular, this chapter indicates how the expected *and* real functions and meanings of grandparenthood may be molded and shaped by current patterns of divorce. Family reorganization precipitated by losses of the noncustodial parents and the challenges of blended and reconstituted families with step-grandchildren are reflected in her research.

In addition, Johnson comments on expectations and functions as influenced by the age, work status, marital situation, and health of grandparents. Her study suggests that age is by far the most important variable in predicting patterns of grandparent behavior, a finding similar to that of Burton and Bengtson. Nevertheless, Johnson notes the considerable variation in response of the grandmothers and the style in which they perform their role.

Cherlin and Furstenberg's study, based on a nationally representative sample of families in which a divorce had occurred, describes the variety of styles in grandparental involvement. They were able to categorize their respondents in terms of five styles of grandparenting: detached, passive, supportive, authoritative, and influencial. That there is no single or dominant style of grandparent behavior is evident from their data. Some grandparents were deeply involved with their adolescent grandchildren, and many others (though passive in style) derived considerable satisfaction from being around to watch their grandchildren grow up.

Cherlin and Furstenberg found little evidence that social class was related to grandparenting styles. Geographical distance, personal relationships, major life events, and values appeared to have greater effects. There was evidence of racial contrasts in grandparenting styles, with Black grandmothers more likely to retain authority over the rearing of children. Their data also provides suggestion that the grandparental role changes as they and their grandchildren age: "fun-seeking" styles are less evident in older grandparents, with mutual assistance and passive styles more pronounced.

When is the grandparent status important? The study by Aldous provides an explicit commentary on changing structures, expectations, and functions in grandparenthood. She addresses how grandparents, contrary to their own preferences, assume caretaker roles and functions when vulnerability, neediness, or changes in the middle generation occur. Both she and Johnson emphasize the nebulous nature of grandparenthood, noting the value discrepancies and competing commitment with family *versus* the voluntaristic or individualistic preferences.

Specifically, Aldous tests the hypothesis that the aging parents will have closer ties with their adult children (who have children) when the adult children are divorced; otherwise, grandparent status will not make a difference in intergenerational contacts. Her findings support this hypothesis. The critical variable in predicting differences in adult parent-child contact is not simply the status of grandparenthood; rather, it is the need for instrumental and emotional aid displayed by adult children who have children and are divorced. This study suggests that grandparenting is not an unconditional temporal continuation of parental roles. Parental roles are never lost; but grandparent roles may be supplanted, complemented, or expanded. In her data, at least, grandparenting becomes a major activity, an important status, only when there are problems in the younger generation.

5

GRANDPARENTING OPTIONS IN DIVORCING FAMILIES
An Anthropological Perspective

Colleen L. Johnson

Research on grandparents indicates the ambiguous and inconclusive conceptions of their status and roles. Although biologically determined, grandparenthood has been described as a derived status only weakly regulated by social norms (Troll, 1981). Not surprisingly, then, grandparenthood is depicted in terms of a variety of styles that reflect the voluntary and personally determined nature of the role (Robertson, 1977; Neugarten & Weinstein, 1964). Although the role may have been characterized by some as having little social significance in the modern family, there is widespread popular interest and profuse sentiments about grandparenting today. Practical books on how to be a grandparent are appearing (Dobson, 1981) and the media frequently depicts the legal battles centering on the rights of grandparents. Thus, one must ask whether grandparents in actuality play a far more important role in the contemporary family than current research approaches have unearthed. With the family system undergoing major changes with frequent divorce and remarriage, perhaps family researchers have been slow to recognize that grandparents are increasingly necessary as a stabilizing force in the American family.

Further understanding of the grandparent's status in the contemporary family comes from an anthropological analysis of the American kinship system. At least three factors emerge that distinguish the American system from most cultures throughout the world (Apple, 1956; Schneider, 1968). First, there is a wider structural separation between generations in the American family system, which results in more autonomy and privacy in the nuclear family and subsequently a more remote status for the grandparents. Second, unlike most kinship systems cross-culturally, our system is not regulated by explicit rights and obligation. Although there is some normative consensus on the parent-child and the husband-wife dyads, other kinship relationships, including the grandparent-grandchild dyad, are more voluntary and rest upon personal initiatives and options at any given time. Third, the American value system—espoused at least by nonethnic Americans—encourages independent and personal freedom, often at the expense of family responsibilities and dependence upon others. Where family allegiances are required, the priorities of one's nuclear family of procreation are mandated over those to grandparents and other members of the family of orientation.

Given these characteristics, one can conclude that the American family system and its kinship extensions are flexible in normal times and permit much freedom for individuals to enter into and leave relationships. With divorce and remarriage, the optional nature can become even more accentuated and can lead to a number of problems. As Paul Bohannon (1971) has pointed out, divorce is only a problem in those societies where the household is formed around the husband-wife relationship to the exclusion of kin. In such cases, the kinship unit cannot provide a "safety net" for the children. For the grandparents, who already have an ambiguous status in families, their roles are even more nebulous in families of divorce. There are few clear-cut rules on what they should do, yet any of their actions are constrained by the parents of their grandchildren, one of whom is no longer formally a relative.

Nevertheless, many insights can be gained by the study of the status of the grandparents during a period of family reorganization following divorce. Given the voluntaristic principle of relationships and the weak normative regulation at least in nonethnic families, questions arise on the nature of the attachments between generations. On one hand, one might argue that intergenerational relationships are not sufficiently regulated by specified norms and rules to the extent that stable, predictable relationships are formed (Cherlin, 1978). On the other hand, one might take the opposite view that the weakness of the normative regulation has advantages, for the optional and situationally determined relationships can create inexhaustible potentials of sociability and supports without burdensome obligations (Furstenberg & Spanier, 1984).

In personally constructing their role, grandparents must make decisions on three types of critical tasks they perform in the divorce situation. First, they must determine how active they should be with children and grandchilren in providing supports during a period of high needs. Second, because any decisions hinge on the wishes of their former children-in-law, they need to decide how that relationship should be regulated and either maintained or severed. Third, in the area of values, grandparents must take some stance on the common value discrepancies between generations and often come to terms with the more permissive lifestyles of their children. They also must determine their own role in transmitting family values to their grandchildren. In such an open situation, it is assumed that decisions are not made randomly, but stem at least in part from the value configuration of the family.

Factors constraining the grandparents' actions are found in the objective social characteristics—their age, kinship relationship (maternal or paternal), and their competing commitments stemming from work, marriage, and voluntary associations. In the first section of this chapter, I will present variations on these situational constraints on the grandparental role. Second, from this base, I will analyze the steps by which individuals personally construct their role of grandparent and how they respond to the situational demands and determine how active to be, what services to provide and so on. Here the situational determinants stem from the divorce of a child and factors influencing the grandparents' participation in the reorganization of the child's family. Third, I will examine "grandparenting as an idea," which refers to the more subjective, culturally determined elements that are expressed in grandparents' interpretations of their role in their children's families. I assume that grandparents' conception of the role is related to their values and norms, personal histories, and experiences as they are framed by the broader cultural context in which they live. Here this cultural context focuses on White, middle-class, suburban settings in Northern California.

SAMPLE AND METHODS

This chapter stems from a larger research project on the role of grandmothers after the divorces of their children. In this project, 49 parent-adult child dyads were interviewed, in addition to ten additional grandmothers who specifically requested that we not interview their child. Although the sample is small and perhaps generalizable only to White, middle-class, suburban families, the ethnographic interview techniques provide the contextual data that can augment survey research and suggest the emergent dimensions of grandparenting in the contemporary United States.

Most of the grandmothers were selected from divorce records of middle-class suburbs in the San Francisco Bay Area. The divorcing offspring was contacted first and a request was made to provide access to his or her parent. Opportunity sampling added a smaller group of grandmothers, and they in turn referred us to their divorcing child. Permission to participate rested on agreement of both generations and consequently represents a sample in which the generational tie was maintained more or less amicably. The factor of generational co-operation possibly represents a sampling bias, but one that was unavoidable if both generations were to be interviewed. In this chapter, only the grandmothers' interviews are used in analysis; the inter-generational relationship will be reported separately. Although grand-fathers also participated in the interviews, the findings here are confined to the grandmothers.

In order to control for expected variation by social class and ethnicity, we confined the sample to middle-class, White families. Approximately half of the grandmothers are maternal and half are paternal. The lineage link was used as a selection criteria instead of custody arrangements because the high numbers of cases of joint custody reported in California would result in further subdivision of an already small sample. Resulting custody arrangements were as follows: maternal, 49 percent; paternal, 7 percent; joint, 20 percent; and undecid-ed or mature children, 24 percent.

The sample was also stratified by age, with half of the grandmothers under 65 years and half 65 years and older. The interviews were conducted less than three years after their child's separation. By design, all grandmothers had divorcing offspring residing in the area, but in a few cases, the grandchildren had recently moved away. The mean age of these grandchildren was 10.3 years with a range from infancy to 34 years.

In-depth interviews were conducted. With the exception of objective measures of social contact and aid, interviews were focused on gathering qualitative data. A list of questions was used to guide the interview, although respondents had considerable leeway in determining the course of discussion. Projective stories of common situations arising from divorce were also used to probe the values of the grandmothers as they commented on the family changes associated with divorce.

VARIATIONS IN THE
ACTIVITIES OF GRANDMOTHERS

On the whole, few grandmothers appeared excluded, or excluded themselves, from the lives of their children and grandchildren. Their relationships with the younger generations were generally amiable and, in many cases, supportive. For examples, 59 percent of their children said that their lives would be more difficult if their parents were not in the area.

The most important source of variation in grandparenting behavior appears to be the age of the grandmother and the grandchildren. Grandmothers under 65 years of age were twice as likely to see the grandchildren at least weekly than were the older women. Most of the under-65 women are "on-time" grandmothers, with 93 percent having grandchildren with a mean age of 12 years or younger. These younger grandmothers are also more likely to be married, healthier, and to work. Although they are not significantly in more contact with their divorcing children, they do see grandchildren much more frequently than older women do. Older women, on the other hand, are experiencing age-related changes in their marital status, health, and work status at a stage when they are also having a decline in grandparenting activity. For both age groups, however, these patterns most likely existed before the child's divorce. Neither group was likely to report an increase in contact with the younger generations following marital dissolution.

The kinship linkage by maternal and paternal lines is of less importance than age as a determinant of contact with grandchildren. Although maternal grandmothers tend to be in more frequent contact with children and grandchildren than are paternal grandmothers, the differences are not significant. Paternal grandmothers, however, evidently are able to compensate for the potential social distance from grandchildren if their sons do not have custody. Significantly more paternal grandmothers retain at least weekly contact with former daughters-in-law than maternal grandmothers retain with former sons-in-law.

Such a pattern of retaining the in-law linkages following divorce reflects a contemporary blurring between consanguineal and affinal relatives (Furstenberg & Spanier, 1984). Where enduring social ties are formed with in-laws, they can become equally or more important than blood ties. These patterns also reflect the flexibility of our kinship system, which, as Furstenberg (1981) notes, opens the door to diverse solutions. One such option is the continuation of the ties with former children-in-law. When that child-in-law can provide access to grandchildren while one's own child cannot, then the relationship might become more significant than the consanguineal bond.

Understandably, the middle generation, the parents of the grandchildren, play a major role in mediating between grandparents and grandchildren. The strength of this linkage appears to hinge on the quality of the relationship between the grandparents and their adult children. Active grandmothers reported a more intimate relationship with their children; they also reported less conflict with their children than the less active women. Compatibility in values also was prominent when the intergenerational relationships were strong, particularly where there was approval among the grandmothers of divorce and cohabitation.

Even though younger grandmothers are much more active, they also have many more competing commitments. In at least ten cases, these women were adapting to their own divorces and remarriages. With the demands of a new husband, or in adjusting to the post-divorce period, there were considerable distractions preventing attendance to grandchildren's needs. Over half of the younger women had living parents who in many cases required social support. These women then were experiencing the "middle generation squeeze" (Hess & Waring, 1978), in which both generations were demanding more from these already overcommitted women.

Patterns of exchange between generations were markedly asymmetrical, leading one to conclude that most of the rewards and benefits from grandparenting must be intangible. The amount of aid flowing from grandparents to grandchildren was twice as much than was given in the reverse direction. This situation was particularly prominent among the younger women; of the total number of services extended by grandmothers, 80 percent was provided by the younger grandmothers. For the older women, there was more symmetry in the exchanges between generations, although these grandmothers still gave more than they received. In those cases where the grandmothers' needs were high, their children were not always able to meet these needs because of the divorce-related demands. These findings raise several questions. Do the inequities in reciprocity act to undermine the relationships between generations? Does the older woman's increasing inability to bestow benefits on divorcing children and grandchildren account for their greater distance from the younger generation?

It was also found that older grandmothers were significantly less family oriented in their social network activity than the younger ones. They spend more time with friends and tend to turn to them for support. Again, this finding could be associated with the stage of the family cycle when the services required by young children—which served to maintain contact—are no longer needed.

In summary, it is apparent that the type of grandmother who extends help to the divorced child and her grandchildren is a younger grandmother who also has an active life of her own. She has an intimate although sometimes conflictual relationship with her divorced child and accepts his or her increased dependence on her. After the divorce, she gives twice as much aid as she receives in return. In contrast, those women who most likely experience greater isolation from children and grandchildren following divorce are likely to be older, widowed, and in poorer health. They have a more distant relationship with their children, but unlike the younger grandmothers, they do receive almost as many supports from children as they give in return. These older women also tend to have personal networks dominated by friends rather than family. For older grandmothers, then, one can conclude that the divorce of a child is less likely to enlarge the content of their family roles. On the contrary, it possibly lessens their involvement in their children's families, a situation that is in marked contrast to the grandmothers in middle age.

GRANDPARENTING CHOICES

Sociodemographic factors account for only part of the variations in grandparenting; other differences between families can be traced to given situations in which one is permitted to make decisions. Goode (1956) has described the divorce process as a period of "social limbo" where, in the absence of structural imperatives, diverse alternatives are possible. Divorce generally creates the need for additional resources to buttress the overburdened custodial parent. Grandparents, however, are not compelled to respond; they have an opportunity to be supportive or unhelpful, aloof or involved in their child's family, and to act as mediators between divorcing parents or sources of conflict. The outcomes for them are also diverse. On one hand, they can restore content to their family roles of parent and grandparent by increasing their involvement with their children and grandchildren. On the other hand, they can suffer social losses from the divorce process as aid and supports from children of divorce decrease due to the extra burdens the divorce has imposed upon their child.

The divorce situations usually results in overburdened parents and increased needs of grandchildren, particularly younger ones. Most grandparents responded with money, baby-sitting, and other forms of assistance. Although some children complained of their parents' lack of assistance, it was a rare grandparent who refused to provide any help to children and grandchildren. In fact, grandparents of all ages tended to see themselves as meaningful figures who, in their stable situation, could selectively offfer nurturance and guidance. Because the divorce of parents created disruptions in family life, the grandmothers saw themselves as a "back-up" person whose home was a "safe harbor" or an "island of security" for grandchildren of all ages.

These views of their potentials did not always correspond with what they actually did. In fact, a passive and remote grandmother was just as likely to extol and sentimentalize grandparenting as a woman who was actively involved in giving help. Generally, grandmothers pointed out that they were the ones who had time to observe and listen to children and merely be there if they were needed. They described these functions as passive, however, and ones that were not usually self-initiated. Because grandmothers waited to be asked to help, the more symbolic dimensions were not always accompanied by objective activities.

In some cases, involvement in the lives of their children and grandchildren was forced upon the grandmothers unwillingly. Although most grandmothers wanted to help their grandchildren, very few wanted to replace their children by becoming surrogate parents. There were situations, however, where grandparents responded to the imperatives of the situation and took on functions normally designated to the parents. In eleven families, the grandmothers took over child care, household duties, chauffeuring, and setting up doctor's appointments on a regular basis. Invariably, this major involvement occurred because there was no one else to assist. Usually parents and grandparents viewed this arrangement not as a permanent and socially approved response, but as one that was the only solution at a given time.

In a second situation, grandmothers could make decisions based upon their personal preferences on how to deal with the other set of grandparents who might be competing for the attention of the grandchildren. The divorce situation can compound the problems of allocating time to each set of grandparents. Either with joint custody or generous visitation rights to the noncustodial parent, the grandchildren's schedule is often crowded with spending alternate days or weeks with each parent. If these schedules must be further subdivided to include two sets of grandparents, some problems arise. It was not uncommon to find young children rotating between four homes, their mother's, father's, maternal, and paternal grandparents.

One solution to this custody arrangement was the formation of a coalition of grandparents. In several cases, both maternal and paternal grandparents worked together in easing the potential confusion these arrangements entailed for the grandchildren. They cooperated in arranging schedules, taking turns being on call for the grandchildren, and planning joint holiday gatherings. Either both parents of the children would be included in these arrangements or grandparents purposely excluded one parent who was "blamed" for the divorce.

In keeping with the flexibility of the boundaries of the American kinship system, a third type of arrangement was made. Some paternal grandmothers formed coalitions with former daughters-in-law. In fact, conflict between paternal grandparents and their son's former wives was less common than between maternal grandparents and former sons-in-law. Many established a working relationship with former daughters-in-law and assisted them in caring for the grandchildren. Where strong friendships existed after the divorce, grandmothers excluded their own sons, even when they voiced objections to these coalitions. The justifications were based upon the best interests of the grandchildren. Because former daughters-in-law were viewed as a special kinship relationship, "the mother of my grandchildren," this relationship was often preserved after the divorce.

Grandmothers can also decide to be inactive with the divorce, or correspondingly their children can decide not to go to their parents for support and sympathy. This option was elected invariably when the relationship historically had been conflictual or distant. As no clear picture emerged that indicated how these arrangements were normatively determined, I assume that decisions more often were made based upon an individual's response to a given situation. The fact that the outcomes often stemmed from the element of personal choice accounts for the wide variations in grandparenting. As one result of this flexibility, the divorce of a child creates an expanded network for the grandmother as often as it deprives them of relatives, for they can retain relationships with relatives of divorce as well as form new relationships with relatives of remarriage.

THE CULTURAL DETERMINANTS OF GRANDPARENTING

In making choices among the options available to these grand-mothers, their perceptions and interpretations of the situation enter into the processes of determining courses of action. These decisions are in part related to the cultural or evaluative elements. In a previous article (Johnson, 1983), a cultural analysis was made of the grandmother's role. Rather than focusing on behavioral outcomes, it analyzed the more subjective material centering on how grandmothers conceptualize the role and determine their actions. In contrast to the wide variations in the grandmothers' behavior, the ideas on grandparenting were more patterned.

One relevant pattern that was discerned relates to their age norms. In response to questions on how they see themselves as grandparents, most grandmothers were in agreement on their conceptions of an ideal type of grandmother that they use as a standard for evaluating their own behavior. This type is a kindly woman who is old, domestic, and nurturing. This image was rejected by most, however—often with great vehemence—because this type of woman was too old, too old-fashioned, and too family-centered. Instead the preferred type of grandmother was one who was young, fun loving, and had a life of her own outside of the family.

Irrespective of their chronological age, these women espoused the norms of middle age and the norms of the liberated woman. An Auntie Mame seemed to be more compatible to contemporary times and the world of their grandchildren. She is one who satisfies her grandchildren's needs for pleasure as well as her own. Whereas the traditional grandmother might slave over the stove all day providing delicacies for the grandchildren, this modern woman plays with them and then takes them to MacDonald's for dinner. Some respondents insisted they were more like a friend or "pal" than a grandmother. In keeping with the middle-aged norms of these women, many also insisted "I'm not typical," "I'm too young to be a grandmother," or "Just because I'm a grandmother doesn't mean I am old." Such conceptions indicate that grandmothers today are not necessarily less active, but it does suggest that they have shed some of the maternal and domestic functions of the role.

A second pattern found in this cultural analysis concerns the norms of grandparenting as they are distinguished by their proscriptive and prescriptive elements. Although researchers have suggested that the role is not strongly normatively directed (Troll, 1981), the respondents in this study reported a detailed list of rules they use to regulate their own behavior. Most frequently mentioned were proscriptive rules warning against being intrusive into their children's families. One *should not* be interfering or give unwanted advice. The emphasis on proscriptive norms suggests that although grandmothers have options open to them in defining their role, their actions are constrained by the mandate on the autonomy and privacy of the nuclear family in each generation and ultimately rest upon the wishes of their children and children-in-law. Thus, the flexibility in our family system can facilitate a compatible, personally defined role, but it also creates an ambivalent situation in which the grandparents' interventions must be indirect. By most social definitions, they should be involved, yet their involvement can also risk negative sanctions for being intrusive.

Another set of norms commonly mentioned were proscriptions on being judgmental. In order to preserve their relationship with their children and grandchildren, these grandmothers concluded that they must not exert their own values on them—which might condemn divorce, permissive sexual activities, and cohabitation, all innovations common among their children and children-in-law. By exhibiting restraint in commenting upon these arrangements, they generally were able to preserve amiable relationships and thus retain access to their grandchildren. In fact, among the many functions and activities grandmothers potentially assign to the role, that of transmitting traditional values of family life from generation to generation was rarely mentioned among these women.

VALUE CHANGES BY AGE AND GENERATION

On the whole, the divorcing parents typify the major changes in morality in twentieth century Western cultures. These changes, in the view of Anthony Quinton (1983), largely entail emancipation from the Victorian ideal of hard work, foresight, prudence, self-reliance, and deferred gratification. One form of the new morality he describes is a permissive one that emphasizes consumption, enjoyment of material things, and an uncritical endorsement of wants and impulses free from censoriousness. In other words, there is a deemphasis on controlling one's impulses and deferring gratification in order to meet long-term goals.

California is often identified as a region where social and political movements, the drug revolution, and alternate life styles have originated. The middle-class, nonethnic Americans—those most affected by these movements—are similar to the sample of divorcing parents in this study. Thus, they most likely represent a variant in American values most applicable to Quinton's discussion of the new morality.

Although the values have not been systematically studied in this region of the country, the media frequently report on the egocentric, permissive life-styles of this area as one that perhaps indicates future national trends. In these middle-class, nonethnic communities on the West Coast, the self-actualization movement is widely endorsed and essentially involves giving priorities to personal needs over family responsibilities. Reports on the reasons for divorce illustrate these values. In fact, a frequent assumption discussed in the interviews was that family success and stability hinged upon the personal happiness of the parent. The majority of the divorcing offspring reported that the divorce was not initiated for conventional reasons such as adultery, substance abuse, physical abuse, or often even incompatibility. Instead, the divorcing parents often described their actions as initiated in a search for personal happiness, "to find myself," "to do my own thing." Many had gone through various therapies of counseling that ideologically are based upon the self-actualization movement.

The grandparents' responses to these contemporary values appear to be related to their age. In this sample, there are two cohort of grandmothers who, because of the dates of their birth, bring differing family experiences to grandparenting. The older grandmothers, born before 1918, married and started their families during the Depression and the war years. Like others in their age group, they had less education and economic resources than the younger grandparents. As a whole, they also did not raise their children during the high familism of the 1950s, a time when "togetherness" was an explicit value and the more permissive psychological child-rearing techniques were endorsed. Neither their background nor their education prepared them for the self-actualization movement of the 1960s and 1970s, so with this older group, there are often sharper contrasts between their values and their children's. In keeping with the norm of noninterference, however, they are no more likely to impose their own views on the younger generation, although these are the grandmothers who in old age turn to friends rather than family for diversion and support. It is possible that this withdrawal from family is an expression of such a value gap between generations.

The younger grandmothers, on the other hand, were born during the Depression and were maturing throughout the war years. With adulthood, they profited from the easier access to education and economic prosperity after the war. They began their families in the 1950s, a period when family values received the highest precedence. Also, their children were raised in keeping with the Spockian era, a time when inhibitions were reviewed as psychologically detrimental. At the same time, these children were growing up on the West Coast and being exposed to the many movements of the 1960s—the new sexual morality, the drug culture, anti-establishment views, and the rejection of the family as an oppressive institution. Today this cohort of grandparents is the most active in the lives of their children and grandchildren. It is possible that the activity of the younger grandmothers is a continuation of the pattern of high familism established earlier. Also, because they were generally tolerant parents, they are now tolerant grandparents. They also are less judgmental than the older grandmothers in regard to the permissive and sometimes hedonistic lifestyles of their children.

Although younger grandmothers tended to be nonjudgmental, the emphasis on self-interest and the search for self-actualization generally eluded both age groups. Few expressed the value that "one should do one's own thing" or put one's personal happiness above the interests of children and family, values commonly expressed by their children. Although most did not condemn divorce, they tended to favor marital stability, even though it entailed unhappiness. One comment was fairly typical, "We just took more from each other. There was no counseling in those days—you know, the kind that teaches you how to be selfish."

The grandmothers usually accepted their self-sacrificing role in the family, but it was common to detect a note of envy as they described their children's freer lifestyles. One grandmother, also recently divorced, described her married life as being absorbed in her husband's career advancement and family activities. "I really feel that the togetherness the 1950s promoted was a mistake. If I had had my own interests then, perhaps it would have been better for all concerned, and I would have been happier."

These belated reservations on family life are also evident in their attitudes toward grandparenting. These women expressed some resistance to repeating the parent role. A frequent comment was, "I've paid my dues." In fact, a hesitance in taking initiative with grandchildren possibly is traced to ambivalence in regard to the responsibilities it entails. As one grandmother summarized this attitude, "If I do too much, I might have to do it all. If I do too little, I might lose them." Others commented that it was now time for them to think of themselves and enjoy a life of their own. Such conclusions were particularly prominent among younger grandmothers even as they were responding to the demands of both older and younger generations. It is interesting to note that such reservations were also common in a more traditional, Midwestern sample (Aldous, this volume), a finding that suggests broader national trends.

CONCLUSIONS

To review the grandmothers' responses to their children's divorces, my research found that age is by far the most important variable in predicting patterns of grandparent behavior. Younger grandmothers, even when they are married, employed, and facing numerous competing commitments, are far more active than older grandmothers. Nevertheless, there is much variation in the responses of the grandmothers and the style in which they perform the role. This chapter has explored the broader social and cultural context of grandparenting in order to account for this variation and to understand the contradictory views on grandparenting today.

When one places the grandparents' status and roles in a cross-cultural perspective, the ambiguity so often noted in the literature is understandable. Grandparents, their children, and grandchildren are not only structurally separate from each other, they are normatively mandated to be independent and at all times to avoid being a burden on each other. Because there are few clear-cut rules and many opportunities to make personal decisions on courses of action with the grandchildren, there is great variability in the styles of grandparenting. Instead of the norm of obligation, this dyadic relationship rests upon voluntary moves of both partners. When divorce occurs, the status of the grandparent can become even more uncertain. At a time when they are more necessary as a stabilizing force in the family, most grandparents must enter uncharted territory and make decisions as they go along.

Among the many options open to them, grandmothers can selectively retain ties with former daughters-in-law and, by doing so, retain the link to their grandchildren. They can minimize a potential generation gap with grandchildren by rejecting traditional dimensions of the role. They can take them to fast-food chains instead of slaving over the stove all day. They can be a fun-loving figure who makes few demands on children and grandchildren. They can also decide to establish distance from grandchildren and pursue their own interests.

Such patterns create a new family form that has uncertain implications for the future. On one hand, given the ease with which many grandmothers can adapt to and even profit by the nonconventional family forms, one can assert that the purported strengths of the traditional system merits reevaluation. Although the voluntaristic principle of relationships might lead to unstable relationships, it also potentially can be one of today's family strengths. As Furstenberg (1981) has pointed out, without kinship rules of closure, the divorce situation permits the opportunity for diverse forms of the family in which grandparents can function as mediaries and participants in numerous family units. Without structural imperatives on which relatives are to be retained and which are to be sloughed off, grandparents hypothetically can construct a family system that is suited to their preferences and needs without entailing burdensome obligations. In actuality, however, grandchildren—particularly younger ones—are the connecting link, so these options are more readily available to middle-aged rather than older grandmothers.

On the other hand, it can be argued that optional relationships are inherently unstable. Although the flexibility in the family system might expand the extended family, grandparents respond to the needs of the situation only on a temporary basis. In the absence of obligatory norms, there are no assurances that an enduring, supportive relationship with grandchildren will persist, even though emotional ties remain strong. Intergenerational relationships can be broken off at will after the crisis of divorce had subsided or when competing commitments arise.

In turn, grandmothers have few expectations for their children and grandchildren in the event their own needs increase. In fact, feelings of burden do not arise in any generation, because actions are voluntarily initiated and curtailed according to the situation at hand. The inherent instability is one cost that is balanced by the benefits of personal choices in creating rewarding intergenerational ties. In many respects, the situation of the contemporary grandmothers in the subculture studied here portrays one type of solution to the basic dilemma of American family life, one in which the individual must balance the costs and rewards accruing in meeting the need for personal freedom, on one hand, and the need for attachment to family, on the other.

6

STYLES AND STRATEGIES
OF GRANDPARENTING

Andrew Cherlin
Frank F. Furstenberg

There is a great amount of variation in the kinds of relationships that American grandparents have with their grandchildren. Some grandparents are actively involved in their grandchildren's lives, but many others are quite passive and distant. In addition, as we will show in this chapter, the relationship can vary from grandchild to grandchild. Some grandchildren may live far from the grandparent, other grandchildren may live with parents who don't get along with the grandparents; and still others may no longer be living with the grandparent's son or daughter as a result of divorce. Under circumstances such as these, grandparents sometimes devote most of their attention to a few grandchildren—or even to just one. This strategy—which we call selective investment— allows them to act like grandparents and feel satisfied with their role, even though they aren't as close to the rest of their grandchildren.

The variation in the styles and strategies of grandparenting is consistent with the general principles that determine the nature of kinship ties in American society. Individuals are allowed to exercise a great deal of discretion in their relations with kin. In his classic account of Amerian kinship, Schneider (1980) characterizes our system as highly voluntaristic. Blood and marriage circumscribe the available pool of kin, but within this pool it is up to individuals to cultivate and maintain ties. Kinship, therefore, has an achieved as well as an ascribed dimension.

This discretionary feature of American kinship is especially salient when divorce and remarriage occur. Our study, which will be described

Authors' Note: *This study was supported by grant AG02753 from the National Institute on Aging.*

below, was originally designed to investigate what happens to the ties between grandparents and grandchildren when the grandchildren's parents divorce. We found a wide range of responses. Many grandparents became heavily involved in their grandchildren's lives, sometimes to the point of becoming surrogate parents, whereas others drifted apart from their grandchildren. There were no fixed rules about how grandparents should react to a divorce, although a pattern did emerge: With some exceptions, the ties between maternal grandparents and their grandchildren were maintained or strengthened after a divorce; but the ties between paternal grandparents and their grandchildren were often weakened. This difference emerged because mothers usually retain custody of their children after a divorce and many divorced fathers have infrequent contact with their children (Furstenberg, Nord, Peterson, & Zill, 1983). It is therefore more difficult for paternal grandparents to retain close ties to their grandchildren after the disruption of the parents' marriage.

In this chapter, however, we will focus on the more general issue of variation in the grandparent-grandchild relationship in intact as well as disrupted families. There have been a number of attempts to classify the styles and meanings of being a grandparent (Neugarten & Weinstein, 1964; Wood & Robertson, 1976; Robertson, 1977; Kivnick, 1982). All find a diversity of responses that form a continuum from substantial involvement to remoteness. These and other studies (Troll & Bengtson, 1979) also suggest the widespread acceptance in the United States of what we might call the "norm of non-interference": the idea that grandparents should not interfere with the parents in the rearing of the grandchildren.

The previous studies have provided much useful information, but they also have been quite limited. They have tended to be exploratory; geographically, socially, and ethnically limited; and small in size. They cannot tell us whether styles of grandparenting vary systematically by age, ethnicity, or other social and economic characteristics. Moreover, these studies leave us with a rather static view of grandparenting, as if we could pin a label on a grandmother shortly after her first grandchild was born ("fun seeker" or "distant figure") and be sure that the label would remain accurate for all her grandchildren for the rest of her life. As that seems implausible, we need to think more about whether there is a life-course of grandparenting and about the ways in which grandparents may simultaneously maintain different kinds of relationships with different grandchildren. In this chapter we hope to provide some insight into these unresolved issues of styles and strategies of grandparenting.

THE STUDY

In 1976, data were collected from a nationally representative sample of households containing children between the ages of seven and eleven. The child and his or her primary caretaker—the child's mother in more than 90 percent of the cases—were interviewed. In 1981, all of the children whose parents' marriages had been disrupted by 1976 and a random subsample of children from nondisrupted homes were reinterviewed. The parent of the child also was reinterviewed. During the 1981 interview, the parents were asked to provide the names, addresses, and telephone numbers of the child's grandparents. For currently married grandparents, one spouse was systematically selected to be interviewed. Telephone interviews were conducted by the Institute for Survey Research at Temple University between February and April 1983 with 510 grandparents—82 percent of the names on the final list. In addition, we reinterviewed a small subsample of the grandparents using in-person, semistructured interviews that were taped and subsequently transcribed. We will draw upon these qualitative interviews to interpret and illustrate our quantitative findings.

The 510 grandparent interviews—which form the data for this chapter—constitute not a national sample of grandparents but rather the grandparents of a national sample of children. The children in question—whom we refer to as the study children—were almost all between the ages of 13 and 17 by 1983. Our study presents data, then, on grandparents who have teenaged grandchildren and who therefore may be older, on average, than the typical American grandparent. Our focus is on the relationship between the grandparent and a teenaged study child; it is possible that the relationship between these grandparents and their younger grandchildren could be different. We intentionally over-represented grandmothers in our interviews because most of the parent respondents were female and women are deeply involved in kin networks, according to many studies (Adams, 1968).

ACTIVITIES

What do grandparents do with teenaged children? We asked the grandparents many questions about their activities with the study children and then, using the statistical technique of factor analysis, examined the responses to see whether there were clusters of activities that some grandparents engaged in but others did not.

One cluster that failed to emerge in our study was the so-called "fun seeker" pattern—consisting of playful, leisure-oriented activities—that was common among the grandparents Neugarten and Weinstein (1964) studied. This pattern was absent not because our grandparents disliked fun but rather because our survey referred to older grandchildren—13- to 18-year-olds, to be specific. The grandparents in the Neugarten and Weinstein sample, it turns out, were much younger than those in our study and were therefore more likely to have had younger grandchildren. In fact, Neugarten and Weinstein found that the fun seeker pattern was less common among grandparents who were over age 65. They ascribed this age difference to trends over time in people's values or to the aging process. We would suggest, in addition, that the difference emerged because grandparents do different things with younger grandchildren than with older grandchildren. Styles of grandparenting, in other words, change as grandchildren and grandparents age. It's easy and natural for grandparents to treat toddlers as sources of leisure-time fun. But no matter how deep and warm the relationship remains over time, a grandmother doesn't bounce a teenager on her knee.

Instead, our factor analyses suggest that what some grandparents do with teenaged children—in addition to the ubiquitous joking, reminiscing, and so forth—is exchange services; and a minority even manage to have a role in how the teenager is being raised. Two groups of activities clustered together. The first was composed of responses to the following four questions: "Over the past 12 months, has (the child) asked for your help with something (s/he) was doing or making? Run errands or chores for you?" and "Over the past 12 months, have you asked (the child) for help with something you were doing or making? Helped (the child) with (his/her) errands or chores?" The first and fourth items refer to flows of assistance from the grandparent to the grandchild; 36 percent and 41 percent, respectively, of the grandparents responded affirmatively to these two items. The second and third refer to assistance from the grandchild to the grandparent; 61 percent and 42 percent, respectively, responded positively to these two items. We formed a scale with a range of zero to four by summing the number of positive responses to these four questions. Most grandparents and grandchildren had a limited exchange of services; but about one-third answered positively to at least three of the four questions, and about one-sixth answered positively to all four. Grandparents who had very frequent contact with the study child or who were younger were more likely to exchange services. Social class and race, however, appeared to make little difference.

The second cluster of activities that emerged in our analysis measured the extent to which the grandparents were able to exert the type of influence over the grandchild that is typically reserved for parents. The cluster was composed of the responses to the following five questions: "Over the past 12 months, did you discipline (him/her)? Give (the child) advice? Discuss (his/her) problems?" "When you see the child do something you disapprove of, do you correct (him/her) often, sometimes, hardly ever, or never?" and "Do your children consult you before making an important decision about (the child) often, sometimes, hardly ever, or never?" A scale of parentlike behavior with a range of zero to five was formed by summing the number of positive responses to the latter two items. The most common score was zero and the least common was five, reflecting the lack of authority in these matters among most grandparents. Still, nearly half scored three or more and more than one-fourth scored four or more.

The grandparents with higher scores on this scale are of particular interest, for they have been able to surmount, at least partially, the powerful norm of noninterference. As with the exchange scale, grandparents who had very frequent contact with the study child or who were younger reported greater amounts of parentlike behavior. In addition, however, race had a strong effect that was not present for the exchange scale: controlling for other effects—including education and income—using the statistical technique of multiple regression, Blacks scored one point higher on this five-point scale than did Whites. It appears that Black grandparents—particularly Black grandmothers—retain more authority over the rearing of their grandchildren. Furthermore, grandparents of study children not living with two biological parents scored 0.4 points higher, other things being equal, as they filled the vacuum left by the absence of a parent. And as with exchange, social class made little difference.

STYLES OF GRANDPARENTING

These two activity scales demonstrate the kinds of activities that some, but not all, of the grandparents in our sample did with the study children. Our analyses of the correlates of these scales suggested that frequent, or at least regular, contact was a critical determinant of the level of activity. In this section, we combine information from the two scales and from the question about contact ("In the past 12 months, about how often have you seen the child?") to identify the different styles of grandparenting that appear among the grandparents in our sample. Any such classification is somewhat arbitrary; the reader should view the categories given below as illustrative and the percentages as approximations. Moreover, as our discussion of selective investment will show, it is likely that a grandparent can follow different styles with different grandchildren. Still, our telephone survey and follow-up interviews lead us to believe that the styles listed below capture meaningful differences in the ways the grandparents interacted with the study children.

To classify the grandparents according to style, we first divided the scores on each scale into two parts: scores of zero, one, two, or three on the scale of parentlike influence were considered "low"; scores of four or five were considered "high." On the exchange scale, scores of zero, one, or two were considered "low," and scores of three or four were considered "high." Thus, in order to score high on either scale, a grandparent had to respond positively to most of the relevant questions; this rather stringent rule reflected our impression that some grandparents tended to exaggerate the amount of exchange or influence they experienced. We also classified all grandparents according to whether they saw the study child at least once or twice a month versus less often.

On the basis of these distinctions we divided the grandparents into three groups. The "detached" grandparents were those who scored low on both scales and had seen the study child less than once or twice a month over the previous 12 months. The "passive" grandparents were those who scored low on both scales but had seen the child at least once or twice a month. And the "active" grandparents were those who scored high on one or both scales, regardless of how often they had seen the study child.

The percentage of grandparents who were categorized in each of these three groups were as follows: detached, 26 percent; passive, 29 percent; and active, 45 percent. The distinction between detached and passive grandparents seemed critical to us for, as we will illustrate below, some inactive grandparents had only a fleeting, ritual relationship with the study children's daily lives. As we mentioned above, the percentages shouldn't be taken too literally, but they do suggest that roughly one-fourth of the grandparents were detached, one-fourth were passive, and half were active.

The active category, in turn, can be decomposed into three sub-groups. Those who scored high only on the exchange scale we will call "supportive"; those who scored high only on the scale of parentlike influence will be called "authoritative"; and those who scored high on both scales will be called "influential." This further breakdown leads to the following distribution of our sample: detached, 26; passive, 29; supportive, 17; authoritative, 9; and influential, 19.

Thus, we have categorized the grandparents as having one of five styles of grandparenting. As Panel A of Table 6.1 shows, the detached and passive grandparents were substantially older than other grandparents and the influential grandparents were substantially younger, suggesting that the aging process may have determined, in part, the levels of activity. Panels B and C of Table 6.1 reveal that the detached grandparents had much lower levels of contact with the study child (a fact that follows from the definition of this category) and lived much farther away—63 percent lived more than 100 miles away. Thus, a clear majority of the detached grandparents faced a strong geographical barrier to a more active role—and yet 15 percent lived within 10 miles of the study child. About half of the passive, supportive, and authoritative grandparents had seen the study child once a week or more during the previous 12 months. It would seem, then, that moderate frequency of visiting is compatible with a passive style or a moderately active one.

The influential grandparents had much higher frequencies of visiting and lived much closer—15 percent, in fact, lived in the same households with study children. The influential style, as might be expected from the previous analyses of the two scales, is closely tied to very frequent, almost daily contact. As for family-oriented values, the detached grandparents scored sharply lower on a scale that measured family rituals ("In your family, are there special family recipes or dishes? Are there family jokes, common expressions, or songs? Are there ritual or special events that bring the family together?"), although even among this remote group most were able to acknowledge some family rituals.

How these differences affected the relationship with the study child is suggested in Panel E in Table 6.1, where the answers are displayed to the question, "Is your relationship with the (study child) extremely close, quite close, fairly close, or not very close?" Given the widespread norm in our society that family relationships should be close, it was difficult for a grandparent to admit to an interviewer that her relationship with a

TABLE 6.1
Percentage of Selected Characteristics of Grandparents by Style of Grandparenting

	Detached	Passive	Supportive	Authoritative	Influential
A. Age of grandparent:					
Under 65	30	33	44	44	58
65 or older	70	67	56	56	42
B. Frequency of visits with study child					
Once per week or more	0	49	54	51	80
Less than once per week	100	51	46	49	20
C. How far away study child lives:					
Co-reside	0	1[a]	5	4[b]	15[a]
0-10 miles	15	66	56	42	57
11-100 miles	22	31	21	25	17
More than 100 miles	63	3	18	28	12
D. Score on family ritual scale:					
0-1 (low)	28	16	19	15	11
2-3 (high)	72	84	81	85	89
E. Closeness to study child:					
Is your relationship to the child:					
Extremely close or quite close?	62	74	82	80	90
Fairly close, or not very close?	38	26	18	20	10
Weighted n	(160)	(182)	(109)	(57)	(118)

NOTE: p < .05 for Chi-squared values.
a. Total adds up to 101%.
b. Total adds up to 99%.

grandchild was not close. Thus, even among the detached, a majority responded "extremely close or quite close." But a clear trend still emerged: The detached grandparents were most likely to admit to a "fairly close or not very close" relationship; the passive grandparents were next most likely; the moderately active (supportive and authoritative) less likely; and the influential grandparents least likely of all.

There were no systematic differences in style according to educational attainment, consistent with the low to modest effect of social class we have noted above. But there were sharp racial differences: Of Black grandparents, 63 percent were either authoritative or influential—two styles in which grandparents retained substantial parentlike authority—compared to 26 percent of Whites and 33 percent of other Nonwhites. Only 8 percent of the Black grandparents were classified as passive. Part of this retention of authority, which is extraordinary given the strength of the norm of noninterference elsewhere, can be explained by the higher prevalence of single-parent families among Blacks. In these families grandparents are often called upon to take on a pseudo-parental role. But even among Black grandparents whose grandchildren were living with two biological parents, a majority were classified as authoritative or influential. These differences provide further evidence of the prevalence of strong Black grandparents (especially grandmothers) who play a major role in their children's and grandchildren's lives.

There were more modest sex differences in style. Grandfathers were more likely to be classified as supportive or authoritative and less likely to be detached or passive. This may reflect typically male patterns of relating to family members. But given the small number of grandfathers we were able to interview, we cannot rule out the possibility that the less active grandfathers were less willing to grant an interview, which would bias our sample toward the more active ones.

SOME EXAMPLES

THE DETACHED GRANDPARENT

Mrs. Myers, a recently widowed middle-class woman, lives in a northeastern city. While raising her four daughters, she urged them to be self-sufficient and independent in case they were faced with crises such as the death of a husband or a divorce. But partly because of these values, she seems to have created an emotional distance between herself and her children and grandchildren. The last time Mrs. Myers saw any of her nine grandchildren was at Thanksgiving, three and a half months prior to the interview. Three of her daughters (and four of the grandchildren) live out of state. The fourth daughter, the mother of the study child Jessica, 18, and four other children, lives only about 15 miles away; but Mrs. Myers reported that she saw Jessica less than once every two or three months during the previous year. Mrs. Myers feels she has a "nice relationship" with her daughters, but she said "I don't think they tell me everything when there are real problems. . . . Sometimes I bite the end of my tongue off to keep from asking questions." As for Jessica and her other grandchildren, she said, "I don't feel real, real close with any of them. . . . Maybe I haven't handled Jessica the way I should have. . . . I should have made more time for her in my life." When asked what it has meant to her to be a grandmother, Mrs. Myers replied in formal, unemotional terms:

> Well, I'm grateful that I've lived long enough to see the children. And I'm grateful that my children are carrying out the principles, the goals, the ideals that I wanted to put into them. And I hope that my grandchildren put it into their children. You know, to lead the good life, be educated, and to continue your education long after you get out of school.

It seems clear that Mrs. Myers is a remote figure in her grandchildren's lives, much to her current regret. Her parting words to the interviewer were, "If you think of any way to help me deal with my granddaughter, please let me know."

THE PASSIVE GRANDPARENT

Mr. and Mrs. Schmidt live on a farm in a northeastern state; they have three children, nine grandchildren, and three great-grandchildren, most of whom live nearby. Years ago, Mrs. Schmidt's daughter Janice was seriously ill and Mrs. Schmidt kept Janice's daughter Vera, the study child, for months at a time. Now, she sees Vera, 14, once or twice a month. The last time the Schmidts had seen any of their grandchildren was three days prior to the interview. Despite the proximity of their extended family and the regular contact, the Schmidts are careful to keep their distance from their children's and grandchildren's lives. Mr. Schmidt explained:

> Sure, we appreciate our grandchildren, and we do anything we can to help them along, and things like that. But we don't, possibly like some people, some people I think go overboard, maybe they do too much for their grandchildren and things like this. I think they ought to be a little bit left on their own. . . . I don't think the grandparents should interfere with the parents.

The interviewer read the following story to all the grandparents in our follow-up interviews, and Mrs. Schmidt's response shows how she takes whatever interaction she can get but doesn't press for more:

> *Interviewer:* Here's an account of some situations that happen to grand-parents, and I'd just like to read them to you and get your reaction. . . . Mrs. Smith lives a half-hour's drive from her son, daughter-in-law, and two grandchildren. Mrs. Smith is unhappy because she doesn't get to see the grandchildren as much as she would like. Sometimes a few weeks go by between visits. She realizes that both her son and her daughter-in-law work full time and that the grandchildren are busy with school activities. But she thinks they could make more of an effort to see her. What, if anything, should she do about it?
>
> *Mrs. Schmidt:* [laughter] We run through that right now. All the kids is into everything, you know? Like I was always used to being by myself so much, that if they can come it's all right, and if they can't, they have to live their lives.

There is even some suggestion that the Schmidts might feel a bit bur-dened by all their grandchildren and the responsibilities they entail.

> *Interviewer:* So, are there any other thoughts you have about being a grandmother that I didn't ask you?
>
> *Mrs. Schmidt:* I don't know what. I'm just getting too many to keep track of. They're nice to have and so on, but I said when Christmas time come, what in the world are you supposed to do?

Mrs. Schmidt's remark, even though said partly in jest, suggests some ambivalence about her relationships with her grandchildren. But for many grandparents, probably including the Schmidts, the passive style is seen as rewarding and proper. Some passive grandparents even have very high levels of contact with their grandchildren and seem quite pleased with the relationships. Consider Mrs. Waters, who lives in a suburb of a Midwestern city. She lives three houses away from her daughter and four children, one of whom is the 15-year old study child, Linda. Years earlier Linda and her mother had lived with Mrs. Waters for two years after the mother's divorce. Mrs. Waters says she is "extremely close" to Linda, whom she now sees three or four times a week. Yet her visits with Linda are brief, often momentary, as when Mrs. Waters stops by her daughter's house and Linda is going in or out. Linda, who Mrs. Waters says is "very, very busy," never calls her grandmother, nor do they sit down and talk very often. Mrs. Waters explains this as normal behavior for a teenager. She doesn't expect more, and she is satisfied with her relationship with Linda and her older sister Rachel, 18. Although Mrs. Waters speaks wistfully of the time when the grandchildren were younger and would stay overnight at her home or need help with homework, she accepts the fact that those days are over because the grandchildren are older: "Now that's gone because here's Rachel, she's 18 years old; who wants to go and stay with their grandmother at 18 years old [laughter]?" Still, Mrs. Waters derives great satisfaction from her past and present involvement with them. Being a grandmother, she says, has been "a terrific thing. These children have been my life."

THE INFLUENTIAL GRANDPARENT

Mr. Sampson, who has been a widower for 20 years, lives in a middle-class neighborhood of a northeastern city. His grandchild Bob, the study child, has recently gone off to college. Bob and his family live just a half-block away. Before Bob left for college, Mr. Sampson typically saw him two or three times a week.

Interviewer: How do you (and Bob) usually spend time?

Mr. Sampson: Mostly just talk. Unless there's something we wanted to fix up and all. . . . And if he has some problem, he'll come over to see me. . . . And if I need some help, like getting some screens down for putting screens in for the summer, I'll get him to help me bring those down. . . .

You know, we used to take tremendous numbers of trips together and things. I've had him up into Canada, I've had him down in Florida, I've had him out at the lake.

Mr. Sampson pointed out that he had a lot of time to spend with his grandchildren because he was widowed. He gives Bob advice, "like about his relationship in college, that he's going to watch smoking and dope and stuff like that." And if any of his grandchildren do something he disapproves of, "I will very nicely tell them I don't think it's right. And they have never resented that too much on anything." When an interviewer read Mr. Sampson the story about the grandparent who is unhappy because he doesn't get to see enough of the grandchildren, Mr. Sampson, in contrast to most passive grandparents, suggested that the grandparent in the story probably could make more of an effort to go see her grandchildren.

But even influential grandparents must modify their relationships as the grandchildren grow up. Mr. Sampson was well aware that Bob was becoming an adult, and he seemed to have come to terms with the impending change this would bring to their relationship. When asked what it meant to him to be a grandfather, he replied:

I would hate like thunder not to be one. . . . No, to me it is really part of my life and I would miss a terrible lot of activity, a terrible lot of pleasure and everything else if I did not have grandchildren. . . . All the trips we used to take, it was fun for me, I enjoyed it. . . . I wanted to do it. . . . And I would miss that if it weren't. Of course, I'm missing it now, but I realize that I can't keep up this activity because they have their own lives to lead. And I think that's one thing, grandparents sometimes make a slip on that: they don't realize that the kids are growing up. You've got your own life to live, I don't care what it is. I've lived mine, they've got theirs coming up. Of course I may miss it; I do. I miss the boy because he's away, I don't see him. On the other hand, to help that I get into a tremendous amount of activities of my own.

A minority of the influential grandparents (15 percent) were living with the study child, often after their daughters' marriages broke up. These grandparents typically took on the role of a surrogate parent—an intense, rewarding experience, to judge from the interviews, but one that also could be burdensome. When asked what it was like to live with your grandchildren, one grandmother replied, "Well, it's heaven and a hassle, I guess you'd put it." Mrs. Williamson, a 63-year-old Black grandmother from a southern city who lived with her daughter and her granddaughter Susan, 16, described a typical day:

> In the morning, Susan's mom is the first to leave the house. . . . Sometimes she will wake Susan up before leaving. If not, she will say, "Mom, don't forget to wake Susan up!" So I will make sure that Susan is up. I prepare Susan's breakfast. Mornings that I have to be at work by eight o'clock, I will leave Susan here; she knows what time she is to catch her bus. . . . When we come in in the evening. . . . Susan usually gets in about ten minutes 'till four. Her mom and I get in about four thirty. . . . I prepare all of the meals. . . . I am the one that will insist that [Susan] eat a good meal, take your vitamin. Susan will do the dishes. Then, after that, there's a period of looking at television, then Susan will get into her books. And she is going to finish that homework before going to bed.

Susan, Mrs. Williamson says, "will ask my opinion quite often before asking her mom's." Being a grandparent is "wonderful," Mrs. Williamson told the interviewer, and there were no disadvantages she could think of to having her granddaughter live with her.

STRATEGIES OF GRANDPARENTING: SELECTIVE INVESTMENT

So far we have examined the relationships between the grandparents and one particular grandchild. Some of the grandparents saw the study child frequently, exchanged services, gave advice, and, in general, seemed to have established intense, warm relationships with the study child. But what about the other grandparents—largely those from the detached or passive groups? Was their greater emotional (and often geographical) distance from the study child typical of their relations with their other grandchildren, or did they have close ties to others? Through design or circumstance, did they evolve strategies to compensate for the weak ties to the study child?

We asked the grandparents, "When was the last time you saw any grandchild?" (Grandparents who lived with the study child were automatically classified as having seen a grandchild "today.") The detached grandparents were much less likely to have seen any grandchild recently than the other grandparents: Half had last seen one a week or more ago; about one-fourth had last seen one a month or more ago. Yet detached grandparents had more grandchildren (12), on average, then did the typical grandparent in the sample (11). Some detached grandparents, then, appeared to be isolated from all of their grandchildren. But others were not: More than a third of the detached grandparents (who, by definition had infreqeunt contact with the study child) had seen a grandchild that day or the previous day.

Consider Mrs. Grant, a "detached" grandparent who lives in a northeastern city. She doesn't get along well with her daughter-in-law, who is the mother of two of her grandchildren, William, 16, and the study child, Delia, 13. Although she lives only a short drive away, Mrs. Grant rarely see Delia, who she describes as close to her mother. She told the interviewer that her relationship with Delia was "not very close." Yet Mrs. Grant sees Delia's older brother William much more often. She feels protective toward him, for he "has always been very, well, he was what you'd call one of those nervous-type babies. I went up and stayed with [the mother] after he was born." Even now, she says, William "gets on his mother's nerves." So Mrs. Grant took a particular interest in him; and now, she says, "he just loves to come here and be with his grandparents." In fact, William wants to attend the local university and live with his grandparents. Mrs. Grant is pleased but torn by this request. She's 72, her health is not great, and she said, "I'm just not up to that responsibility." Thus, although Mrs. Grant may be detached from Delia, she is much more actively involved in William's life. Being a grandmother has its rewards for Mrs. Grant, but the stress of her relationship with her daughter-in-law has taken its toll. "It's just not worth being a grandmother if you have to go through all this hullaballoo, you know. . . . I get a bit fed up."

Nevertheless, Mrs. Grant's situation shows that grandparents often turn their attention toward particular grandchildren in order to compensate for unsatisfactory relationships with others. We asked the grandparents the following question: "It's not unusual for grandparents to like some grandchildren more than others. Do you have a favorite grandchild?" We felt it would be difficult for grandparents to admit to playing favorites; most prefer to say "I love them all." Yet 30 percent were willing to admit that they had a favorite. (In Mrs. Grant's case, it was William.)

Take, for example, Mrs. Sabatino, who lives in a suburb of a midwestern city. She was classified as a "supportive" grandmother on the basis of her telephone interview, but probing during the follow-up interview suggested that the help was slim—"passive" probably would be the more accurate classification. "I really can't say we do things for him," she said of the study child Christopher, nor could she cite much that Christopher had done for her. She sees him once or twice a month, but when asked whether she felt close to him, she replied, "No, not really, I mean we see him a lot, but not as close as maybe some people would be to their grandson."

However, Mrs. Sabatino does have a favorite: her granddaughter, Nora, 23. Nora, her first grandchild, spent a lot of time at her grandmother's home when she was young. Then Nora's father died. Mrs. Sabatino helped Nora adjust to the loss, and they have remained close ever since. According to Mrs. Sabatino, "We have a very special relationship." This close tie to one grandchild seems sufficient for Mrs. Sabatino; it allows her to think of herself as a person who has good relationships with her grandchildren. When she was read the story about the grandparent who was unhappy because she didn't get to see the grandchildren as much as she would like, Mrs. Sabatino responded:

> I don't think there's really much that she can do. She should just wait and see when they can see her. . . . But I don't think she should feel, if she has a good relationship with the whole family, I don't think she should feel hurt.
>
> *Interviewer:* So you would advise her to . . .
>
> Just see them whenever she could and be content.

Mrs. Sabatino, it seems clear, thinks of herself as someone with a good relationship with her whole family. Her strategy of grandparenting seems to be to maintain at least one very close relationship and accept the lack of other close relationships—as with Christopher—as nothing personal. This allows her to express considerable satisfaction about being a grandmother:

> For one thing, I know it's the continuity of the family going on. And it's somebody to love, somebody that comes to see you and that you go to see. And I think it makes you feel that you're not really getting that old.

Thus, it appears to us that many grandparents invest more heavily in their relationships with some grandchildren than with others. There are many reasons why selective investment may be common: Some grandchildren may live closer, some may have parents who get along better with the grandparent, or some may be more in need of help because of a family crisis. Moreover, some may just be more appealing to the grandparent because they are the first born, the last born, or the most outgoing. Consequently, the payoff is likely to be greater for investment in some grandchildren than in others. Often, we suspect, a close tie to one or two grandchildren, coupled with a more distant, ritualistic relationship with the rest, may be sufficient to make grandparents satisfied with their role. They may generalize to all their grandchildren their satisfaction with their relationships with their favorites. Thus, it may not be necessary for grandparents to have equally intense ties to all grandchildren in order to feel good about being a grandparent. Furthermore, equally intense relationships might even be burdensome for an older person with lots of grandchildren. Consciously or not, then, some grandparents have evolved a strategy of selective investment in which a few close ties to grandchildren suffice—in which the part substitutes adequately for the whole.

Given the flexible nature of the American kinship system, grandparents often can choose the grandchildren to whom they pay more attention and can change loyalties as they and their grandchildren age or change places of residence. To be sure, there are constraints on their ability to choose: geographical distance, poor relationships with the middle generation, the limited number of grandchildren they may have, and so forth. Still, this strategy of selective investment fulfills the function of allowing older persons to act as grandparents and to feel as though being a grandparent is an important part of their lives. It may also give grandchildren, who may not have close relations with both sets of grandparents, a better opportunity to experience intense ties to at least one grandparent.

Within families, then, all grandparent-grandchild relations are not equally close, despite the oft-repeated (and usually true) statements of grandparents that they love all their grandchildren. Instead, one often finds wide differences in the strength of the grandparent-grandchild bond, differences that appear to serve the needs of both grandparents and grandchildren to have meaningful, intense relationships with at least some members of the opposite generation.

CONCLUSION

That there is no single, dominant style of grandparenting is clear from our sample of grandparents. At one extreme are the "detached" grandparents, as we have labeled them. Some of them seem to be remote from all their grandchildren—truly distant figures for whom intergenerational ties, by choice or circumstance, play a small role in life. Older, less imbued with familistic values, perhaps far removed geographically, or emotionally estranged from their children, these people are grandparents only in a symbolic sense. They are recognized by kin and friends as grandparents, but they do little more than fill slots in a geneology. Other grandparents, however, are detached from some but not all of their grandchildren. They may have little to do with the teenager in our study, but they have regular, rewarding contact with other grandchildren. Having adopted a strategy we labeled "selective investment," they focus their efforts and emotions on one or more of the grandchildren who live nearby or are especially personable or in need of help. In this way, they are able to act as grandparents and to compensate for weak ties to other kin.

Thus, a grandparent can be simultaneously detached and involved. Mrs. James, for example, who lives in a northeastern city, has nine children and 40 grandchildren. With such a large family, she can compensate for relationships that are dormant. She sees little of the study child, Henry, who lives with one of her daughters about 20 miles away; but she resides with another daughter and her children, with whom she is deeply involved. Personality differences and geographical mobility constrain the choices of grandparents like Mrs. James concerning involvement with kin. But the flexibility of American kinship patterns allows grandparents like her to selectively take on the grandparent role when and where they can. Grandparents often cannot manage an active, involved role with all of their grandchildren, but in our society they need not do so in order to regard themselves—and to be regarded by others—as "good" or "normal" grandparents. They can achieve the status of grandparenthood by investing in a small proportion of the possible kin ties open to them.

The "passive" grandparents we identified differ from the detached grandparents by their regular contact with the study children. Despite their inactivity, they may serve useful functions merely by being around. They may, for instance, be the "family watchdogs," in Troll's (1983) phrase, who stand ready to offer assistance when needed but otherwise are loath to interfere in the raising of the grandchildren. Most passive grandparents, we believe, derive substantial satisfaction from their relationships with their grandchildren. They consider the regular but often superficial contact with their teenaged grandchildren to be acceptable, proper, and unavoidable given the nature of adolescence. Although they may be nostalgic for the days when the grandchildren were younger, they also can derive satisfaction from watching them mature. Some of the passive grandparents in our study selectively invested in other grandchildren to compensate for the increasing independence of the teenaged study child. The passive grandparents, we submit, best fit the popular image of American grandparents: the loving older person who sees the grandchildren fairly often, is ready to provide help in a crisis, but under normal circumstance leaves parenting strictly to the parent.

We found other grandparents who take on more active roles. They exchange services with the teenaged grandchildren or, in some cases, advise, discipline, and even help rear them. At the extreme are the "influential" grandparents, who see the grandchildren quite often and are major figures in the grandchildren's day-to-day lives. The influential grandparents are younger and perhaps therefore more energetic; and they tend to have a familistic value orientation. But the key prerequisite for this style of grandparenting is frequent, almost daily contact with the grandchildren. Indeed, a sizable minority of the influential grandparents resided in the same home with the study children, where they often took on a pseudo-parental role. It is therefore a style that is not open to the large number of grandparents who cannot—because of distance, health, or poor relations with the middle generation—visit so regularly. It is a style that seems to be quite rewarding—90 percent of these grandparents reported that they were "extremely close or quite close" to the study children. But it also can exact costs: It demands a great commitment of time, energy, and sometimes money. It is a style that we often celebrate and mythologize (as if it were the common arrangement in some bygone era—an unproven assertion); but it can be both a joy and a burden for the grandparents involved—"heaven and a hassle," as one grandparent said. On balance, though, we received the impression that the heavenly aspects outweighed the hassle for most of the influential grandparents in our sample.

We found litle evidence that social class made a difference in grandparenting styles. Black grandmothers were much more likely to retain some authority over the rearing of the grandchildren. We say grandmothers rather than grandparents because we were not able to talk to many Black grandfathers. (Of our 51 interviews with Black grandparents, 44 were with grandmothers. Our lack of success in gaining interview access to Black men may be an indicator of their lesser role.) As mentioned above, the authority of Black grandmothers holds up nearly as well when the grandchildren are in two-parent homes as compared to one-parent homes. From our follow-up interviews, as well as from some preliminary interviews at a predominantly Black senior citizen's center in Baltimore, we received the impression that a strong grandmother is an accepted part of Black family patterns. Perhaps this role dates back to family disruptions during slavery or perhaps it is a more recent reaction to high rates of marital disruption or to the difficult economic position of Black men. Regardless, the Black grandmothers with whom we spoke often evinced a degree of authority, intensity, and warmth that made manifest their central roles in their children's and grandchildren's lives.

Although our study focused on grandparents with teenaged grandchildren, we were able to present evidence suggesting that the grandparental role changes as grandparents and grandchildren age. There is, then, a life course of grandparenting, although this life course can follow several diverse patterns. Early on, some grandparents offer substantial assistance in the form of baby-sitting, gifts, or even coresidence, and they seek leisure-oriented fun from their young grandchildren. The pattern of assistance continues for some, although it is transformed from baby-sitting to direct exchanges of services with the grandchildren. As grandchildren enter adolescence, the "fun seeking" style seems to fade. It can be superceded by mutual assistance, advice-giving, and discussions of problems; or it can be superseded by a passive style in which the grandparent still sees the teenaged grandchildren regularly but is increasingly removed from their world. And as the grandchildren enter adulthood, the grandparents prepare to let go of the relationship, just as parents do. Perhaps the relationship is strengthened again when the grandchildren marry and renew the cycle by producing great-grandchildren.

The styles and strategies we have described in this chapter show the kinds of relationships that emerge when the grandchildren are adolescents. There has been speculation that this lifecycle stage is a low-point in grandparent-grandchild relations. Perhaps so. But we found some grandparents who were deeply involved with their adolescent grandchildren and many others who, though passive in style, derived substantial satisfaction from being around to watch their grandchildren grow up.

7

PARENT-ADULT CHILD RELATIONS AS AFFECTED BY THE GRANDPARENT STATUS

Joan Aldous

There is currently an upsurge in interest in the grandparent status among both social scientists and social critics. A popular book has come out on the topic (Kornhaber & Woodward, 1981), and the results of several studies of grandparent-grandchild contacts are beginning to appear (see chapters by Johnson and Cherlin and Furstenberg, this volume). Until now, the literature has been fairly meager, focusing primarily on the characteristics of the grandparent status (Kahana & Kahana, 1971). It includes Neugarten and Weinstein's (1964) work on styles of grandparenting as well as reports of the relative importance of the grandparent roles in life satisfaction as compared with other roles (Blau, 1973; Kivnick, 1982; Robertson, 1977; Wood & Robertson, 1976).

The question, therefore, arises as to why this current interest in grandparenthood exists. It is true that demographic changes have allowed people more years to occupy the grandparental status and its attached roles (Uhlenberg, 1983). Moreover, with many people retiring at age 65, they have more leisure time to enjoy being grandparents. Thus, without much fanfare, grandparents and grandchildren have more time to enjoy each other than does the middle-parent generation. The customary absence of responsibilities that grandparents and grandchildren have with respect to each other also encourages an intrinsic pleasure in the relation, further strengthened by blood ties.

Author's Note: *This research was funded by the National Institute of Aging grant 12938. Rodney Ganey provided valuable statistical advice. This is a revision of a paper presented at the Wingspread Conference on Grandparenting and Family Connections. I wish to thank David Klein, the co-principal investigator in this project, for the use of the data, and Michael Weldh and Elizabeth Klaus for their suggestions concerning an earlier draft.*

NO POSTPARENTAL PERIOD

But today's high divorce rates probably have more to do with the increased attention to grandparents than either longevity or "leisure years" factors. Troll (1983) has labeled grandparents "family watchdogs" because they step in to help the children and grandchildren when they are in trouble. Parents serve as guardians of their children's welfare while the latter are under their roofs. Even when children leave home to establish financial independence and to form their own families, this parental solicitude does not stop. The term, "postparental stage," therefore, is a misnomer, because parents do not move out of the parental status and its cares with the departure of adult children from home. And unlike watchdogs, parents do not limit their concern to raising an alarm. When trouble comes, they are affected not only emotionally, but they attempt to lessen it for both their children and their grandchildren. Trouble often comes as a break-up in the grandchildren's families due to the divorce of their parents. Social critics (Kornhaber & Woodward, 1981) and lay persons alike perceive family elders as being able to take over the child care, confidant, and financial agent roles the absent spouse customarily played.

Given these functions of grandparents in a time of prevalent divorce, grandparenthood—always sentimentalized—may now be taking on the "blowsy piety" Featherstone (1979) previously associated with the family. Social critics along with "media" people appear to be assigning grandparents the responsibility for maintaining intergenerational family continuity that the middle generation cannot be counted on to do. The grandparents are to maintain the generational integrity of the family because of their concern for each succeeding link. A commendable concern for the well-being of children among some of these persons is linked to their holding such traditional values as women's primary responsiblity to care for the young. This value, of course, is consistent with grandparents' behavior. As Johnson's and Cherlin and Furstenberg's studies, summarized in this volume, show, it is grandmothers and not grandfathers who tend the cross-generation ties.

But now, older women are active in other roles. Two-fifths—44.1 percent of women 55 to 64 years (Fullerton, 1982)—are in the labor market. Some have children still at home or elderly parents needing assistance. (The latter was true of a fourth of Johnson's San Francisco Bay grandmothers.) Others are relishing the freedom from having children at home, enabling them to spend more time with their husbands. Women can find the loyalties associated with being wives, mothers, and children competing with the demands of grandparent roles. They may, consequently, show little preference for these roles when grandchildren are not in difficulty.

If this is the situation, there will be variation, depending upon the marital and parental statuses of their children, in how active incumbents are in the status of grandparent. It may well be that the sentimental picture of parents being more attached to families of adult children who are themselves parents is incorrect. Only if these families are broken will the parents devote more attention to them.

INTERGENERATIONAL CONTACTS
AND THE GRANDPARENT STATUS

Research that has been done on intergenerational relationships has consistently shown that geographical proximity and female gender of child are related to more frequent contacts between parents and their adult children who have left home (Adams, 1968; Aldous, 1967; Lee, 1980). But there is little material on how the marital and parental status of the adult children affect contacts with their parents. One study using a national sample of children showed more involvement of the grandparents when the children's parents were divorced, suggesting closer parent-adult child ties under these circumstances. The grandchildren were more likely to be living with grandparents following divorce and, in all cases, the latter were engaged in more child care and other services for the child (Cherlin and Furstenberg, this volume).

Such a finding is consistent with custodial parents' needs. These parents, usually mothers, are busy attempting to earn a living. They need the help of their parents for the nurturance services they cannot afford to give to children in monetary or temporal terms. Thus, the marital status of the middle generation, the grandparents' adult children—not necessarily the presence of grandchildren—may determine the emotional and contact closeness of the oldest and middle generations, as well as the oldest and the youngest generations. Whether or not ever-married adult children who are themselves parents are divorced becomes central in determining the importance of the grandparent status.

It is necessary, however, to disentangle the effects of marital and parenthood status of adult children on their ties to their parents. During the postdivorce adjustment period, the divorced childless may be more needy of parental emotional support than the divorced with children. The latter's children can return love as well as receive it from divorced parents. The divorced with children, however, require instrumental and financial assistance to keep their households organized. Parents, therefore, may have to be in more frequent contact with their divorced children regardless of their parental status than with their other adult children, even if these other children are parents. Thus, after remarriage when the formerly divorced are less needy of attention, extra parental solicitude, according to this argument, should not continue.

If we look more closely at the notion of the grandparent generation as guarding the welfare of their descendants, however, it is also necessary to take into account never-married children. Presumably younger and not yet established in occupational and spousal or parental roles, the never-married may well need special attention. This could include parents' financial aid due to the job inadequacies of the never-married and parents' emotional support while the latter look for a lasting intimate relationship. To examine fully how the marital status of adult children affects parents' contacts with them, therefore, we need to include never-married children in any study.

The following hypothesis seems to be in agreement with the available literature on the relations of parents and their ever-married children. If divorced adult children have children, parents will show preference for them with respect to contacts. There is little available data, however, to provide the basis for hypothesis concerning how marital status along with parental status in the younger generation affects intergenerational relations. The neediness of adult children, as indicated by their marital and parental statuses, rather than the children's parental status itself, is hypothesized to determine parents' attention.

STUDY DESIGN

This study looks at the grandparent status through an investigation of the relation of aging parents and their adult children. If this status is a central one to aging parents, it should be a major factor influencing intergenerational contacts. After all, the frequency of contacts and to a certain extent their quality between grandparents and grandchildren—particularly young grandchildren—depends upon the mediation of the parents (Hagestad, 1981, p. 36). To examine what part grandparent roles play in parent-adult child contacts, we have data on the contacts parents in the middle sixties had with their adult children who had left home. Consistent with the rationale discussed above, these couples' adult children were divided for comparison purposes into the never-married, the childless married, the married with children, the remarried with children, the childless divorced, and the divorced with children.[1] Thus, analyses of the influence of marital as well as parenthood statuses on intergenerational activities are possible.

The data come from a larger study on kinship interaction and family size. As a result, the sample was drawn from a population where there was a greater probability of larger families being located than would be the case with a sample from the general population. The sample consisted of married fathers who had graduated from a large Catholic university in the years between 1936 and 1940 and lived in five midwestern SMSAs. The men were asked to participate, along with their wives, in an interview study.[2] The number of children in the 124 families sampled ranged from one to 11, with an average family size of just over six persons. The fathers had a median age of 64 and the mothers had a median age of 62. Professional, technical, or managerial occupations were common among the men with over 75 percent of those who were still employed holding jobs of this sort. Almost one-third of the fathers had already retired, but bivariate correlations analysis did not reveal significantly different findings for the two groups of employed or retired husbands/fathers. These parents were still young enough to be in reasonably good health and to have sufficient financial resources. Thus, the intergenerational contacts that did occur were relatively voluntary, and the effect of grandparenthood was not confounded with these other factors. Of the 124 couples, 28 percent (34) still had children at home, and in an equal number of couples one or both spouses had living parents. Some of the sample, therefore, were still involved in parenting and being adult children at the same time they were grandparents.

The "launched" children averaged just over 30 years of age. Ten percent of the 330 children ever-married had experienced divorce. Although the currently divorced groups with or without children (13 and 10, respectively) and the remarried with children (10 in number) were small, they can provide illustrative findings about the effects of children's marital and parental status on ties to their parents.[3]

Husbands and wives were interviewed together about the kind and number of contacts they had with their children who had left home. Each spouse also separately completed a questionnaire designed to obtain information on sociometric issues, and on the different feelings of husbands and wives about the relationship with each of their children.

The indicators of intergenerational contacts follow: instrumental services—providing transportation, care during illness, help with housework, help with shopping, child care, gift giving or paying bills of $50 or less value, and gift giving or paying bills of over $50 value; emotional support—providing comfort, and writing letters or telephoning sociability contacts—informal home visits, getting together for the holidays, going out together, taking vacations together, and participating together in church or community activities. For these indicators, the data consist of frequencies of contacts initiated by parents and refer to the period of the previous 12 months.

Analysis of variance was used to compare the effects of marital and parenthood statuses of adult children on parent-child contacts. The design matrix included a blocking factor for family membership. This was done to take into account the presumed effect of family membership on children's behavior, where children from one family fell into different marital or parental categories. The design allowed for partitioning the effect of family membership from the total sums of squares and should result in a better estimate of the mean square error for the comparison of means (Box, Hunter, & Hunter, 1978, p. 208). The Scheffé test was selected for the comparison of means, because it holds the design error rate to the specified alpha level of .05 and is exact even for unequal group sizes.

FINDINGS

The findings support the study hypothesis that parents show greater solicitude for their divorced children who have children. The findings, however, also uphold the larger rationale that parents continue to serve as family guardians when children are grown, and the comparative needs of their children, as indicated by their marital and parenthood statuses, have much to do with attention parents give. Differences in geographical proximity do not explain these results, as the various categories of children all lived roughly the same distance from their parents.

As Table 7.1 shows, parents were more attentive to their never-married children's instrumental needs than to such needs among their married children with children. Parents were more apt to provide financial aid to their single children as well as to help them with transportation. Couples, however, were more likely to provide child care to grandchildren whose parents were divorced and not remarried than to those whose parents were married. Moreover, parents more often gave comfort to divorced, not remarried children with children and helped them with housework than was true in their contacts with the never-married or first-time married with or without children. There were generally no differences in the number of joint activities shared by parents and their children. These included informal home visits and getting together for holidays, occasions usually involving the youngest generation and so, presumably, of particular interest to couples with grandchildren. The remarried with children did go out more with their parents than did the married with children.

There was also some suggestion that the remarried with children initiated more contacts with their own parents. They provided more comfort to the couples in our study than did the divorced with or without children. The same group also helped out more in times of illness than did the never-married, the divorced with children and married children whether or not they had children. The never-married, however, did more housework for their parents than did the first-time married with children. In other contact areas, marital or parental status did not affect the younger generation's getting in touch with the older.

GENDER DIFFERENCES IN CONTACTS
WITH ADULT CHILDREN WHO HAVE CHILDREN

It might be argued that gender of child is a confounding factor in the findings. Perhaps the hypothesized greater intimacy of parents with children who have made them grandparents appears only among daughters. These children customarily remain in closer touch. To see if gender does have an effect on the findings, the marital status groups were differentiated according to gender. As would be expected on the

TABLE 7.1
Parent-Child Contacts by Children's Marital and Parenthood Status

	Group 1 Never Married N=115 $\bar{X}$	Group 2 Divorced Childless N=10 $\bar{X}$	Group 3 Divorced with Children N=13 $\bar{X}$	Group 4 Married Childless N=75 $\bar{X}$	Group 5 Married with Children N=222 $\bar{X}$	Group 6 Remarried with Children N=10 $\bar{X}$	Significant Differences Among Group
Parents to Child:							
Gifts, paying bills value $50 or less	5.09				2.91		1 over 5
Gifts, paying bills value more than $50	2.90				1.41		1 over 5
Transportation	11.22			1.07	2.86		1 over 4, 5
Housework	0.75		9.38	0.92	2.45		3 over 1, 4, 5
Child care	N/A	N/A	28.38	N/A	9.20	8.90	3 over 5, 6
Comfort giving	8.52		18.92	4.95	6.39		3 over 1, 4, 5
Child to parents:							
Care during illness	2.11		0.00	1.01	1.65	9.10	6 over 1, 3, 4, 5
Housework	10.97				4.03		1 over 5
Comfort giving		2.80	5.46			17.33	6 over 2, 3
Joint activities:							
Going out together					4.82	9.40	6 over 5

basis of previous research findings, parents and daughters do tend to be more involved in each others' lives than parents and sons. (There is no significant difference in the two gender's geographical proximity to their parents' residences.) Marital status of children, however, continues to make a difference, as Table 7.2 shows. Parents are most solicitous of their divorced daughters who have children. They help them significantly more with housework than they do with their first-time married sons and daughters with or without children. Child care is the other instrumental service they most often provide to divorced daughters with children. They favor them over first-time married sons and daughters with children and remarried sons with children. Parents also show concern for their never-married daughters, who receive more comfort than married, childless sons. The amount of comfort parents give divorced daughters, however, is significantly greater than the comfort they give the never-married, regardless of gender, and all other groups except divorced, childless sons and remarried daughters.

Never-married daughters, in turn, along with remarried daughters are most likely to give parents modest gifts or monetary aid, as compared with never-married sons and married sons with children. Remarried sons, however, are more active than never-married children and divorced or married children regardless of gender or parental status, with the exception of divorced, childless sons and remarried daughters in giving care during illness. When it comes to giving comfort to parents, married daughters who are childless are more assiduous than married sons who are childless. Married sons with children also give more comfort than the latter although somewhat less than childless, married daughters.

AGE OF GRANDMOTHER AS A DIFFERENTIATING FACTOR

Johnson (1983) found that younger grandmothers were more involved with their grandchildren whose parents were divorced and so, presumably, with their children. The greater energy and financial resources of these often employed grandmothers would seem to account for the findings. Thus, age of the older women may affect whether they differentiate contacts with children who are parents. In this study, the indicators are not categorized according to whether only one parent is

TABLE 7.2
Parent-Child Contacts by Children's Marital and Parenthood Status, and Gender

Contact Indicator	Group 1 Never Married Sons $N=65$ $\bar{X}$	Group 2 Never Married Daughters $N=50$ $\bar{X}$	Group 3 Divorced Childless Sons $N=4$ $\bar{X}$	Group 4 Divorced Childless Daughters $N=6$ $\bar{X}$	Group 5 Divorced Sons with Children $N=6$ $\bar{X}$	Group 6 Divorced Daughters with Children $N=7$ $\bar{X}$	Group 7 Married Childless Sons $N=36$ $\bar{X}$	Group 8 Married Childless Daughters $N=39$ $\bar{X}$	Group 9 Married Sons with Children $N=114$ $\bar{X}$	Group 10 Married Daughters with Children $N=108$ $\bar{X}$	Group 11 Remarried Sons with Children $N=6$ $\bar{X}$	Group 12 Remarried Daughters with Children $N=4$ $\bar{X}$	Significant Difference Among Groups
Parents to Child:													
Housework	0.40	1.20				15.14	0.94	0.90	2.35	2.56			6 over 1,2; 7-10
Child care	N/A	N/A	N/A	N/A		41.29	N/A	N/A	8.81	9.62	8.00		6 over 9-11
Comfort giving	5.82	12.04		5.67	4.50	31.29	2.06	7.62	4.74	8.09	1.20		6 over 1, 2, 4, 5, 7-11; 2 over 7
Child to Parents:													
Gifts, paying bills value $50 or less	2.63	4.46							2.66			7.75	12 over 1,9; 2 over 1,9
Care during illness	3.12	0.80		0.00	0.00	0.00	1.86	0.23	1.32	2.00	15.17		11 over 1,2, 4-10
Comfort giving							5.25	14.26	12.23				8 over 7; 9 over 7

involved. To see, however, if older age of wives modifies the findings, the sample was divided at the median age of the wives, 62 years of age.[4]

Although the Ns in the case of the divorced and remarried children are small, Table 7.3 indicates that where differences appear, couples with younger wives are more involved. Again, however, there is no indication that being able to play grandparent roles is a primary factor in keeping parents in contact with their adult children and, through them, with their grandchildren. There does continue to be greater intergenerational activity between parents and divorced children with children as compared to married children with children. When the activity involves instrumental services requiring physical effort, couples in which the wives are younger are generally more involved. This is true of parents helping out in times of illness and with child care.

It should not be overlooked, however, that couples in which wives are younger in some instances continue to favor their never-married children as compared with couples where wives are older who have married children with offspring. This was true of financial aid.

When it comes to children doing things for parents, couples in which the wife is young more often receive children's help. The never-married are more active in giving less costly financial aid and gifts than the married with children and older mothers. The married childless with younger mothers also are more active in this respect than either the never-married or the first-married groups with older mothers. The never-married with younger mothers also help more with housework than the married with children regardless of the age of the mothers. When they have younger mothers, the divorced childless are more active than the same group with older mothers and the never-married and the first-married with and without children and regardless of the age of the mothers in giving gifts or help involving more than $50. The first-married with children and younger mothers more often provided comfort than the never-married with older mothers. There were no differences, however, among the various groups of children in the joint sociability or participation measures.

DISCUSSION

The findings support the hypothesis that grandparents have more contact with adult children who are themselves parents, only when the

TABLE 7.3

Parent-Child Contacts by Children's Marital, Parenthood Status, and Age of Mothers

	Group 1 Never Married Mother Less Than 62 N = 68 $\bar{X}$	Group 2 Never Married Mother 62 or More N = 47 $\bar{X}$	Group 3 Divorced Childless Mother Less Than 62 N = 4 $\bar{X}$	Group 4 Divorced Childless Mother 62 or More N = 6 $\bar{X}$	Group 5 Divorced with Children Mother Less Than 62 N = 5 $\bar{X}$	Group 6 Divorced with Children Mother 62 or More N = 8 = $\bar{X}$	Group 7 Married Childless Mother Less Than 62 N = 40 $\bar{X}$	Group 8 Married Childless Mother 62 or More N = 35 $\bar{X}$	Group 9 Married with Children Mother Less Than 62 N = 79 $\bar{X}$	Group 10 Married with Children Mother 62 or More N = 143 $\bar{X}$	Group 11 Remarried with Children Mother Less Than 62 N = 2 $\bar{X}$	Group 12 Remarried with Children Mother 62 or More N = 8 = $\bar{X}$	Significant Difference Among Group Means
Contact Indicator													
Parents to Child:													
Gifts, paying bills value $50 or less	5.25												1 over 10
Gifts, paying bills value more than $50	3.49												1 over 10
Child care	N/A	N/A	N/A	N/A	47.80	16.25	N/A	N/A	15.61	5.66	2.50	10.50	5 over 6, 9-12
Care during illness	1.18	0.23			21.20		0.55	0.29	0.47	0.88			5 over 1,2,7,8,10
Child to Parents:													
Gifts, paying bills value $50 or less	4.00	2.60	4.00				5.18	2.49		2.50			1 over 10 / 7 over 2,8,10
Gifts, paying bills value more than $50	0.25	0.81		0.17			0.23	0.66	0.47	0.63			3 over 1,2,4,7-10
Care during illness	1.50						0.43	1.69	1.27	1.86		11.38	12 over 1,7,8,9,10
Housework	15.16								4.62	3.71			1 over 9,10
Comfort giving		6.13							13.53				9 over 2

latter are divorced. These findings also suggest that the encompassing rationale, the adult children's need for parental attention as reflected in their marital and parental statuses, is the explanation for intergenerational contacts. Whether or not currently married children are parents appears to make little difference in the frequency of intergenerational contacts. Couples are in touch with these adult children about the same amount whether or not the children had made the couples grandparents. That status in itself did not affect their involvement with their adult children. Thus, there is value in taking into account the marital and parental statuses of all adult children in research on intergenerational relations.

Complementing their parents' attention giving, comparative resources appear to determine the children's concern. Instrumental assistance is needed by never-married children who are more apt to be in the initial phase of occupational careers and have not yet assumed family responsibilities with the attendant emotional support. Financially less secure, these children benefit from parental monetary help and help in transportation. These children reciprocate when their mothers are younger with the primary resource they have, energy. They provide physical assistance with housework, and return the financial aid they receive with less costly attentions.

The divorced with children—although not those without—are the other group of adult children seeming to need parents to watch over them. This watchful care extends beyond providing housework and child care and includes giving support. Parents attempt to bolster their morale as well as to supply the day-to-day physical maintenance needs formerly met in the marital union.

Other children who have less need for their parents' attention have resources that they can give their parents. The remarried are a particularly interesting example of this. The study is not longitudinal and the number of cases is small. The findings, however, suggest that the divorced with children who are the particular recipients of their parents' concerns attempt to even the balance after being remarried. They are more apt to provide comfort than those who are in their first marriage with children. They also are more apt to take care of their parents when the latter are ill than all other groups except for the divorced childless. The remarried more often go out with their parents than do children with offspring who have been married only once.

The latter result is the only findings, whether controlling for gender of child or age of mother, where parents appear to differentiate in joint activities involving sociability according to marital or parental status of children. Such intergenerational activities that would be likely to involve the third generation—and so enable couples to play grandparenting roles—do not occur disproportionately. Thus, being a grandparent does not appear to favor get-togethers of parents and adult children who are themselves parents.

Other results are more consistent with current thinking. Daughters, to a greater degree than sons, are socialized to retain more intimate ties with parents. They are expected to go outside their own families of procreation for sympathy and understanding in times of joy and stress. This greater freedom to seek out emotional support and to show dependency is reflected in the present results, but is affected by marital status. Parents are more solicitous of their daughters who are divorced and with children than their married sons or daughters with children. Parents provide the most comfort to these divorced daughters and the next most to their never-married daughters. The former, however, are most likely to receive parental instrumental assistance.

When it comes to children and their initiation of contacts with parents, it is often—although not always—daughters who are more active. Never-married and remarried daughters are more likely to provide less costly gifts or financial assistance than are never-married sons and marrieds sons busy with their own children. Married daughters who are childless closely followed by married sons with children give more comfort than married, childless sons.

These results with respect to sons are particularly interesting. In contrast to previous findings emphasizing the primacy of daughters in intergenerational contacts, this study shows the continuing relations of parents and sons. The involvement is specified by marital and parental status, not usually controlled in other studies, which may account for the differences in results. Parents here generally do not provide sons with comfort regardless of marital and parental status. Gender roles, with their emphasis on male self-reliance, can be responsible for the lesser emotional dependencies of the sons. But, married sons with children, more settled in their intimate relations, give comfort—something married sons without children are less likely to do. Although the cases are few in number, remarried sons in this sample indicate concern for their fathers and mothers through care for them during their illness.

Couples where wives are younger tend to be more active in instrumental services for their children and, seemingly as a result, are more apt to be favored with attention from their children. The one exception is care during illness, in which the remarried give the most attention to parents when the mothers are older, and so presumably more apt to need such care.

The critical variable in intergenerational contacts, these data suggest, is not the status of grandparent. Rather, it appears to be the need for instrumental and emotional aid displayed by adult children who have never-married or who have children and are divorced. The attendant parental caretaker roles represent a continuation of roles parents played when children were young. Parents of adult children, however, do not differentiate in instrumental and sociability contacts and emotional support between married children who have children or who are without children. This equity of treatment suggests that it is situational stresses in the middle generation that activate grandparent roles. To this extent, grandparents can safeguard intergenerational continuity. The middle generation in turn stays in touch in ways permitted by available resources.

The question remains, however, whether current demographic and societal changes will lead to other roles taking precedence among the heterogeneous group of persons in the grandparent status. Grandmothers appear to be emphasizing the voluntary nature of their roles and increasingly want the same distance from grandparenting their husbands enjoy. The sample couples in the present study, for example, were very specific in their desire to structure parent roles as they chose. When asked how they would feel about their adult children returning home, they were generally negative. Just 29 percent of the 440 comments the wives made and 25 percent of the husbands' 445 comments indicated unqualified approval of this eventuality. And it was not only their fear that the return would be due to divorce, a particular concern among these overwhelmingly Catholic couples. In their replies, they would sometimes begin by remarking that it would be all right for children to move in for a temporary period. But they would generally hasten to add that they would want their children to reestablish their independence. Parents wanted to lead their own lives now. As one husband remarked, "Gosh, I wouldn't want it at all. I think if they moved back it would be difficult. Somehow I would feel I had to tell them what to do, and you can't tell them what to do when they are 30." And a wife exclaimed, "Oh, God, I wouldn't like it. It would be awful. I'm tired of waiting on people."

Grandparenting, this research shows, is not an unconditional temporal continuation of parental roles. Parental roles are never lost, but grandparent roles may be supplanted, complemented, or expanded. It is a matter of choice. And parents do not overlook their single or childless offspring. Grandparenting when it is a major activity is generally due to problems in the younger generations (Troll, 1983). Grandparenting then loses its voluntary nature and becomes a burden. Sentimentalizing grandparenthood, therefore, is only possible when it is a status whose roles individuals choose to enact.

NOTES

1. The remarried with children were included although our data did not indicate whether the children are from the previous or present marriage. (There was only one case involving a person remarried with no children.) There is a dearth of information on whether the posited greater parental concern for the divorced carries over to their remarriage. The present data provide some information on this issue.

2. Among those couples contacted who were eligible to participate, complete data were collected from 53 percent. Lack of time and ill health constituted the primary reasons for couples' failures to participate in the study.

3. It is more difficult to obtain statistical significance in tests of differences among group means where some of them have small Ns. Such results, if present, indicate quite different means.

4. This age division provided the greatest number of cases for the analyses. As only 34 of the women were employed at the time they were interviewed, the customary age of 65 for retirement was a less critical factor in the decision. Geographical proximity did not differentiate the groups.

PART III

GRANDPARENTHOOD, PERSONHOOD, AND THE LIFE COURSE

Contemporary grandparents are diverse, in their characteristics and behavioral styles; part of this diversity can be traced to changing structures, expectations, and functions of the social context. But grandparents are people, too. Part of their diversity lies in individual differences, in their psychological configurations and interpersonal connections. Here again the symbolic meanings of the grandparental role are crucial.

The primary emphasis of chapters in this section is on individual development and personality dimensions of the grandparent role. The authors, speaking from clinical experience in psychiatry and psychology as well as developmental psychology, discuss how the grandparent role emerges from psychosocial development. They discuss issues such as the subjective meaning of the role, emotional attachments to it, role abdication, and the voluntaristic versus the obligatory nature of the role.

Troll speaks to the contingent nature of grandparenting, how it is a process that is shaped by the synchronicity of its timing with previous expectations and other life processes. Its meaning and behavior are determined, she writes, by complementary issues in psychological and social development, as well as by marital, filial, work, or parental status.

Kivnick addresses grandparenthood and its relationship to mental health in terms of three interrelated components: meaning, behavior, and satisfaction. She argues that, though these three components are interrelated, it is necessary to focus on each separately in order to adequately understand grandparenting behavior. For example, the meaning of grandparenthood in her clinical sample can be seen in terms of five dimensions: role centrality, valued eldership, immortality through clan, reinvolvement with personal past, and indulgence. The dimensions are of differential importance to each individual, and these relative levels of dimensional importance are likely to shift as the individual ages and life circumstances change.

Kornhaber discusses grandparenting in terms of its significance to the psychiatric and social well-being of family members, as well as to society. He posits that grandparenthood provides an avenue for vital emotional and social connections to occur between and within generations, lest pathology prevail. But he calls attention to a "new social contract" based on the irrelevancy of intergenerational connections. His chapter discusses grandparental role abdication, grandparental rejection of grandchildren, lack of commitment to the functions of grandparenthood, and individualistic and narcissistic personality traits as factors that pose threats to the stability, continuity, and emotional bonding of multigeneration families.

Gutmann's chapter presents grandparents as "wardens of culture." He speaks to the value of enlisting grandparents, as conveyers of culture to aid in reversing malaise and deculturation. He disagrees with Kornhaber's assertion of a "New Social Contract," at least in terms of its pervasiveness. Inherent in Gutmann's chapter is a view (not unlike that promulgated by Margaret Mead) that elders, the living repositories of change, can be actively engaged to provide younger groups with the knowledge, skills, and experiences that will foster age-integrated society, as well as to be a contributing force in ensuring social equilibrium.

8

THE CONTINGENCIES OF GRANDPARENTING

Lillian E. Troll

Let us not make the mistake of thinking that grandparenting is like parenting at an older age. Among the many differences is the fact that whereas parenting tends to shape and alter all other parts of life, grandparenting tends to be shaped by other events going on in life. People usually—at least nowadays—make a decision to become parents and then keep on making decisions about how to be parents. People rarely make decisions to become grandparents. No matter how eager they may be to become grandparents, they must abide by other people's decisions in this respect. In fact, many of their future decisions about how to be grandparents are colored by other people's decisions, too. Grandparenting is a contingent process.

This means that grandparenthood can be either a gift or a curse, a reward or punishment for what one has done or been earlier. Many grandparents, no doubt, interpret grandparenting as a reflection upon the quality of their parenting. If their children make them grandparents too early, they must have done something wrong. If their children never make them grandparents, they must have done something wrong. If their children do not raise their grandchildren as they—the grandparents—would have wished, they—the grandparents—must have done something wrong. It is not, therefore, a worry-free state to be a grandparent. It has lots of meaning and drama. But because grandparenthood is primarily a contingent situation, its meaning and drama can be imbued with the helpless feeling of a nightmare or a dream.

The following pages constitute a largely speculative treatment of the effects of timing of grandparenting, timing within an individual grandparent's other life processes. It is notable that grandparenting, even more than parenting, is a far from unitary mode of interpersonal interaction. From the pioneering work of Neugarten and Weinstein (1964), who separated out five styles of grandparenting, to essential replications of this finding by Robertson (1977) and Kivnick (1982), stress can be put upon the multiplicity of grandparental behaviors and meanings. Empirical work so far is preliminary and descriptive in nature. It is hoped that this chapter, along with the others in this volume, can suggest directions for future research. With Joan Aldous (this volume), I raise the question, "Why is there a heightened interest in grandparenting at this point in time?" Answers to this can point to the importance of families in the lives of today's Americans, contrary to the prevailing myths that the family is dying.

TIMING

Grandparenting is shaped by other events of a person's life. Its onset can be alternatively too early, on time, or too late. What else is going on determines how it feels and how it is enacted. In other words, timing is important. There are three aspects or components of personal timing to consider. One is the expected or anticipated time. Another is the normative or "ought-to-be" time. The third is the context of other life circumstances. Let us consider these separately.

EXPECTED TIME

To phenomenologists, space and time are the two most significant parameters of experience. Our ideas about how much time we have to live—how much time in which to do what we expect to do—determines most of our life decisions and interprets most of life events. We each have a "time line," if you will, with markers on it of what events have or will occur, when they should have or will happen, and in which order.

Just before he died (more or less when he expected to) Ray Bortner (1978-1979) sketched out a short essay on his concept of "Expected Life History." He left it with Daniel Levinson, who fortunately sent it to the *International Journal of Aging and Human Development*. It was published there in 1978-1979. Bortner proposed that at any moment of our life, we could describe what we expect will happen to us in the future.

Did we or do we expect to marry, to hold a job, to have children, to be divorced, to be widowed, to be rich, to be poor? When did we or do we expect to marry? What kind of job do we expect, or did we expect? How many children did we expect, and what kind of children—beautiful, strong, brilliant, sickly, whining? What kind of home did we expect? And so on.

For present purposes, individuals also had or have expectations for grandparenthood. When did we expect to become grandparents? How many grandchildren did we or do we expect? Will they be like our children, or better—or worse? How will we feel about them? How often will we see them? What will they do for us? These expectations will, of course, be derived from our observations of our parents and grandparents, and of our friends and age-mates, as well as deductions from our own past lives.

We might expect to duplicate the experiences of our forebears, or to fare better than they, or—if we are pessimistic by nature—to fare worse. And expectations like these shape our experience. If we expect to become a grandparent at 50 because that was when our parents did, we may be dismayed to become one at 35, or despairing if we aren't one at 75. If we expected at least half a dozen grandchildren but have only one, we could feel deprived. If we have 15 instead, we could feel overwhelmed. If we expected to see our grandchildren about once a month, we might be distressed if they come to live in our house, or equally distressed if they only visit once a year.

NORMATIVE TIME

Bernice Neugarten (Neugarten, Moore, & Lowe, 1965), among her other numerous and important contributions to the field of life span development, pointed to the significance of age norms; that there is a right time for things to happen or for one to do things, and a wrong time—either too early or too late. If events are too early or too late, one is an age deviant, and that is shameful. There is a right time to become or to be a grandparent. Generally, it is too early to be one before about the age of 45 in American middle-class society today. By the same token, it is too late to have to wait for one's first grandchild until after one is 60.

I was intrigued that my mother-in-law let her hair grow in gray after my oldest daughter—her first grandchild—was born, when she was about 50 years old. She had turned gray in her 20s and dyed her hair red for over 25 years. It occurs to me now that she may have felt right about becoming a grandmother then and also felt that it was appropriate for her as a grandmother to have white hair. This implies that she would have remained a symbolically more youthful redhead if she had been made a grandmother five or ten years earlier.

SYNCHRONOUS EVENTS

At the time that I acquired the title "grandmother," I was back at the university completing my dissertation, with an academic job waiting for me. My children were all "finding themselves," or in their own words of that era, "getting their heads together." I had separated from my husband. My father was dying. One whole era of my life was ending and I was beginning a whole new era, becoming interested in many new and exciting pursuits. Thus, at that time, being a grandmother had minimal significance. When my sister became a grandmother for the first time, she was at a point in her life when it made a big difference. Like me, her children had all "left the nest" but, unlike me, she wasn't sure what she wanted to do next. After almost a quarter century of housekeeping and child rearing, she had not found a niche outside the home that absorbed her. Her husband was starting a new career, but she was still heavily involved as his helpmate. My first year as a grandmother was spent revising my dissertation and learning how to be a college teacher. Her first year was spent sewing baby clothes, writing letters to her daughter—the baby's mother—and waiting for new photographs. In one respect we were alike, however. We both spent a lot of time and money on planes: My granddaughter was in Vermont and hers was in California and we both lived in the Midwest.

In the early years of gerontological research, the mid-1950s, Neugarten and Peterson (1957) gathered respondents' prevailing ideas about life timing. They found that people generally used five categories or divisions in conceptualizing movement over time: health and physical vigor, job careers, family, personality characteristics, and social responsibilities. Not only was there remarkable agreement about the ages at which different milestones were supposed to occur, but there also seemed to be agreement that the timetables differed among these separate five pathways. Twenty years later, in a thoughtful chapter in the

Handbook of Aging and Social Sciences, Neugarten collaborated with Hagestad in discussing age and the life course (Neugarten and Hagestad, 1976). One of the important issues they addressed is the amount of synchronicity or asynchronicity among different life careers or pathways.

Life span developmentalists have questioned the suitability of terms like "life cycle." The original title for this chapter had been, "The Intersection Between Family and Individual Life Cycles," but this wording presents two problems. One is that the term "cycle" suggests that at the end of life we come back to our beginnings, which is potentially impossible. It was partly to counter this fallacy that in the first paragraph of this chapter much stress is placed upon the point that grandparenting is not equivalent to parenting. The other problem with this original title is the implication that family development is a distinct form of development, outside individual development. The 5-pathways classification of Neugarten and Peterson (1957) is relevant here. Individual development takes place along many tracks, family aspects constituting one, although I do not want to deny the multiplicity of family development itself. It would be appropriate, for example, to use a term like "life careers" to refer to all the different tracks or paths along which we move.

There are intersections between the careers of grandparenting and the other ongoing careers of individual development. Grandparenting itself is one of several family careers, which also include coupling—and sometimes uncoupling, parenting, and filial tracks, as well as other family careers like sibling and grandchild. It is not necessarily a later stage in a sequence that includes parenting as an earlier stage because most grandparents remain parents at the same time they add on the becoming and the being of grandparents. Now let us examine the timing of grandparenting as an intersectional process involving synchronous events.

HEALTH AND VIGOR

Grandparents in poor physical health and vigor can, if their grandchildren gather about them, tell them stories and give them advice. They can also, if they are financially fortunate, give them gifts and money. But they are not able to have the same interactions with them as more vigorous grandparents. It may be harder for them to appear at birthdays, graduations, and weddings, for example, or to take them to the zoo, Disneyworld, or Europe—or even, perhaps, to the local supermarket. If the problem is mental health—Alzheimer's disease or depression—they would probably have difficulty communicating meaningfully, at least from the perspective of their grandchildren.

On the other hand, older grandchildren and those who live nearby are in a postition to provide care for physically needy grandparents, as well as to entertain them and comfort them. Recent surveys have shown that young adult grandchildren are even more likely to say they would take care of their grandparents if necessary than their parents are to say they would take care of *their* parents—the same older people. But as Brody (Brody & Lang, 1982), wryly notes, we do not know how much these grandchildren really will do when the time comes. Most care of sick old people is provided by spouse and children, after all. When I observed (Troll, 1981) that there were marked age differences among grandparents in the number of their spontaneous mentions of their grandchildren, I wondered if the oldest grandparents—those over 80—who mentioned grandchildren much less than younger grandparents—in their 50s, 60s, and 70s—found the high activity patterns of grandchildren more than they were comfortable with or could cope with. This is presuming that grandparents over 80 are not as vigorous as those who are younger. This would be true particularly if their grandchildren were very young and consequently high in activity level. Following a 2-year-old around all day is not likely to be a preferred activity of slow-moving 90-year-olds.

Two studies have looked at health and grandparenting specifically, but both concern grandchildren who are at least in their teens: Cherlin and Furstenberg (this volume) and Troll and Stapley (in press). Cherlin and Furstenberg did not find health related signficantly to contact with grandchildren once distance was controlled—although their data do suggest that contact may be lower among those grandparents over 75 and in poor health. Unfortunately, their sample included too few grandparents over 75 to be sure of this. Similarly, in the Troll and Stapley analysis of three generations between 12 and 92 years of age, the number of spontaneously mentioned health problems by the grandmothers was not related to either happiness or distress on the part of their granddaughters (though it was to their daughters' distress), nor was it related to these granddaughters' spontaneous references to family members in their conversation—that is, to salience of the family in their thoughts. There was a sex difference, however. Grandfathers' mentions of health problems were correlated negatively with their grandsons' family salience scores, and these salience scores were in turn related to the affect of the grandsons. That is, grandsons of ailing grandfathers were *less* likely to refer to family members in their conversation than were grandsons of healthier men.

Most other studies require us to infer the effects of health or biological processes upon grandparental processes from the probability that poor health increases with age. Thus Neugarten and Weinstein (1964) reported that younger grandparents had more diverse styles of grandparenting than older ones; older grandparents were largely either formal or distant in their interactions with grandchildren. Johnson (this volume) mentions that the older grandparents in her study (over age 65) had less contact with their grandchildren and also gave them less help than did those under 65.

Unfortunately, although age may index health, it also indexes birth cohorts, and we do not know the effect of historical differences in attitudes towards grandparenting. Therefore, it is important to get more specific data based upon health per se. Another problem with age as an index of health is that it is also related to age of grandchildren. A final note on the intersection of health and grandparenting is that mentioned by Kivnick (this volume). Although health may influence behavior, she suggests, it may not affect the meaning or centrality of grandparental interactions or feelings. It is not unlikely that those grandparents whose health is deteriorating may increase the centrality and meaning of their grandchildren, who would be the key to their immortality. Obviously, the issue is complex, and we need more information before we can do more than speculate.

JOBS

One of the differences between my sister's and my own introduction to grandparenting had to do with employment. I was getting ready to start a new and challenging academic career whereas my sister had long resigned herself to remaining within the traditional feminine domain of home and community.

For a long time, family theorists believed that grandparenting was really a grandmothering activity, at least until grandfathers retired from their jobs, because it was perceived as centered in the domain of the home. Grandmothers were not seen as having jobs. Until very recently, in fact, jobs and family careers have been seen as in opposition to each other. Fathers were not expected to devote much time to parenting because of the demands of jobs, and mothers who were employed must somehow be "overloaded," in conflict, or neglecting their children.

In part, the issue boils down to quality versus quantity. It has been found repeatedly that quality of parenting—of mothering, particularly—is the effective factor in good child rearing, not quantity. Contributors to a 1963 volume on employed mothers (Nye & Hoffman, 1963) showed that satisfied mothers, whether satisfied with working or with not working, had higher-achieving and better-behaving children than did mothers who were not happy with their employment status. Would not this principle apply to grandparents, too? Grandparents who had more time because they were not involved in other activities like working need not enjoy their grandparenting any more than grandparents busy at work.

Oscillations in labor force participation over the past few decades have affected both men and women, blue-collar as well as white-collar workers. I use the word "oscillations" because changes that not long ago looked like linear or long-term trends are perhaps now more likely to look like irregular and short-term effects. Retirement for a while was getting earlier, mostly affecting men. At the same time, women were surging back into the marketplace. At present, it is hard to assess the effects of these changes upon grandparental relations.

Unfortunately, not only do we have little grandparenting research, but census information that has kept us up-to-date about fluctuations in age of marriage and age of birth of first child and last child has not included age at birth of first grandchild, not to mention of last grandchild (Norton, 1983).

The effects of job status—employed, nonemployed, retired, and so on—upon grandparenting are probably wider than influences upon available time. They also include amount of money and energy for entertaining, gifts, and travel, and, perhaps more important, the esteem and status in which grandparents may be held by their children and grandchildren. Elders with money and recognition in the wider world could occupy a different position in the family from those who have only a limited pension and family roles; they could be viewed in a much different light by their grandchildren.

Cherlin and Furstenberg (this volume) found no effect of grandparental labor-force status upon contact with grandchildren. Johnson (also in this volume), on the other hand, found that employed grandmothers had more contact, although Aldous (this volume) reminds us that those who are employed are probably younger and also have younger grandchildren. At any rate, contact per se is probably not the most important dependent variable. What we want to know are the intersections between job careers and the grandparental career, the style and meanings of grandparental relationships. Just as health may affect the centrality of such relationships, so might employment. Kivnick (this volume), in fact, notes that retired women report a higher centrality of grandchildren in their life than do nonretired women. If younger, employed women find more energy and time to interact with their grandchildren, older, retired women may put a lot more stress on just *having* grandchildren and more psychological weight on the time spent together. It is interesting that the centrality of grandchildren to the grandfathers in Kivnick's sample was not affected by their retirement status. Many family theorists have speculated that men would become more affiliative with their children and grandchildren as they become older—or retire, though so far there is no empirical support for this hypothesis. We might remember that when Maas and Kuypers (1974) followed up the Berkeley and Guidance Studies parents into their later years, they did not find any evidence for an increase in family orientation. Those men and women who had been highly oriented toward their family in old age; those who had focused upon jobs or community involvements in youth remained focused on instrumental and formal preoccupations in old age.

When we earlier considered health, we looked for an index of health, namely chronological age. In considering employment, we must resort to an even more tenuous index, using a combination of both age and sex. Until we have more direct information about relationships like those in Kivnick's data—supplemented, we hope, by the grandchild's perspective—we should not try to look for empirical confirmation of our guesses about what shifts in the occupational career might do to grandparent-grandchild relationships.

FAMILY

The existence of other family involvements should have an influence upon grandparenting. We know that those who are not currently married tend to be more involved in extended family relations than those who have a spouse (Troll, Miller, & Atchley, 1979). Some grandparents have nobody in the world to whom they are important or for whom they care except their grandchildren, and presumably, of course, their children. Others are involved with spouse, siblings, cousins, nieces and nephews, not to mention friends, business associates, neighbors, club co-members, and so on.

Many grandparents today also have their own parents living. If so, they are likely to be highly involved with them, particularly as their health declines. Not that such involvement would detract from the salience or centrality of their grandparental involvement, though. In the three-generational analysis cited above (Troll & Stapley, in press), middle-generation daughters of ailing mothers tended to speak more often of younger family members—presumably their own children and grandchildren—than did middle-generation daughters of healthier mothers.

Widowhood, particularly for women, is common among older grandparents. Although grandfathers whose wives die are likely to remarry shortly, grandmothers are not (Troll, Miller, & Atchley, 1978). In one way or another, this should influence grandparental interaction. As Kivnick points out (this volume), whether it increases the centrality of grandchildren or decreases the interactions with them depends upon other factors in the relationship and other processes going on at the time. Parron (1982, personal communication) in a followup of her research on golden-wedding couples, found that women who had been heavily involved in a wide variety of social (including parental and grandparental) relationships while their husbands were alive tended to reduce these involvements after they were widowed.

The prevalence of divorce today adds another complication. Grandparents—most obviously, grandfathers—may have a new wife and new infants, confusing if not distracting from their grandparental feelings and interests. Both men and women may have acquired new stepchildren whom they are trying to raise. Additionally, grandparents who divorce and remarry may face divided loyalties and rivalries from their children that could distance them from their grandchildren, given that the middle generation serves as the "lineage bridge" between generations (Aldous, 1978). Through new combinations of the families of their children, they may have to assimilate "ready-made" grandchildren into their fold.

Accumulating research on families in which child-rearing parents divorce shows the benefits to the grandchildren—the children of the divorced parents—of grandparental involvement (see Troll, 1983 and Cherlin and Furstenberg, this volume). Similar findings exist for grandparental involvement with teenage mothers and their children. Although the majority of grandparents might well prefer to avoid this kind of involvement, the consequence of being "surrogate parents"—to use Neugarten and Weinstein's (1964) term—is undoubtedly to heighten the centrality of the grandparental relationship for all family members involved. It is worth noting that when Neugarten and Weinstein interviewed grandparents in the early 1960s, "surrogate parents" was a relatively rare style of grandparenting; it is probably much less rare today.

PERSONALITY

Although the evidence of systematic personality changes during the adulthood is not altogether convincing (see Troll, 1982; Costa & McCrae, 1976; Siegler, 1980), many people do experience major life events that could produce significant personality changes during the years of grandparenting. Thus, some might become more energetic and assertive than they had been earlier (Neugarten & Gutmann, 1964), and others less so. A woman who had been a gentle, self-sacrificing mother, for instance, could turn into a domineering grandmother who controls interactions with clarity and determination. Conversely, a controlling mother could become a doting, permissive grandmother. A distant, Jovian father could become a tender, cuddly grandfather.

Current personality theorists present contrasting models of adulthood changes. One school suggests that middle and later adulthood is a time for consolidation, integration, and intensification of earlier characteristics. This would mean that the person, or, if you will, the "self," would remain the same over time; that each person's essential nature would become even more dominant as he or she gets older. Erikson (1950), for example, speaks of the acquisition of ego integrity as the major issue beyond those of early adulthood, intimacy, and generativity. As mentioned above, Maas and Kuypers (1974), looking at longitudinal data, saw remarkable stability of lifestyles and pursuits. Costa and McCrae looking at other longitudinal data, also saw stability in many personality dimensions, but noted that men, when young, tend to be centered on feeling, when middle-aged on thinking, and when older on integrating feeling with thinking. Kuhlen (1964) shows expansion in goals during the early years of adulthood and constriction thereafter. Thus, grandparents would have the same kinds of feelings and even behaviors as they had when they were parents, and even, perhaps, be more consistent about them.

Although this first group of theorists stresses continuity, a different group of life span developmentalists feels that there is convincing evidence for the existence of a significant midlife personality change at some time between the ages of 35 and 60. The personality characteristics on which this second group focus are usually linked to sex-role behavior. Men's and women's differences are seen as most extreme and most stereotypic ("masculine" and "feminine") in young adulthood, the time of producing and raising children (Gutmann, 1975). In middle age, both men and women are seen by these theorists as returning to an earlier androgyny, to the kind of diversity and nonstereotypy that characterized them in childhood. In middle age, individual differences would be more obvious than sex-typed conformity. Neugarten and Gutmann (1964) perceived three different kinds of mastery styles in the fantasy productions of adults: That of young adulthood, of middle age, and of old age. Livson (1977) and Monge (1975) have data that support the distinction between young adulthood and middle age. Gutmann (1975) and his colleagues provide both cross-cultural and American research.

How would we expect to see essential stability, or alternatively, midlife or old-age change in the style of grandparenting? As noted above, essential stability would be manifested in persistence of parental style into grandparenting as most people—at least those who are middle class—would still be in a stage of active mastery, according to Gutmann's view. Men would be leery of nonmasculine attributes like sensitivity and passivity, and thus more likely to be distant, controlling grandfathers. Women would be primarily passive in mastery style as well as sensitive and affiliative, and would thus nurture and maintain closeness with their grandchildren. According to this model, after a midlife transition, these grandparents would change their style—or, if they only become grandparents in later years, would be different kinds of grandparents. Grandfathers in their fifties and sixties would be more sensitive than those who were younger and grandmothers would be more assertive. When both grandmothers and grandfathers are old, according to Gutmann, they would evince "magic mastery" styles. This might lead them to fantasize about their grandchildren—to be less realistic about them than they were about their own children. They could see them as more ogre-like than they really are, or alternatively, more angelic.

If such major transitions are accompanied by distress, as many theorists believe, this would affect family relationships like grandparenting in a variety of ways. The joys of cuddling or interacting with grandchildren could soothe, or the noise and confusion of grandchildren could exacerbate tense feelings.

SOCIAL RESPONSIBILITIES

The later years of the aging process are sometimes marked by progressive disengagement from societal involvement. Thus, although grandparents in their thirties, forties, and fifties are likely to be even more engaged in extrafamilial activities than they had been earlier, those in their sixties on would be "letting go." Most evidence suggests that this disengagement is not *from* the family, though, but *into* the family (Troll, Miller, & Atchley, 1978); that much of the energy previously used in outside activities would be diverted to family activities. To some extent, family responsibilities might be felt even more acutely by older grandparents. The men and women who were involved in trying to influence and in being influenced by their young adult grandchildren (Hagestad, 1978) might exemplify this trend. Softening this trend, of course, would be the ebbing of total energy.

MULTIPLE INTERSECTIONS

So far, each of the five processes has been considered singly and separately. This is possible in the laboratory, of course. In vivo, health can be deteriorating at the same time that occupational changes are occurring. Family involvements can be changing at the same time that societal involvements are decreasing. Personality changes can be going on at the same time that occupational, health, and family processes are going on. The effect of combinations of intersections are almost impossible to predict. We must await more data, at any rate, before we can speculate.

SYSTEMATIC CAUSES OF DIVERSITY

Only brief mention will be made of systematic causes of diversity in intersections between grandparenting and other life processes. For one thing, other chapters in this volume deal more directly with them. They also have been alluded to earlier in this chapter. We do need to note, however, that sex differences dominate all categories. Men are most likely to be in poor health at an earlier age than their wives. Women, although not as likely to be employed as men, are more likely to find retirement difficult (Atchley & Corbett, 1977). Men are more likely to be married in later years; women who lose their husbands are less likely to find a new one. Women are more likely at all ages to be close to their children and grandchildren. Early grandparenting is more likely to occur for parents of teenage women because teenage fathers are not customarily involved in child rearing.

Social class is, of course, another major source of diversity. Lower class people are more likely to become early grandparents, to need to become surrogate parents more often, and to face multiple economic, health, and behavioral problems in their children and grandchildren than are middle-class grandparents. Economic conditions in society expand or contract poverty, add or subtract ameliorative social support, increase or decrease employment for both men and women of different ages, push people together into shared households and forced intimacy, or enable them to spread out for greater comfort and autonomy.

CONCLUSION

This ad hoc itemization has suggested some conditions for diversity inherent in grandparenting. And diversity is the most salient observation in the research so far. Multiple styles of grandparenting have been found by all investigators, from Neugarten and Weinstein (1964) through Robertson (1977) and Kivnick (1982). This diversity, in fact, suggests that grandparenting is not really a role in the classic sense, that its chief meaning derives from family systems rather than from individual characteristics.

As I noted earlier (Troll, 1983), grandparents could best be viewed as "family watchdogs." Grandparenting is generally a secondary activity in most grandparents' lives unless they have reason to believe that their values are not being handed down, or unless trouble in the lives of their children leads them to pitch in to help. It is, therefore, not surprising that research has found that those older people who are most involved with their families have the lowest morale. It is true that grandparents are not necessarily old but one suspects that at any age, finding your children and grandchildren in trouble does not make for happiness. Besides, it is much more fun to do your own, new thing and be with your own friends than to repeat earlier behaviors, no matter how enjoyable they were the first time around.

This chapter then, has dealt with the contingent nature of grandparenting, how it is a process shaped by the synchronicity of its timing with previous expectations and other ongoing life processes. Physical, psychological, and social development all determine its meaning and behaviors. Marital, filial, and parental status and events may shape grandparenting, as may employment or social involvement. Healthy, vigorous, and intelligent grandparents probably interact with their grandchildren quite differently from physically weak or mentally confused grandparents. Married or employed grandparents may be very different from those who are widowed or retired. To lump together all people between the ages of 30 and 100 whose child has given birth to their grandchild is by way of creating a meaningless category.

9

GRANDPARENTHOOD AND MENTAL HEALTH
Meaning, Behavior, and Satisfaction

Helen Q. Kivnick

In thinking about the grandparent role it is helpful to differentiate among three components: (a) the *meaning* of the role, (b) the *behaviors* characterizing the role, and (c) the degree of *satisfaction* experienced in the role. This chapter discusses the three role components and some of their interrelationships. It then considers these components in terms of such general conceptualizations of mental health as well-being, perceived control satisfaction, and life-cycle development.

The quotes and case-study observations that appear in this chapter are drawn from research in which 30 grandparents participated in a series of five open-ended, life-history interviews, and 286 grandparents completed a lengthy, interviewer-administered questionnaire. Interviews varied in length from less than one hour to more than three hours, with a mean of one and a half to two hours. This study addressed issues of grandparenthood meaning to grandparents, grandparenthood importance throughout the life cycle, and relations between grandparenthood meaning and grandparent mental health (Kivnick, 1982a).

GRANDPARENT ROLE COMPONENTS

THREE COMPONENTS

Perhaps because all three grandparent role components are difficult to measure, many studies refer simply to the "grandparent role" without

Author's Note: *The research discussed in this chapter was primarily supported by NIMH grant MH32155-01 and NIHR grant G008006801. Data analysis was assisted by PHS Biomedical grant RR05182-04.*

systematically differentiating among its components or investigating their interrelationships. However, though meaning, behavior, and satisfaction are clearly related, they are, just as clearly, different from one another (Kivnick, 1984). A particular role behavior may have very different meanings to different people. For example, taking grandchildren to favorite restaurants has been discussed in the following ways by different grandparents participating in my research interviews: "I'm so proud to be able to show him off to my friends—how much he looks like me"; "It's my duty as a grandmother to teach them to behave like little grownups"; "I'm too busy to spend time thinking about what might suit his fancy. When he comes to me I take him along on whatever I had planned to do—to the Club or out to lunch, or whatever"; "I get a bang out of arranging what I know will be a real treat for her." Although these grandparents all refer to the *behavior* of taking their grandchildren to restaurants, the *meaning* of this behavior varies considerably among them.

Conversely, very different behaviors can have similar meanings to different people. For example, the following activities were described by grandparents in my study as occasioning feelings of identification with the grandchild: watching him in a basketball game once in a while; taking her to ice skating lessons each week and watching how well she does; baby-sitting for them in the evenings when they do their homework; being there to watch each new grandchild born and hear the first cry; keeping a collection of up-to-date photos of the grandchildren on the desk in the living room. Although these activities might be evaluated as quite different from the standpoint of grandparent behavior, they could all be classified in the same way in an analysis of grandparenthood meaning.

In an attempt to clarify grandparenthood meaning, five dimensions were empirically derived as follows: (a) *Centrality*—grandparenthood as central to grandparents' lives; (b) *Valued Elder*—passing on tradition and being valued in that capacity; (c) *Immortality Through Clan*—patriarchal or matriarchal responsibility, identification with grandchildren, and family immortality; (d) *Reinvolvement With Personal Past*—grandparents reliving their own earlier lives and identifying with their own grandparents; and (e) *Indulgence*—attitudes of lenience and extravagance toward grandchildren. These dimensions have to do with what it means to grandparents to be grandparents, with how grandparents think about this experience. The dimensions are conceptualized as being simultaneous in nature, but hierarchical in personal importance.

That is, the overall meaning of grandparenthood to any grandparent is viewed as comprising all five dimensions. Within this overall meaning, the dimensions are of differential importance to each individual, and these relative levels of dimensional importance are likely to shift as the individual ages and as life circumstances change (Kivnick, 1982a, 1983).

These dimensions are reflected in the different meanings discussed by research subjects, above, as underlying the behavior of taking grandchildren to a favorite restaurant. The grandmother who enjoys introducing grandchildren to the grown-up world of nice things may be expressing the importance she attaches to the dimension Valued Elder. By comparison, the grandfather who enjoys arranging treats may be expressing Indulgence.

INTERRELATIONSHIPS AMONG COMPONENTS

Attaching a great deal of importance to a particular dimension of grandparenthood meaning does not necessarily imply grandparent well-being or satisfaction. For example, consider 74-year-old Mr. Goodman, a research subject to whom Valued Elder is the most important grandparenthood dimension. For years he looked forward to taking his grandchildren to synagogue, teaching them the Hebrew blessings, and passing on his own involvement with religion. His only child, a son, married a Catholic woman. Mr. and Mrs. Goodman, senior, made no effort to modulate their disapproval and disappointment with their son's choice of a partner. Rather than come to accept their daughter-in-law as a loving partner to their son, they have continued to hope that the marriage would break up. It is not surprising that this older couple is not particularly welcome in their son's home, and that their daughter in-law offers them little access to their grandchildren. Thus, although Valued Elder is an extremely important dimension of grandparenthood meaning for this grandfather, he is unfortunately dissatisfied at the severely limited ways he is able to express this importance. This dissatisfaction in a dimension of primary importance leads to disappointment in his experience of grandparenthood as a whole.

Differentiating grandparenthood meaning from grandparenthood behavior, and differentiating both of these from grandparenthood satisfaction, can lend valuable clarity to our consideration of the overall grandparent role—with regard to both research design and clinical intervention. Failing to differentiate among these components can perpetuate confusion on a variety of levels.

Grandparenting behavior is the role component most easily observed and most frequently described and measured by researchers. Some consider such within-family grandparent roles as troublemaker (Abraham, 1913; Campbell & Bubolz, 1982; Fox, 1937; Fried & Stern, 1948; Rappaport, 1958; Strauss, 1943; Vollmer, 1973) or surrogate caretaker (Deutsch, 1945; Lajewski, 1959; Von Hentig, 1946). Other studies focus on grandparenting styles such as formal or fun-seeking (Neugarten & Weinstein, 1964) or friendly mutuality (Radcliffe-Brown & Forde, 1950). However, because such research does not explicitly differentiate among the three role components, a finding of no association between a particular form or frequency of grandparenting behavior, on one hand, and a measure of psychological well-being, on the other (Wood & Robertson, 1976) may easily be misinterpreted as indicating no association between grandparent mental health and grandparenthood as a whole.

Perhaps, indeed, grandparenthood behavior is *not* associated with grandparent mental health. Perhaps, instead, as suggested by the example of Mr. Goodman above, grandparent mental health is associated with role meaning, or with satisfaction in a dimension of meaning that is particularly important. Differentiating among role components will help us both to clarify these associations and to understand the overall grandparent role.

GRANDPARENTHOOD AND MENTAL HEALTH

PERCEIVED CONTROL

Troll (this volume) has emphasized grandparents' distressing feelings of passivity and helplessness attendant with the timing of becoming a grandparent, and also with related family interactions. She discusses these feelings in terms of what would, in the terms of this chapter, be regarded as the component of role meaning: grandparenthood as a gift or a curse, or grandparenthood as an after-the-fact evaluation of parenting effectiveness. Let us also consider these feelings in terms of role behavior and satisfaction in relation to the issue of perceived control (Kleiber, Veldman, & Menaker, 1973; Schulz & Hanusa, 1980; Gatz & Siegler, 1981).

Certainly grandparents have little (if any) control over the timing of becoming grandparents. It is also true that a grandparent is likely to have minimal control over such grandparenting-related factors as geographic proximity to grandchildren, instinctive affection for and from the children-in-law who are the grandchildren's parents, divorce in the middle generation, middle-generation parenting styles, and more. It is also quite possible that the grandparent may have little control over the personal meanings that each of these factors holds. In view of the chronic depression that can result from perceived helplessness (Abramson, Seligman, & Teasdale, 1978), it is important to note that despite these uncontrollables, the individual may exert a considerable amount of influence on the kinds of grandparenthood relationships he or she will have. That is, the grandparent can exert considerable influence over his or her grandparenting behaviors, in turn influencing derived satisfaction, and perhaps affecting meaning as well.

For example, Mrs. Johnstone, a 67-year-old widow who expected to live around the corner from her grandchildren and to have casual daily contact with them, is extremely distressed that all four of her children have taken jobs and made their homes several hundred miles away from where she has always lived. If she persists in feeling that her children have abandoned her or in thinking that the only satisfying way to be a grandmother is to give the grandchildren cookies and milk on their way home from school each day, she may well continue to experience grandparenthood in terms of helplessness and deprivation.

However, this subject does have other alternatives. In spite of her disappointment, she can try to develop creative grandparenting behaviors involving the telephone, the camera, and the mails. She can try to reorganize her time and money to permit more frequent visits to her children than had previously been the norm. While visiting she can offer to stay with the grandchildren, in order to provide their parents welcome relaxation and time alone. In her own community she might volunteer as a teacher's aid in an elementary school. She might decide to do after-school child supervision work, or to teach baking in a local Y, church, or other organization. None of these behaviors is likely to be easy or to feel natural, at least at first. None can wholly eliminate her distress at disappointed expectations. However, any one of them—and a multitude of other behaviors—might offer her the opportunity to exert direct control over her grandparenting behavior, both mitigating her feelings of helplessness and enabling her to experience real satisfaction in the grandparent role.

Unmet expectations by role partners may cause distress at any stage of the life cycle. Consider the 30-year-old, unhappily single, professional woman who expected to be married and have children by her mid-twenties; the male executive in his mid-thirties who expected his wife to maintain the home front, follow him around the country and up the corporate ladder, and who now finds that she will not leave the job she loves; the unemployed middle-aged steel worker who expected to work hard for the reward of living his life in the middle class; the young or middle-aged victims of unexpected accidents or age-inappropriate diseases, who had planned on being healthy and active for several more decades; the divorcee who has been abandoned without warning by her marital partner; and others. In all of these cases, we recognize shattered or otherwise unmet expectations as causing distress. However, in these cases and others we expect that the individuals will find a way to cope with realistic distress, to act on the basis of existing circumstances, and somehow to proceed with the business of living their lives.

To a surprising extent people seem willing to tolerate disappointment and helplessness in grandparenthood—although they are likely to be far more assertive in responding to other kinds of dissatisfaction. Perhaps this passive toleration is a function of a societal expectation that older people accept what comes to them. Perhaps the peripheral status to which many people relegate grandparenthood somehow suggests that related disappoinments are of little consequence and must therefore be endured; perhaps adaptation and accommodation are viewed as strategies appropriate only with respect to central life issues. Perhaps the peripheral status of grandparenthood leads people in all generations emotionally to seek disengagement from the relationship rather than experience its full disappointment or conflict. People may simply be unaccustomed to recognizing disappointment in grandparenthood as a feeling either worth attending to or subject to modification. Perhaps grandparents feel entitled to having grandparenthood expectations met. Perhaps they feel that it is the younger generations who should accommodate, if any accommodating is to be done.

It is understandable that unmet or disappointed grandparenthood expectations may be a source of real distress—to grandparents and to middle-generation parents, as well. In fact, however, grandparents are not nearly as helpless as they may either feel or behave in this regard. Family systems theorists acknowledge that members of *all* generations influence relationships and processes within the family (Terkelsen, 1980; Walsh, 1980; Walters & Walters, 1980).

This reciprocal, intrafamily influence may provide grandparents a valuable defense against perceived helplessness and its deleterious consequences, as mentioned above. The longstanding nature of family relationships provides a unique context in which grandparents can use the control they do wield to maximize various kinds of life satisfaction. That is, within the family disappointed grandparents may well be able to assert control in developing behaviors that will fulfill underlying role meanings, resulting in role satisfaction that was initially thwarted. The fact that people may not now optimally exercise this control does not minimize the potential advantages that might accrue from so doing.

LIFE-CYCLE DEVELOPMENT

Clinical work suggests that in considering any life process (e.g., grandparenting, parenting, working) in relation to mental health, we must place the behavior in a life-cycle context. How do requirements and risks for mental health vary across the life cycle? At different life stages, how do various life processes facilitate or inhibit healthy psychosocial development—and vice versa?

According to Eriksons' formulation of the life cycle (1950, 1982), an individual progresses through a sequence of eight developmental stages, each one characterized by a focal psychosocial tension, the dynamic balancing of which represents the essential psychosocial challenge of the stage. Recent elaboration of this formulation places new emphasis on lifelong processes of pre-facing and refacing not currently focal tensions (Kivnick, Erikson, & Erikson, 1983). Thus, an essential component of psychosocial old age is to renew an age-appropriate balance for all seven earlier tensions. Recent elaboration also emphasizes the importance of vital involvement in the material and psychosocial world to development at all stages.

In Erikson's (1982) terms, grandparenting represents an age-appropriate involvement through which the grandparent may reface issues directly related to parenting (Generativity versus Stagnation), and perhaps less directly related to such other tensions as Identity versus Identity Confusion; Industry versus Inferiority; Autonomy versus Shame and Doubt. Other life processes in which the grandparent participates also represent opportunities to renew earlier psychosocial balances. Thus, the grandparenthood experience and its interaction with other life processes must be understood as one aspect of the grandparent's overall struggle to develop the robust senses of caring and wisdom that represent psychosocial "goals" of middle and later adulthood.

Reciprocally, from the grandchildren's point of view, relations with grandparents can facilitate essential psychosocial development at all stages of the life cycle (Kivnick, 1982), as relationships with all adults can facilitate childhood development. In addition, interacting with grandparents can provide opportunities for children to do essential pre-facing of the psychosocial tensions that will become focal later in their life cycles.

CONCLUSION

The grandparent role and its relation to mental health and psychosocial well-being comprise an extremely complex issue. This chapter has sought to begin at least to organize—if not to simplify—this complexity, first by considering the overall grandparent role in terms of the three interrelated components of meaning, behavior, and satisfaction; and second by considering these components in relation to various aspects of mental health and psychosocial well-being throughout the life cycle.

As grandparenthood is a role in which the majority of adults in our society participate for many decades of their lives, understanding this role and its intersections with other life processes can make a major contribution to our understanding of well-being throughout adulthood.

10

GRANDPARENTHOOD AND THE "NEW SOCIAL CONTRACT"

Arthur Kornhaber

The central argument of this chapter is that a new social contract between parents and grandparents has subtly and slowly come into force in this country. The effects of this contract have sheared apart the three-generational family and critically weakened the emotional underpinnings of the nuclear family. The contract—one that has never been signed or even orally agreed upon—consists simply of this: A great many grandparents have given up emotional attachments to their grandchildren. They have ceded the power to determine their grandparenting relationship to the grandchildren's parents and, in effect, have turned their backs on an entire generation.

A colleague and I have conducted natural history interviews with more than 1000 grandparents since 1975. The results of these inquiries indicate that an emotional disconnection has evolved between the generations, a lack of vital connections. Elsewhere (Kornhaber & Woodward, 1981), we described processes of interaction between grandparent, parent, and grandchild generations along with the emergence of the new social contract. This contract has had an effect on the grandparent-grandchild bond, the emotional bonds between all family members, and the relationship between the family and society.

The realization of this new social contract evolved slowly as a result of cumulative inquiries into the nature of the grandparent-grandchild relationship over a period of time. After interviewing the first 100 grandparents and grandchildren in two sites—their home and in a clinic setting—it became evident that close grandparent-grandchild relationships, "vital connections," were few and far between. At present, approximately 15 percent of the 1000 or more of those interviewed relate a close emotional bond between grandparent and grandchild. A great majority of the families that were interviewed report that they arranged their lives and generational interactions on the basis of the new social contract.

The new social contract is a recent historical event that began to unfold during the economic upheavals of the Great Depression when multitudes of men had to leave their families to find work. This breakdown of the family and its current manifestation affected the emotional life of all three generations. It has removed grandparents from their grandchildren as well as from their natural role as involved parents. This new arrangement of intergenerational interactions has been labeled a contract because it is an agreement, most often mutual and unstated, between grandparents and their adult children that the grandparents will no longer be involved in the rearing of grandchildren.

> The evidence provided by such grandparents leads us to assert the existence of a powerful counterveiling force which vitiates the instinct to grandparent and, with that instinct, the primordial bond between grandparents and grandchildren. This force is rooted in history, not biology and is manifest by thoughts rather than feelings. We call it "the new social contract." It is social because it is based on attitudes which have been learned and digested from family experience in a changing society. It is contractual because it assumes that parents can and should decide whether and to what extent grandparents will nurture their grandchildren. And it is new because it has developed within the lifespan of the current generation of grandparents. (Kornhaber & Woodward, 1981, p. 2)

The new social contract is so powerful that it can be implemented by one party if the other offers no strong protest. The terms of the contract (not mutual support, but independence) are both the result and cause of a state of unprecedented animosity between many parents and grandparents unknown to their forbears. We believe that vigorous action must be taken to nullify this contract, which is so full of peril to the emotional life of both family and nation.

It should be emphasized that the picture presented of the nation's emotional health is not one of unmitigated gloom. Although millions of people live by the terms of the pernicious social contract we have described, others—those with "vital connections"—still strongly adhere to what we term a "natural arrangement," an unstated agreement that family members should be permanently attached and should live within a three-generational family structure (the opposite of the new social contract). We have found that in the great majority of cases observed, people from families observing natural arrangements are happier, better adjusted, and lead more fulfilling lives.

In the following pages a description is presented of the ways that family members relate to one another, and we learn how the people who live under these arrangements feel.

CLINICAL INVESTIGATION BY
EMOTIONAL HISTORY: METHODOLOGY

The investigation of emotional attachments is a difficult and complex process. Not only did we wish to examine what happened to individuals in terms of their emotional attachments (sociological dynamic), but also how they felt (emotional dynamic) about what happened and how their attitudes and behavior adapted to the event (psychodynamic). In order to do this, we spent a great deal of time with each subject (a minimum of three hours). We were aware that information collected in this fashion can be of limited validity because of its subjectivity and vulnerability to the preconceived bias of the investigator. Generalized conclusions drawn from this type of investigation can only be regarded as "speculative." Personal insights derived from this method can be very helpful to the researcher and the subject. In spite of these pitfalls, we proceeded with our investigation using the technique of "emotional history" because it was the only clinical method that enabled us to peer into issues that were closed to examination by other investigative techniques.

As stated earlier, over 1000 grandparents have been interviewed since 1975. These interviews were carried out in diverse settings—local and national, in our clinic, private homes, and during the course of grandparents' meetings. For example, with regard to socioeconomic background, the sample was composed of 20 percent who were categorized as upper class, 40 percent who represented middle-class lifestyles, and 40 percent of lower socioeconomic status. Generally, these grandparents were White (76 percent). The remaining were from a variety of ethnic backgrounds, namely Black (10 percent), Hispanic (8 percent), Asian (5 percent), and American Indian (1 percent). Geographically, the bulk of the grandparents were from the eastern United States (50 percent).

Some were from the Midwest (30 percent) and the West (20 percent). The latter included north-south boundaries.

Since 1979, my colleagues and I have been involved in the Grandparent Clinical Project, recruiting grandparents to assist their families in times of stress. In addition, we started the Foundation for Grandparenting. Its intent was to teach people the importance of grandparenting and to help reconnect the generations. As part of this goal, we have been involved in the grandparents' visitation rights movement in order to assure the integrity of the grandparent-grandchild relationship when parents die or divorce.

The following example illustrates the inherent complexities faced in researching this topic. In this case, we were investigating infant-grandparent relationships. The question was, "How did parents view grandparenting styles?"

> An 18-month-old child had grandparents from different cultures. One set was Latin, the other Nordic. Her Latin grandparents tickled, frolicked with and cajoled her. Her Nordic grandparents (who loved her no less) let her "be." Her Latin mother thought her in-laws were "cold and hard," while her Nordic father thought his in-laws were "driving her crazy." The youngster was perfectly content with both sets of grandparents. (Kornhaber, in press)

This is only one example of the complex variables affecting the grandparent-grandchild relationship. Indeed, there are many complicated situations, such as "special" grandchildren—the first born—and grandchildren who resemble a given grandparent physically or temperamentally. There are "rejected" grandchildren—infants of "despised" in-laws and children who resemble the "other side" of the family.

In spite of procedural complexities, the "emotional history" technique provided a valuable clinical tool that allowed (with the subject's permission) a privileged three-dimensional view (biological, psychological, and social) of the subject's internal universe.

THE NATURAL FAMILY ARRANGEMENT

In the normal course of things, every time a child is born, a grandparent is born and a new three-generational family is formed. This is a natural and organic relationship manifested in people's minds, expressed through their attitudes and behaviors, and experienced as emotions. This is a biological given that has occurred since humankind's beginnings.

In this situation, a natural family arrangement is forged—child, parent, and grandparents (and great-grandparents). The sum of these individuals creates another entity—the three- or four-generational family that may be visualized as a pyramid.

In this system, each generation rests upon the previous one—one supporting the other, each emerging telescopically from the preceding one. In the best of all worlds, the "natural family" would live in a society that would, in its turn, accommodate itself to the needs of the individual and the family—in such a utopian state of affairs, the individual's community or larger society.

Briefly summarized, the results of our study indicate that the grandparent-grandchild bond is second only in emotional importance to the parent-child bond. When enacted, its benefits enrich the lives of all family members. Grandparents and grandchildren affect one another, for good or for bad, just because they exist. Problems passed on from grandparent to parent are *not* directly passed on from grandparents to grandchildren (although children are profoundly affected by their grandparents' attitudes toward their parents). This clinical observation has been instrumental in establishing grandparents' right to visitation.

The study also showed that children with close relationships to at least one grandparent were different from children with intermittent or infrequent grandparent contact. These youngsters with close relationships to grandparents had a sense of belonging to a family and community. They were not ageist because of their contact with older people who loved them. They were not sexist because they saw grandfathers and grandmothers who had similar activities. Children with close grandparents did not fear old age because their grandparents served as positive role models. Grandparents offered these children an emotional atmosphere of acceptance for just being alive—a place to go, apart from the world of their peer groups and their parents, to learn about other times and other ways of living. Thus, these youngsters felt deeply connected to their families and were highly socialized. They had a sense of shame: They knew that their behavior reflected upon their families. They lived in a loving and emotionally secure world.

Another important suggestion made by the study was that grandparenting is an instinct manifested by thoughts, feelings, and actions, and is affected by the culture. Before the child is born, many future grandparents mentally rehearse future grandparenting. The way in which a given individual experiences grandparenthood is based on his or her experience as a grandchild, the attitudes of the society toward grandparenthood, his or her own altruistic orientation, and the grandparenting behavior of his or her own parents. When a grandchild is born, new grandparents experience strong feelings and unique thoughts. There is an urgency to make contact with the new child, a need for intimacy that initiates the "vital connection."

Grandparents' roles are unique. They are similar to parents' roles because a grandparent has already been a parent, and can fulfill that role. They are different because a parent cannot be a grandparent. These roles deepen and broaden as grandparents and grandchildren spend more time with one another. They are also interchangeable—some roles may predominate at a given point in their relationship. At first a grandparent's role is titular, conferred by the birth of a grandchild. Immediately, a grandparent becomes a living ancestor and a role model for the child. When an intimate relationship is established, a grandparent becomes a living historian and family archivist. As mentors, grandparents teach children in an atmosphere of acceptance with a great deal of time and attention. A grandparent's "curriculum" is often taught nowhere else.

As nurturers, grandparents are the second line of defense—a safety net for the child—when parents fail. The nurturing role of grandparents is twofold—indirect, by supporting the child's parents, and direct, by caring for the child. When grandparents and grandchildren spend a great deal of time together, grandparents become magical wizards, heroes, and romantic figures in the eyes of the young child, and cronies to the older child. These roles give meaning to elders' lives and exemplify generativity in its most powerful form—the application of a lifetime of wisdom and experience to a relationship with their progeny.

NATURAL FAMILY ARRANGEMENTS: WHERE GRANDPARENTS AND GRANDCHILDREN FLOURISH

Elders in our study who were able to design and implement natural families were altruistic by nature, had a deep philosophical and spiritual commitment to their families, and placed an emotional priority on their lives. They were connected to their family origins and often to their religion, and provided for the future of the family. They were generous, giving freely of their time and possessions to family members. Children were especially important. The self-image and self-esteem of these people were based on their importance to the family rather than to social status or role. A blacksmith who was a "good son" was more revered by his family than his brother who made a great deal of money but relinquished his family. This supports the concept of "personal" forces in grandparenting reported by Wood and Robertson (1976).

These elders protected and provided for their families and supplied their families with a strong set of values that were a countervailing force to societal values. This "social immunity" was especially prevalent in the young. They supplied a powerful image and source of security for younger family members and thus were greatly loved, respected, and revered. They were the opposite of the lonely elder as described by Erik Erikson (1950), who ends his life in "despair and stagnation."

Not only were these individuals respected by their families but they were often well-known in their communities and expressed their altruistic orientation toward life in their churches, temples, and their community agencies. We could not identify any specific religious, sexual, or political commonalities among them. One of the most important things that they did have in common was the gift of "generativity" (Erikson, 1964), the nurturing of and concern for future generations.

THE NEW SOCIAL CONTRACT

Parties to the new social contract view their families in direct contrast to those who live according to a natural family arrangement. Thus, parties to the new social contract are often narcissistic instead of altruistic. They appear to be committed to individuality and "independence" instead of family. They live according to a materialistic, acquisitive philosophy that emphasizes personal pleasure and altruism.

The most devastated victims of the contract are children. Unfortunately, children are hard put to directly interfere with the world around them; they are dependent on the adults who raised them. They are open and vulnerable to the attitudes and behavior of their parents and grandparents toward one another, and are the primary victims of intergenerational wars. A youngster named Alice shared her experiences as a child whose parents and grandparents were parties to the New Social Contract.

> My mother doesn't like it when I am with my Grandma because she thinks Grandma is too bossy. I can't even say anything nice about Grandma to Mom. Grandma is great to me but I guess she is not nice to Mom. I don't understand because I never see Grandma being mean. Anyway, I hardly get to see Grandma because of this. My mother even lies to Grandma when she calls to have me come over. Mom tells her I am busy when I am not. She tells Grandma that she is too busy for us to go to Grandma's for Sunday dinner. Dad wants to play tennis. I want to go, but we don't.

Alice's fears are not limited to the present. She worries about the future. Will she repeat her mother's attitude toward her grandmother? Will she be able to be a grandmother or will her own children block her grandchildren from seeing her?

> I worry that I will treat my mother like she treats my grandmother especially since I don't know why she is like that. How will I know how to be a grandmother if I can't be with mine to see how she does it? I thought families should be happy together and help one another.

Thus, Alice expresses succinctly a feeling of demoralization concerning family life that is so common to children whose ancestors have lived their family lives according to the new social contract. This demoralization is so profound that it infiltrates every aspect of the child's view of the meaning of his or her very existence. Alice continued in a way that is reminiscent of the way that children of divorce often feel:

> Sometimes I am so upset about the way that Mom and Grandma are to one another that I wish I was never born. They would have nothing in common, me,—if I were dead. I am just something to fight over. If I didn't want to see Grandma my mother would never see her again. I am in the way.

Alice's fears are supported by our own observations as well as by others'. For example, another researcher reports:

In addition to its consequences during childhood, the absence of a meaningful childhood relationship with a grandparent may well limit the richness of the relationships that a given individual will have with grandchildren two generations in the future. (Kivnick, 1982)

Deprived of grandparents, children raised under the new social contract are susceptible to identifying with media-learned stereotypes of old age. Thus they become scornful of the elderly and fear becoming old.

Parents are deeply affected by the new social contract. They turn to strangers instead of family when adversity strikes. Many have told us of the loneliness they feel because their own parents aren't available to them. Others complain about the difficulty in raising a family with no respite because grandparents are unwilling to support them. Several divorced people told us that their marriages would have survived if their own parents were available so that they "could have had time together without the pressure of the children."

Grandparents ascribing to the new social contract are not pleased about the added responsibility of becoming grandparents. They are not aware of the future and of their increasing isolation and alienation from their family. Their time is spent in the workplace or with their peers.

For all of these people, emotional bonds are viewed as bondage. Interest in the welfare of family members is perceived as controlling, intrusiveness, or meddling. When conflicts arise, family members emotionally cut themselves off from one another. The family personality is ignored. The family continuity is abandoned. Families who ascribe to the new social contract ignore their common history and have no common future. Most important, grandchildren are never considered.

THE FALL OF THE NEW SOCIAL CONTRACT

THE FUTURE UNDER THE NEW SOCIAL CONTRACT

If the new social contract is not changed, we believe a number of consequences will prevail. The first will be a continued erosion of the quality and quantity of deep emotional attachments between family members and the progressive abandonment of children. (It is interesting that several of the teenagers we interviewed who were born into families adhering to the new social contract joined cults that not only supply a "meaning" to life, but offer "family" attachments.) Family members have become emotionally disconnected from one another. First, fathers left for work; now grandparents are moving progressively away from the middle generation. Increasing numbers of mothers are leaving their young to the care of others. Thus, from the beginning of their lives, emotional connectedness is neither being given nor demonstrated to a great many young children. The new social contract has created a growing number of individuals who devote their time to the rearing of other people's young. The most powerful human emotional attachment of all, the mother-child bond, is now under stress in our culture.

The second doleful consequence is the dismemberment of the family and the replacement of basic family functions by businesses and social institutions. When these institutions take hold, they assume a force of their own and make it difficult for human and family functions to move back into the gap they created. Breast-feeding is a good example of the phenomenon. What was once a substitute for mother's milk has become the predominant form of nourishing the young. Indeed, there was a point when women who wanted to breast-feed their own children were hard put to do so. Another example is the boom in therapy, which has become a growth business. The inexorable human need for human companionship and the disconnectedness created by the new social contract have left a basic human need unsatisfied. This is often exploited by the business of grouping people together for therapy or companionship. People will always seek what the natural family freely offers.

A third, and perhaps the most harmful, consequence will involve the progressive dehumanization of our society as people trained to be isolated and alienated spend more time with the fruits of impersonal technology. Television, video games, and walkman radios are not only intellectually seductive but remove the participant from the real-life emotional events that are the fabric of personal attachments. To take this one step further, it is not difficult to envisage a society in which the dehumanized young, emotionally detached from the aged, could find it very easy to institutionalize "euthanasia" for the useless aged.

REPEALING THE NEW SOCIAL CONTRACT

I hold that the new social contract is an arrangement that should not be tolerated in a civilized society. I submit that society is nearing its threshold of tolerance. An emotional revolution is beginning that will bring down the new social contract.

In recent past, we have seen more and more Americans gaze up from the reflecting pool of their own narcissism to take stock of the state of their emotional world. American fathers are doing this. Long alienated from the nurturing of the children, many fathers are reexamining their relationship to the work place and its emotional cost to them. Many young mothers in our study who have gone to work, out of desire rather than necessity, are in the process of reexamining their priorities (when children are involved). Perhaps nowhere is the emotional revolution more evident than in the recent national movement to establish the right of grandparent visitation when the child's custodian seeks to divorce grandparent and grandchildren from one another (a phenomenon linked to the current high divorce rate and the formation of more and more "reconstituted" families without grandparents). During the course of our research, we came across several grandparents who were fighting for such rights, and learned that not only did most states not have laws allowing grandparents who were deprived of their grandchildren to sue for visitation, but that ageist courts with no knowledge of the importance of the relationship would deny visitation on the grounds that it was in the best "interest" of the child. Researching the issue, we found that visitation was most often denied either because it was inconvenient to the parent or to protect the child from the parent's wrath (if the child wanted to visit with the grandparent against the parent's wishes).

Since that time, thousands of grandparents have banded together, and as a result, 49 states now have laws that assure grandparents the right to sue for visitation In addition, a proposition to establish a federal grandparent visitation law has passed through the House of Representatives and is currently waiting a vote by the U.S. Senate. In a nation where the new social contract is in full force, a handful of grandparents who are committed to their families have spoken out for the importance of family attachments by demanding their right to see beloved grandchildren. One grandparent summed up the meaning of the emotional revolution well:

My grandchildren are what my life is all about now. I never thought about it much before—took it all for granted—the family. Then all this divorce around me. Then my daughter got divorced and remarried this man who didn't want to be bothered—to many grandparents he said to my daughter—so he didn't want me to see my grandchildren. I never signed a paper or voted in my life. I never got involved but when things come to this, when a person like me, who is crazy about her grandchildren, can't see them anymore there is no law or person or anything that's going to keep me away from those kids.

There is no power stronger than a mother's love except for the love of a grandmother—the mother's mother—and this society and the television and the magazines and even the kids have gone far enough and it's up to the grandparents, with a lot of love and in the right way to straighten it out, and by God! I am healthy and I've got the time to do it, and I will.

The Grandparents' Movement has established the role of grandparents as important and necessary. It has validated the importance of the three-generational family system and emotional attachments. Most important, it has taught the young that emotional and family attachments cannot be legislated out of existence. It is, in the best sense, a revolt against the terms of the new social contract. But these are only the first steps. Even those grandparents fortunate enough to have the money to sue for visitation often lose in court. This is because judges, attorneys, and mental health professionals not only are ignorant of the importance of the grandparent-grandchild relationship, but also view the issue in terms of the new social contract. As a result, grandparent visitation is often forbidden "in the best interest of the child," which upon further exploration is a euphemism that really means "in the best interest of the parent." It is the parent who is most disturbed when visitation takes place. Thus, more and more grandparents who were caught unaware and were unwillingly removed from the lives of their grandchildren (through death, divorce, adoption, or negative relationships) have reinvested themselves emotionally in their remaining children and grandchildren. Thus, it is becoming more and more common to see grandparents (who subscribed to the new social contract with their older children) repealing the new social contract with their younger children. This, in our view, is a clarion sign of the emotional revolution and is happening now within the same generation.

CONCLUSION

Although the present state of the family is critical, it is far from fatal. Families are, after all, a natural state for humans. They are recreated every time a child is born. They can never be biologically extinguished no matter how much they are ignored or disdained socially.

The resurrection of emotional attachments and the family is the responsibility of today's middle generation—present and future grandparents—in their personal life, family, and society. Personally, they can create a family for themselves by honoring their own emotional attachments. Socially, they can create and support a government and a society that supports the family and honors emotional attachments of all family members. With the family as a nucleus, a three-generational society may be forged—a society without age segregation or isolation—where all three generations function harmoniously—loving, caring for, and nurturing one another.

No generation before us has ever had the ability and the capacity to change the culture in only one generation, to create a society that fits the way we are as human beings and to nurture all that is good about us. We have, for the first time ever, the chance to do this.

No generation before us has ever had the opportunity to create a world where people can be born and die within the cradle of their families and where families, in turn, can be cradled by society.

It is not just a question of the pendulum of rapid social change having swung too far and now having to swing back to the "old days," because the old days never existed. It is a case of throwing out the virulent new social contract and replacing it with a humane and caring intergenerational society, with individuals who are emotionally nurtured within their own families. This can and must be done by today's and tomorrow's elders, using the grandparent model for a behavioral example.

11

DECULTURATION AND
THE AMERICAN GRANDPARENT

David L. Gutmann

AMERICAN ORIGINS:
THE REPUDIATION OF GERONTOCRACY

We can think of the American grandparent as a gerontocrat manqué; accordingly, any discussion of American grandparenthood should begin by considering the typical American's stance towards gerontocracy in general. There is a common posture, that is, contragerontocratic: In our own lives, or in the lives of our immigrant forebears, we are the people who rejected gerontocracy.

The American immigrant was typically a refugee from gerontocracy, one who had fled from the "old ways" of an "old country," from traditional designs of life monitored by a ring of censorious, gossiping elders in claustrophobic villages. The historic myth on which our culture and even our individual identities is based memorializes the overthrow of the ultimate gerontocrat—the King of Old England—by the band of democratic brothers in New England. These myths and their gerontophobic consequences are enacted in our individual lives. Thus, we try to deny our own aging: In our families, we sunder the three-generation family, split grandparents from grandchildren, and trundle our aged parents off to retirement or nursing homes; and in our politics, even our aged presidents have to deck themselves with the cosmetics and manners of youth.

Americans are the true Promethans: Our covert myth is that we stole the powers of the gerontocrats, and ran away with them to this country. Our covert fear is that the aged, should they ever again become ascendant, would levy on us the punishment of Prometheus. Accordingly, we are mainly at ease with the aged when we deny their latent powers, visualizing them as victims in need of our benign services; when we keep them at arm's length in their own retirement colonies; or when, in perpetuation of the American myth, we leave our elders behind, in the "old neighborhood."

GRANDPARENTS AND THE
REPUDIATION OF CLOSENESS

Thus, gerontologists usually believe that it is the American young who leave the American aged behind, and not the other way around. But now, those few social scientists who study the intrapersonal correlates of interpersonal family bonds are coming up with new and surprising findings: namely, that many aged do not wait passively to be abandoned, but instead initiate their own inner affectional migration away from the young—including their own grandchildren.

This inward defection from intimacy on the part of grandparents was first brought to our attention by the Disengagement theorists (Cumming & Henry, 1961), who argued that the emotional decoupling in aging was a mutual process, that it took place on both sides of the generational boundary, and that it was instigated by the old as well as by the young. More recently, Kornhaber (this volume) reports that the aged are now signatories to what he calls a "new social contract" based on emotional distance between the generations, that has replaced an earlier unity of close-knit, generational bonds. Kornhaber finds, to his dismay, that his grandparental informants are relatively disinterested in intimacy, even with their grandchildren, and take pride in their self-sufficiency, their freedom from "need for the other." However, in the absence of longitudinal data, Kornhaber cannot demonstrate that the contemporary "contract" is particularly new or that it has in recent times superceded a prior, "natural family contract" based on intimacy rather than emotional distance. Indeed, it may even represent a long-established format in American grandparenthood rather than a new departure, in that Kornhaber's older subjects may be reiterating an individualistic, "loner" strain that has long been established in American culture and character.

Let me explain. We may once have been refugees from gerontocracy, but we were also immigrants *toward* a positive, compelling vision. Historically, America always functioned as a major collecting point for a particular human type: that planetary minority of highly individualized, "self-made" people of many racial and ethnic strains, who voluntarily chose to be ancestors, rather than inheritors, and who turned against the guaranteed securities of life in the extended family in favor of a life founded on risk, challenge, and individual rather than collective achievement. Self-selected immigrants of this sort—those who flee the old and established in favor of the new and unformed—turn automatically against received history and received traditions in order to participate in the building of new myths, new histories, and new traditions.

Rooted in time, tradition, and place, the multigenerational family is at odds with essential emigré values; and the clash between the ethos of familism and the ethos of ascendent individuality often shapes and drives struggles and schisms between young and old in the American immigrant family. In effect, the American child is expected to recapitulate the collective myth of separation in his or her development—in this case, from the old folks, rather than from the old country. Presumably, separation from a secure maternal order leads to reestablishment within a new order that one has created for oneself and out of oneself. "Separation-individuation" is the keynote of American development and a major motif of our American psychology about development.

According to some sociologists of the family, the tensions between familism and isolated individuality have led to a compromise pattern in which both sets of priorities are given some scope and are not brought too sharply into conflict. Thus, we have the "modified extended family" and "intimacy at a distance" arrangements encouraged by the car and the telephone, which allow the generations to maintain some physical distance while being available for occasional family sociability and mutual help during emergencies. Thus, when grandparents stress their independence and their fear of burdening their descendants with their senescent dependency, they may well be voicing their pride rather than (as Kornhaber suggests) their despair. In many instances, they may not be defending against rebuff from their grown children; instead, they may be expressing their defiance of age and infirmity. Very much in the American grain they insist on living, despite the blows of fate, by the laws of their own individuality.

Indeed, our research at Northwestern Medical School into late-onset psychopathology indicates that the passionate assertion of independence is the very pivot and fulcrum of self-esteem for many older individuals. They become emotionally ill not because of their self-sufficiency, but because they can no longer maintain their sense of continuity as independent, self-maintaining individuals.

However, despite its virtues, any psychological position has psychic costs, and Kornhaber does well to remind us that children pay a heavy price for our American obsession with autonomy—particularly when we equate autonomy with interpersonal distance and separation. Currently, too many social scientists are trying to liberate adults from the restraints of parental roles; and some—here I must include myself—are similarly engaged in "liberating" the grandparental generation, who are perhaps more entitled to their freedom.

It is good for us liberationists to be reminded that there is no free lunch, and that the unshackling of one group is usually achieved at the expense of another. Typically, despite all the propaganda in favor of day-care centers, it is children who pay the price of adult liberation, particularly the trendy philosophy that equates liberty with unchecked hedonism rather than—as was the case in the older generation—with self-sufficiency.

THE NEW HEDONIC GRANDPARENT

And indeed, this consensual shift in the definitions of liberation may be at the heart of the contractual shift that Kornhaber notes and deplores in the grandparental generation. To repeat, Americans have always equated liberation with social distance, with a muting of the neediness that intimacy entails: The tumbling tumbleweed could be our national plant and the lone cowboy—who needs nothing but his skills to survive and his horse for company—is our national totem. Thus, what may be new is that a significant number of elders have begun to equate liberation not with self-sufficiency and social distance, but with hedonism. What we—and Kornhaber—may be witnessing is the greening of the graybeards; as well as the disastrous consequences—for our children—of this most recent piece of cultural entropy.

Though the now passé ethic of personal independence served the cause of personal freedom, it did not rule out service to others, including grandchildren. Indeed, self-sufficiency is often demonstrated through a rather compulsive, dutiful caring for others, through having dependents rather than being one. But the ethic of hedonism tends to rule out service to others; and when it is adopted by the elders, grandchildren come to be seen as nuisances and even as competitors for the older person's diminished pleasures.

The ethic of self-sufficiency may have entailed some freedom from intimacy; but, unlike the ethic of hedonism, it does not entail freedom from responsibility—particularly, responsibility for others. We should not make the mistake of lumping both versions of elderly liberation together, such that we come to see elderly self-sufficiency and elderly hedonism as part of the same social pathology, equally contemporary and equally destructive to children. In so doing, we not only make a historic error, but we also misread a genuine strength of older people: We mistakenly define their self-sufficiency as though it were a piece of personal and social pathology. However, although we should probably sponsor rather than condemn their independence, we should be concerned about the aggravated consumerism and hedonism that surfaces in Kornhaber's grandparental informants. Inasmuch as the self-indulgence of the grandparents appears to be an echo of the narcissism and consumerism that has recently surfaced in younger cohorts during the "me" decade, then it is probably a new and socially entropic development. It may well be that the hedonism discerned among the old and the neo-narcissism discovered among the young are conjoint symptoms of social phenomena that, although they attack cross-generational family bonds, may have their origins in larger social entities that are prior to the family.

Thus far I have been suggesting that important aspects of the grandparental "contract" are not really so new; and that the self-sufficiency component reflects long-established aspects of American culture and character. I will also suggest that the undeniably new component of the grandparental contract—its narcissistic hedonism—is not a true expression of American culture but is instead a symptom of social entropy: *deculturation,* the breakdown of American culture.

CULTURE AND NARCISSISM

Again, some explanation is called for. To begin with, I see "culture" as standing ultimately apart from the collective norms, trends, and usages that sociologists discover. Thus, a troop of monkeys may have normative, learned ways of behaving that set it apart from other troops of the same species; but it does not have "culture." For me, culture is not represented by what a collectivity is found to be doing at any particular time, but by the actions and objects that the collectivity undertakes or approaches with awe, and with a special excitement. Paraphrasing Redfield (1941), who defined culture as a "system of shared understandings," I see culture as a system of shared and *idealized* understandings. Inquiring about culture, we should not ask, "What car or hair style do you prefer?" but instead, "What, if necessary, are you ready to die for?"

Culture may or may not relate the individual to the marketplace; but a strong culture does relate the individual, via special usages, to the founding myths of his or her special collectivity. A culture's orgin myth speaks of a time when unordinary agents—gods or great leaders—intervened in human affairs to bring about a special people, with a special history and their own defining ways. Culture is a metaphor and transformation of the origin myth; a code for bringing about, within daily circumstances, the unordinary climate of the myth. Through participation in the cultural lifeways, the ordinary individual partakes of the myth, is made to feel—like his or her people—special and unordinary. Thus, as a system of myth-burdened, hence idealized understandings, culture imbues the ordinary practices of life with the tonus of significance, of *meaning*. As such, meanings render palatable the controls, the daily conformities, and even the deprivations on which a decent social life depends.

But the most important function of a shared and signifying culture is to transform the potential stranger into a familiar. Thus, if I share culture with another who is not personally known to me, that other becomes my familiar, my extension, through self-examination. Through knowing myself, I already *know* and can accurately predict a good deal about the other who shares my culture. I know what the other values and abhors. Most important, through self-examination, I know what is *ideal* for the other; despite our differences I become *identical* with the other by virtue of our shared reverences. Because our common culture joins us, I can extend my own self-regard, my own self-love outwardly, to include other. In effect, via culture, the other, the potential stranger, is transformed into a version of self; and narcissistic cathexes, originally directed toward the isolate self, are converted into social bonds.

Thus culture functions to limit the socially entropic effects of individual narcissism, to convert narcissism from antisocial to pro social uses. Culture thus functions to protect the social order, the daily existence and continuity that requires a decent trustfulness among relative strangers. Lacking culture, we become alien to each other, and the order upon which social action depends is not guaranteed from within but must be imposed—usually by some version of the totalitarian police state—from without.

DECULTURATION AND THE GENERATIONAL SCHISM

I submit that in our nation and in this time we are rapidly losing that common core of shared and valued understandings. Not too long ago, values were regarded as *objective*—fixed social realities to be internalized by the individual, but to be created and maintained apart from the individual, by idealized social institutions and their leaders. But in recent times, the process of value formation has been *democratized,* taken out of the institutional province and given over to the individual. Moving thus from the social to the personal sphere, values lose their shared and objective character, becoming private and *subjective.* In effect, we have democratized and relativized the process of value formation to the point where citizens are conceded the right to decide for themselves the question of value: what values should be, and by what standards the citizen should be judged. Unfortunately, the social sciences have played a large and perhaps crucial part in abetting the relativizing and subjectivizing of values to the point where culture no longer entails shared ideals, losing the power to convert strangers into familiars and narcissistic cathexes into enduring social bonds.

When culture is strong, individuals relate to each other in terms of the explicitly *social* categories that emerge readily out of group experience and affiliation: family, neighborhood, ethnic group, religion, social class, profession, and nation. The groupings formed under these categories admit individuals to membership regardless of their age, and to a large degree, regardless of their sex. When culture is strong the social categories, formed out of collective experience, predominate over those formed out of individual, idiosyncratic experience. When culture is strong, those of my social class are my comrades, and all Americans are my fellow compatriots.

But under the conditions of deculturation, narcissistic object choice dictates the lines of affiliation. I can only extend the tonus of familiarity and selfness to those who are like me in the most concrete, immediately sensible respects—those who have the same skin color, body conformation, genitalia, sexual appetites, and same age as myself. In effect, with deculturation, the principles of association are no longer based on shared principles, but become instead racist, ageist, and homoerotic.

As we all know, exclusive age, racial, and sexual groupings based on narcissistic choice are becoming the norm in our society—particularly in our urban centers. The consequences for family life are very much as Kornhaber has described in his chapter. Where the family once united its members, regardless of their age position, the family is now riven along the fracture lines of generational and even sexual difference. Thus, to the degree that family solidarity still persists across the generations, it is mainly between the grandmothers, daughters, and granddaughters of the female line, more and more excluding of men. By the same token, the mistrust between generations that is now a feature of our general social life has invaded the heart of the family itself.

Thus, I do not think that grandparents have under some special social contract acted independently to cut their ties with grandchildren. My hunch is that there is mutual repulsion at work, under the sign of "Don't trust anybody under 30—or over 30." The result is a kind of pseudo-hedonism on both sides, where young and old look to impersonal substances and gratuities—drugs, video, liquor, food, casual sex—to provide the feelings of comfort and security that they can no longer trust intimate others to provide. Under conditions of deculturation, addiction becomes another substitute for the true object choice. Unfortunately, the addictive needs can corrupt the political process as well, such that our children begin to reach out to the totalitarian leaders, and to those other cultists who share with them the adoration of the same leader. When political affiliation is based on narcissistic principles, totaliarianism is a predictable result.

RECULTURATION AND THE ELDERS

Because culture provides meanings that compensate for deprivations, culture makes the human family and adequate human parenting possible. Given a strong culture, young adults will routinely, even cheerfully, enter into the chronic emergency of parenthood, giving up their narcissistic claims for omnipotentiality in favor of the demands made on them by the uniquely vulnerable human child. But as culture loses the capacity to endow deprivation with significance, it is not only grandparents, but also parents who become unreliable and untrustworthy to their offspring. The totalitarian leader, the "Big Brother," becomes more and more attractive as a substitute for the unreliable or absent parent (or grandparent).

Because Americans fear history, received tradition, and gerontocracy, we tend also to be inimical to culture as I have defined it here. As an unintended consequence we may end by replacing culture with totalitarian leaders who will be far more oppressive than the gerontocrats we left behind in the various old countries of our origin. If we are to avoid that consequence, then we have to do more than revive the integrity of grandparenting. We at least have to begin by recognizing that our social malaise has its basis not in the change of culture, but in the loss of culture; and we will have to enlist the elders, who have traditionally been the wardens of culture, to help us and even guide us in this vital process of reversing deculturation and crafting the new myths on which reculturation can be based.

PART IV

GRANDPARENTS, RELIGION, AND THE CONTEXT OF VALUES

One of the many issues that have received little attention in the study of grandparenthood to date concerns the value context of the role—or, in more theological terms, the moral implications of grandparenting. One of the concerns of the two sponsoring organizations that brought together the conference of scholars represented in this volume was the religious aspects of grandparenthood. Ministers and rabbis, Sunday school teachers, and involved laypersons continually encounter issues of religious transmission as well as intergenerational roles. What can the new thrust of scholarship concerning grandparenting say to these practitioners in their positions as counselors and teachers?

The chapters in this section focus on issues of grandparenthood within the context of Judaic and Christian traditions. Written by a rabbi and two priests, they provide an exegesis of the grandparental role with emphasis on how grandparents may be instrumental in achieving transmission across generations of the religious heritage and how grandchildren are important in the "Third Age" of the life course.

Wechsler's chapter discusses the Judaic tradition of grandparenthood. He begins with the recorded experience of Ruth and Jacob as archetypes of what grandparents hope for and receive as blessings in their later years. He notes that "my grandfather" in rabbinic Hebrew means: my old person, my sage. He examines the tension between the Talmudic precept that "what is old is good" and the physical challenges of old age. The expectation of deference ("Thou shalt honor thy father and mother") is important in mitigating the sorrows of old age; but perhaps the key is found in grandchildren, who "restore the grandparent's soul." Grandchildren are essential because they enact the laws of "honoring" in ways not possible for the middle generation, given their other preoccupations and perhaps their own position as children of the grandparent.

Conroy and Fahey focus on the role of grandparents in the transmission of religious heritage. This is a key function of grandparents, from earliest Christian times; they may be more effective transmitters than the parents because of their longer memories of the traditions and their distance from primary disciplinary functions. Conroy and Fahey describe, in very practical terms, some appropriate behaviors grandparents may initiate during seven stages of psychosocial development until their grandchildren become adults. They also examine some problems with respect to whether grandparents can have an influence on grandchildrens' religious socialization in contemporary society. They conclude that issues of religious transmission should, and must, be addressed by behavioral scientists; and that pastoral practice must be informed by scholarly observations on the grandparent role.

12

JUDAIC PERSPECTIVES ON GRANDPARENTHOOD

Harlan J. Wechsler

For a Judaic perspective on grandparenthood, we need to refer to the classical literary sources of the Jewish tradition: the Bible and the writings of the Talmudic period.

GRANDPARENTS IN THE BIBLE

Two Biblical characters, Naomi of the Book of Ruth and Jacob the Patriarch, are described as finding joy from a grandchild in their old age. Naomi is congratulated by women who say: "He shall be to you a restorer of your soul. And he will sustain your old age" (Ruth: 4:14).

Having suffered losses throughout her life, Naomi is, in the opinion of her friends, to be comforted by this grandchild. On the one hand, following the Biblical laws of levirate marriage (Deut. 25:5-6), the child will carry on her son's name, and perhaps it is the certainty of continuity that will restore her soul. On the other hand, to say her grandchild will sustain her in her old age may refer to financial sustenance or to the spiritual consolation she feels.

Naomi nurses her grandson (Ruth 4:16), and the women conclude their congratulatory remarks by saying: " A son is born to Naomi" (Ruth 4:17). Imagine that: "A son is born to *Naomi*"—when the son was born to Ruth, and not her mother-in-law! The Talmud (*Sanhedrin* 19b) points out: "Ruth bore and Naomi brought him up; hence he was called after her [Naomi's] name."

In the Book of Genesis, Jacob is seen in relation to his grandchildren. Jacob, alone among the patriarchs, has the good fortune to be able to bless his grandchildren. He asks Joseph to bring his grandsons to him, noting that they will be like his sons, inheriting his estate. He recalls the death of the boys' grandmother and it is as if the two grandsons finally bring him consolation for that death. The description is poignant. Jacob can hardly see and he asks for his grandsons to be brought close. He kisses them and embraces them, saying to Joseph, "I never expected to see you again, and here God has let me see your children as well" (Gen. 48:11).

Interestingly, Scripture goes on to give the details of a blessing nominally directed at Joseph ("And he blessed Joseph"), while the words of the blessing are actually directed instead at the children:

> Bless the lads
> In them may my name be recalled,
> And the names of my fathers Abraham and Isaac,
> And may they be teeming multitudes upon the earth. (Gen. 48:16)

Here, it is as if Joseph were of significance because of his sons, as if the grandfather saw in them the continuity of his life, the certainty of his own eternity. All that was quite clearly coupled with the simple emotions that brought him to hug and kiss.

The stories of both Naomi and Jacob repeat a motif in kind, if not in detail. The old person has had great cause for sorrow throughout a difficult life. Solace, joy, and hope for the future are engendered by grandchildren.

Elsewhere in Scripture, in Psalm 128, several rewards for fearing the Lord are enumerated. A person will be happy and, moreover, his wife will be a fruitful vine, with his children like olive plants around the table. But even more: "You shall see your children's children, and peace upon Israel" (Ps. 128:6). Here, grandchildren may be a blessing in two ways: One, their presence is indicative of one's own long life, and the verse may simply be saying you will live long, an important blessing in the store of Scriptural rewards. Second, it simply may be that seeing grandchildren is a joy and a blessing. Who need say more? This latter interpretation would be fully consonant with the view expressed in Proverbs 17:6: "Grandsons are the garlands of old men, and fathers are the pride of their sons." In Hebrew the word for garlands is *atarah*, which literally means a crown. It is the grandchild that makes the grandparent feel like royalty.

In addition to these verses referring specifically to grandparents and grandchildren, keep in mind that although the Bible does not have a command to honor one's grandparents as it does command for honoring of father and mother, there is a general command to honor the old:

> You shall rise before the aged and show deference
> to the old; you shall fear your God:
> I am the Lord. (Lev. 19:32)

This verse applies to all the old, and one would expect that basic attitudes toward the old will be reflected in specific relations toward grandparents. Scripture is here very clear what the attitudes should be: Honor and respect as illustrated by rising when in the presence of the old.

THE TERM FOR GRANDPARENT

Perhaps most interesting is the very language that refers to grandparents and the old, for in both the Bible and the Talmud there is no Hebrew word for grandparent. In the examples from the Bible brought above, the English translation "grandfather" is taken from two Hebrew words that are equivalent to "the father of his father." Grandchild is rendered similarly: "the son of his son."

Most people who know modern Hebrew will tell you that the word for grandfather is *saba*, for grandmother *sabta*. But these are recent modern Hebrew usages of Talmudic terms for the old derived from the Aramaic words for white or gray hair. In Rabbinic literature, the most common word for grandfather is *zaqen*; for grandmother, *zeqenah*. But this very word is precisely the same word used for "old person."

One word has a multiplicity of meanings, beginning with grandfather and old person. Yet these meanings only scratch the surface of the term *zaqen*. For *zaqen* refers as well to a sage. A *zaqen* is also a judicial office equivalent to that of judge. A *zaqen* is an elder and is also the title for head of the academy. All these meanings are wrapped up in one single word. The term *zaqen* is, in Max Kadushin's (1965) language, a "value concept." It is value-laden. It is filled with valences, nearly all of which are of a positive force. Thus, to appreciate what a grandparent is we must recognize that the structure of the language yields a word that means many things.

"My grandfather" in rabbinic Hebrew means my old person, my sage. It is as if one were to recognize that there are those who, in general, are referred to as old. But this one is *mine*. There is a relation between this old person and me. My grandfather shares as well in a word that conveys authority and sagacity, judgment and status.

OLD AGE IN THE TALMUD

To understand more about the relations between the generations, it will be most helpful to see the Talmudic view of old age itself. This view is not without its perception of problems.

Rabbinic literature is replete with descriptions of the ailments of the old.

> Appreciate your vigor in the days of
> your youth, before those days of sorrows
> come and those years arrive of which you
> will say, "I have no pleasure in them."
> (*Koheleth* 12:1)

The Rabbis comment that Koheleth's advice refers to old age.

The Rabbis go on to describe what was so bad. The beauty of the face, the forehead, the nose, the skin all disappear. The cheeks lose their glow. Tears seem to well up in a person's eyes. There is difficulty in controlling bladder and bowel functions. The knees, the ribs, the loins all shake; the body is bent. The teeth are gone, the stomach inefficient. The eyes have grown dim. The voice of song seems like only a whisper because the ears can no longer hear well. A person cannot sleep.

The old are said to be filled with fears: fear of heights, for even a small mound appears a high mountain; fear of the road; fear of muggers coming to attack. Poverty, due to inability to work, was the inheritance of old age. Imagine then the several levels of attack upon the self-respect of an individual—physical, psychological, and economic—that are recognized here. Why does a person suffer? Not because he or she has caught an unusual tropical disease for which there is as yet no cure— unless the disease be called that of being human and of getting old.

All this having been said, old age in the Rabbinic tradition is also considered a great gift. In the Jewish tradition, it is a blessing to live. When Abraham makes a convenant with God, he is told "you shall go to your fathers in peace. You shall be buried at a ripe old age" (Gen. 15:15). Longevity is a blessing and is a special gift for the observance of the commandments:

> Let the mother bird go and take only the
> young, in order that you may fare well and
> have a long life. (Deut. 22:7)

This very same approach is found in the Babylonian Talmud (*Megilah* 27b-28a). The question is often asked of an old sage: "By virtue of what have you lived so long?" The sage will normally respond by citing some simple act of ethical or ritual behavior to which most people pay little regard, but that he has observed scrupulously.

Keep in mind that the Bible—and by extension Judaism—is built upon the bedrock of the creation story of Genesis, which understands this world to be the creation of God, a creation that is good. Not only that, but after God creates the animals and especially man and woman on the sixth day, He looks and says that it is *very* good. Those two words, "very good," underlie much Jewish thought. Humankind's existence, the tie to matter though the matter crumble, is very good. And the prolongation of material existence is, at least theologically, very good as well. Where the creation is good, living long preserves the blessed state.

But there is another aspect to the blessing of longevity that may be closer to those benefits appreciated by common sense. For although there may be theological reasons to praise long life, there may be practical reasons to praise it as well. In the Talmudic tradition, the old are compared to fine wine that gets better with age because of one quality they possess: They have studied more Torah (*Mishnah Avot* 4:20). Not only is learning an important reason for respecting the old, but study is an important ingredient in increasing the quality of aging. As Rabbi Yishmael, the son of Rabbi Yosi says:

> Scholars, the older they get the more wisdom
> they accrue. . . . But the ignorant, the older
> they get, the more stupidity they accrue.
> (*Shabbat* 152a)

Here you see the value of old age. It derives its significance from the fact that learning is cumulative and more will accrue with the years. Similarly, without study old age is a progressive decline rather than something good.

What then of the old who are not scholars? If Torah is the source of significance for the old, are the unlearned unworthy of respect? The Talmud raises this question in regard to the commandment to honor the old, and it concludes that *all* the old, regardless of the level of their learning, are included in the commandment to rise before the aged. As Rabbi Yohanan says: "How many troubles have passed over these!" (*Kiddushin* 33a). Life's experiences make their impression and hone the wisdom of the person who accrues more of them as time goes on.

WHAT IS OLD IS GOOD

There is fundamental value operating here, impressive partly because it differs so much from the underpinnings of the modern world in which we live. That value is "what is old is good." Worth in the world of the Talmud was not measured in terms of speed, economic terms, or according to an aesthetic that sees vigor and muscle tone to be what is good. Rav Papa puts it bluntly: "Everything which is old is best, except for dates, beer and fish-hash." Although I hesitate to speculate on the problems of dates, beer, and fish-hash, there is undoubtedly an approach to living here wherein the value of a person increases with age.

This is possible, given the following conclusions: (1) Life is a blessing. The more of it, the more one is filled with blessings—and who could then have enough? (2) Torah fills life with meaning. The act of study, of internalizing God's word, fills a person with self-worth in addition to keeping the mind sharp. (3) Life's experiences provide learning worthy of respect in every human being.

As desirable as these conclusions may be, it is nonetheless true that they become part of a tension, even a contradiction, when believed. For although old age was considered a reward and a blessing, remember that it was also understood to be physically demeaning and debilitating. To resolve such a paradox practically, there need be objective "forces" as one might call them, either activities, relations, or states of mind that operate actively upon both individual and society to balance these opposing ideas about old age in everyday life. To succeed, they will constantly have to reinforce the underlying values of the goodness of each person and the praise for learning.

Indeed, where self-worth is most threatened by the slings and arrows of fortune, there ought ideally to be stable elements—in the Talmudic tradition you would expect them to be laws—that will help inculcate and sustain the values that support the individual aged person and counter a natural loss of self-esteem. There are two such laws: The first mandates honor for the old in general. The second mandates honor and respect for one's own parents. Seen together, they will provide the key to the unique relation between a grandparent and a grandchild.

THE COMMANDMENT TO RISE UP
BEFORE AND HONOR THE OLD

In the Torah, the injunction to honor the old is, as we have seen, found in Leviticus 19:32. To translate rather literally, the verse reads:

> You shall rise up before the hoary head,
> And honor the face of the old,
> And you shall fear God;
> I am the Lord.

On the surface, this is a clear command to honor and respect the old, though the Hebrew words may be read as a mandate to honor scholars. All this is placed in the very serious context of fearing God. In Rabbinic literature (principally *Kiddushin* 32b, *Jerusalem Talmud Bikurim* 3:3, and *Tosefta Megilah* 3:24), two actions are understood to be prescribed: (1) "You shall rise up" (*takum*) and (2) "You shall honor" (*ve-hadarta*). The practical ramifications of both these words are clearly defined.

Standing before the old is said to mean that one must rise when an old person approaches within about four yards of one's presence. It is therefore not necessary to rise when the old person is seen from a distance. It is not permissible to close one's eyes and thereby avoid the requirement of standing. When the person to be honored has drawn near, it is proper to greet him or her and to respond to his or her greeting. This involves a motion of bowing. Gather the picture: One stands and greets the old person while bowing toward him. The action required is a physical one, motivated by conscience (God's demand). It involves a public expression of respect, clearly understood as such (the old person must be in one's presence, remember), using social conventions that communicate respect for the individual.

The second requirement, that indicated by the Hebrew verb *vehadarta,* is more varied in its meanings. The Hebrew here conveys an attitude that bears a value—it can be translated as honor or respect—and it comes from a root that means "beautiful." Honor, respect, make beautiful the face of the old. And Rabbinic literature spells out the practical implications of this as well. Honoring the old person means that one may neither stand nor sit in his or her place; that one should neither speak in that person's place nor contradict his or her words. In addition, one must conduct one's self toward that person with fear and reverence, allowing the old to take precedence when entering or leaving a place.

These prescriptions constitute the meaning of "you shall honor" in the sources. One can see that the prescribed actions are public in nature, using the customs of the time to clearly indicate deference to the old. No monetary expense is required.

HONOR YOUR FATHER AND MOTHER

So far we have considered the laws that are applicable to all the old. The specific actions mandated are those showing public deference in a variety of ways. But first, they are actions. Second, they indicate attitudes and emotions that either give birth to the actions or are intended to be engendered by them.

But the case of the specific old person can be seen more clearly if we turn to the duties incumbent upon children toward their elderly parents. This is the meaning of the Fifth Commandment found in the Decalogue. In fact, the law "Honor your father and your mother" appears twice in the Torah, in Exodus 20:12 and in Deuteronomy 5:16. It is found in a somewhat different form in Leviticus 19:3, where Scripture reads: "You shall each revere his mother and his father. . . ." Note that the Torah says "honor" one time. Another time the Torah says "revere." Therefore, the laws governing relations to parents are elaborated in terms of the meaning of "honor" and "revere."

Honoring a parent requires positive actions such as giving a parent food and drink, clothing, as well as leading him or her in and out

(*Kiddushin* 31b). Note that these positive actions are *not* part of the general law pertaining to the old. The specifics here are a bit ambiguous for they leave unclear who will pay. Does "giving a parent food and drink" mean paying for it, or actually physically serving the parent? Does clothing the parent mean financial responsibility for clothing, or actually helping the parent on with clothes? The Talmud raises these questions and answers them by deciding that it is the personal service rather than the payment that is required by the Torah.

Later commentators raise questions about this conclusion, interpreting the text to apply to the old person who has his or her own means. But the text of the Talmud does not say this. To the contrary, what stands out here is the Talmud's interest in the personal relation between parent and child. It is not enough to honor a parent by sending a check, as we might say today. Proper honor involves personal presence, a child *personally* helping an aged parent, not hiring someone else to do it instead. That is the unique feature of honor.

The law to revere one's parent is, on the other hand, similar to the law requiring respect for the old. The child must neither stand nor sit in the parent's place, nor should the child contradict the parent's word.

THE MEANING OF DEFERENCE

Personal, public acts provide the solution to the paradox earlier described. They come out of a world view in which the universe is created by God and there is an inherent goodness to this creation. Bodily life is good in essence, though in experience there may be significant problems with it. If God's plan requires the body to age, and this brings with it physical and social disabilities, the human being will have good cause to wonder how blessed this created state is. Commandments to the rescue, then. If a person's self-esteem goes down on one tally, it should rise on another. Let the child and the community bolster that flagging sense of self-worth by publicly demonstrable actions that continue to convey the great value of every human being. The mandated actions affirm the theological idea, even when experience would otherwise question its correctness.

Note the significance of social conventions for the communication of respect; and note, as well, the emphasis on *personal* actions toward another human being. It is the person who makes another aware of his or her humanity, and computers, institutions, or government agencies can never really do that. They may play their part in maximizing what they do best (such as providing funds for complicated medical care) but they are not human. Only single individuals are.

Increasing respect for the human being turns a potential cipher and a potential "case" into a person. It turns that person from something insignificant into something grand. It should not be forgotten: Grandpeople are the people who are old.

GRANDPARENTS AND GRANDCHILDREN

Perhaps here we can see, finally, why the grandchild is so important. Why did a child restore Naomi's soul? Why did a little child mean so much to Jacob?

In the Talmudic discussion (*Kiddushin* 31b) concerning the obligation of a child to honor his or her father and mother, one sage, Rabbi Abbahu, tells how exemplary his son Abimi was in fulfilling this command. When Rabbi Abbahu came to visit his son and grandchildren, Abimi himself speedily ran to the door to open it for him crying, "Yes, yes" until his father reached the door. Notice Abimi's piety. He ran faster than the grandchildren and therefore he deserves special praise. Implicitly one learns that a son must be terribly pious to run as fast as a grandchild to greet his grandfather.

What restores a grandparent's soul? The very same thing that restores anyone's soul: respect and honor personally and publicly expressed. The old, because of the realities of aging, need that respect, orchestrated in society and in one's children. But perhaps there is one group that if left on their own need laws to do what has to be done. Perhaps they respect experience and authority that does not come into direct conflict with them—rather they serve as models of what one can ideally respect. Perhaps grandchildren naturally fit this bill and mean so much to their grandparents because it is these children who naturally put them on a pedestal and thereby restore their souls.

13

CHRISTIAN PERSPECTIVE ON THE ROLE OF GRANDPARENTS

Donald B. Conroy
Charles J. Fahey

In the renewed liturgical calendar of the Catholic Church the feast of Jesus Christ's grandparents—Saints Ann and Joachim—is an intriguing addition in the cycle of celebration. This in itself may be just a quirk of bureaucratic change, as what were formerly separate celebrations have been combined into one. But it also may indicate a new sensitivity to the importance of ancestors—and in particular grandparents—in passing on the religious tradition and influencing the values of the coming generations.

This chapter examines the role and function of grandparents from a Christian perspective. In the first section, we look at the various stages of child and adolescent development as they are commonly defined by the behavioral sciences, and present a pastoral and theological reflection on the role of grandparents with respect to the handing on of religious heritage. The intent here is to make observations from the point of view of Christian (especially Catholic) tradition.

In the second section, our purpose is to examine some of the problems presented by the hypothesis that grandparents have a measurable influence on grandchildren. Four issues are considered, beginning with the demographic fact of the rapid growth in the numbers of older people of the grandparental generation. A second issue concerns the diverse, and sometimes complex, social expressions of grandparenting, whereas a third involves difficulties encountered in scientific examination of this area of intergenerational socialization. A final consideration is the need for doing research on the "Third Age" of life, especially grandparenthood, with collaboration between behavioral scientists and pastoral theologians.

APPROPRIATE TIMES FOR
GRANDPARENTAL INTERACTION

From a Christian perspective, a key function of grandparents involves passing on heritage and tradition. From earliest Christian times the household of faith was crucial in transmitting the Christian perspective on life—its origins, memory, and values. Although parents are, indeed, crucial to this process, the grandparents, even more than the so-called "godparents," are strategically placed to be transmitters of the tradition. In some ways, they may transmit even more than parents, as they have longer memories of the traditions. Moreover, grandparents may be tempered by the wisdom of longer experiences and possibly deeper insights into the values to be handed on.

In a sense, Christian grandparents share in a general cultural need to involve "significant older" adults other than parents and those from the middle or parental generation. Those elders can interact with and evoke within the child a sense of religious perspective, heritage beyond the secular world, and history within a value frame of reference.

KNOWING OUR ROOTS

Although the "Roots" experience, occasioned by Alex Haley's book by that name, was notably about a Black family, it also had a Christian and religious theme in which grandparents and ancestors contributed. To know where they stand religiously and to be informed of that heritage is a basic right of every child. Christians are "people of the story" and they need elders to pass on this "story." From a Catholic point of view, beyond even the Scriptures of the Bible, the story is passed on in the people through oral tradition, ritual, and customs. Catholic Christians consider themselves to be a "sacramental" people. Grandparents, in particular, show evidence of being highly significant symbols of the Transcendent.

Grandparents in various degrees fulfill the role of being story-persons. Yet it is not through telling stories so much as *being* "living stories" that they are significant. Simply because they are present to the child, they are signs of the tradition and transcendent. We know from educational theory the power of "modeling" as an effective form of teaching or transmitting values. The enchancement of such modeling in the person of the grandparent should be evident.

At first glance, one's grandparents may seem to be quite ordinary. But their relationship with grandchildren, according to Kornhaber and Woodward's interviews (1981, p. 43), has a heroic effect. Moreover, there is something special in the whole context of being a generation beyond one's parent's generation, as Hagestad (1981) has noted. This tradition stretches back before their parents began to live and touches the "unknown." This numinous aura is all the more attributable to great-grandparents.

With respect to the telling of history as the grandparents experienced it, the importance lies beyond the expertise of the story-teller. Rather, when the grandparent recounts the story, a more immediate connection exists with how they came to be in time and space. This touches their identity and tells the child concretely about his or her own story and origin. It communicates the values of life and reason for existence.

A central element from the Christian perspective on grandparenting is how it "sacramentalizes" life. This can happen when the grandparent embodies the transcendent meaning of life through family rituals and customs. Why so? This kind of "sacramental presence" involves a symbolic representation of the religious reality that has a real effect on our lives (see Martos, 1981).

As the Christian life is generally lived out, there is a wealth of reality unfolding at the various stages of life. This keeps pace with the Church's sacramental life in the parish and relates to the embodiment within the home of the same reality, but in a different way. Psychological and sociological studies (see Erikson, 1950; McCready, 1978) have pointed to at least seven stages of childhood development through adolescence. Dobson (1981) makes use of these with respect to significant periods in understanding the grandparent's role.

Applied theology correlates with these stages and points out significant ways in which the home in general and grandparents in particular can have an impact on the religious and underlying character formation of the child. Several issues are salient for extended study of the religious socialization of the child (Erikson, 1968; McCready & McCready, 1973).

GRANDPARENTS AND THE
TRANSMISSION OF RELIGIOUS HERITAGE

The stages of grandparenting from birth through adolescence have special import for the transmission of religion.

The first stage of development is from *birth to about one year,* when the child begins to walk. Parents' and grandparents' roles at this stage are difficult to distinguish in terms of the religious development the child is experiencing. However, a basis for future explicit moral development is being laid in how the generations are beginning to self-define their role in terms of affective relationship to the child. From a Christian perspective, the more grandparents are reflectively aware of their traditions, its teachings, and its customs in relationship to the developmental needs of the child, the more they are seen to be able to act effectively as role models.

The main Christian sacramental event that happens ritually during the infancy period is baptism, signifying birth into the church community as a child of God. The grandparents' role is in backing up the parents. This can be reinforced in the new Catholic rite of infant baptism when a special blessing is added for the grandparents. The grandparents' role will be indirectly focused on the grandchild and their role more directly will be one of helping and being supportive of the new parents. As grandparents and parents realize their complementary roles, the celebration of baptism lays the basis for future religious socialization.

The second, or *toddler,* stage begins approximately from the grandchild's first birthday to the third year of life. Going beyond the oral-sensory development of the first period of life, the toddler now is in the muscular-anal period where autonomy and self-control are important (Dobson, 1981).

As the development of self-confidence in the child is the crucial task of this period (this is important in religious formation as well), grandparents can reinforce this by letting the child explore his or her world unhindered. Too many negative commands as attempts of exploration are made may inhibit the child, and he or she will learn self-doubt instead. This, too, has religious implications. Self-confidence as well as the basic trust of the first stage in infancy will lay the basis for future prayer attitudes and religious understanding. Along with this, grandparents can begin to tell and read simple stories (including short Bible stories) along with singing basic tunes and melodies (including religious songs).

The third stage is *early childhood*, which begins around two or three years of age. Sometimes called the "first adolescence," because of the disequilibrium of the "terrible twos," the child gets demanding and insists that things be done in a certain way or he or she may display violent emotions with outbursts of tears and temper tantrums. Patience is a grandparental virtue, and the religious grandparent—who may want to teach a child "discipline" too early—may actually undermine the child's development. The grandparent must recognize that this is a transition stage between infancy and preschool stages. It has no negative moral connotation. This is a time when grandparents can take the grandchild to the playground or can select toys and do simple games to help in developing locomotive control and the underlying emotional skills that will be important for future religious development.

The grandparent can now begin in a more earnest way to provide celebrational occasions for the child and young family on such days as Christmas, Easter, and birthdays. Play is very important to the religious as well as the psychosocial growth. Storytelling may begin in earnest and family rituals will often have a life-long impact on the young child. Basic words with religious value or significance can be introduced, too.

Next comes a calmer period that parents and grandparents often enjoy deeply. The *preschool years* extend from three to five or six. There are a number of crucial tasks a child has at this time in terms of greater interaction with the environment, and grandparents can be directly helpful to the child.

Religious customs and ritual celebrations can be genuinely appreciated at this time. Basic emotional responses can take place that are important for the stability of the religious development of the child. Important faith symbols can be introduced within the homes of both the child and grandparents. Examples of these are presented by Veronica Dreves (1981) in her series of preschool religious education books based on White's (1973) research. This series, in fairly wide circulation in the United States and Canada, presents to the grandparent a wide range of possible activities that will make a deep and lasting impact upon the grandchild. Also, Bible stories can be readily understood and imagined by the grandchild at this stage.

In the period of *middle childhood* (ages 6 to 11) the grandparent can continue to play an important role. Storytelling in greater depth will be appreciated. Customs that involve the young person and the grandparents can be a very satisfying experience for both and will lead the young child to a deeper understanding of faith in God and kindness to the human community.

Grandparents at this stage can be particularly helpful in preparing for and celebrating the grandchild's First Communion. Customs such as Christmas Eve dinner, May devotions, and Christian traditions at Easter, Pentecost, and even Halloween are times for religious values to be passed on. Grandparents can explain the meaning of the religious heritage at times of visits to churches and shrines and outdoor festivals. The direct experience, and not didactic teaching, will be the more effective way of dealing with these values and beliefs.

As the stage of *preadolescence* (11 to 13) comes along, grandparents may recede somewhat in the child's social world though they may still be very important in the cultural and religious development of the grandchild. Stories that relate to the grandchild's beginning search for identity are important. These can be such things as incidents from the grandchild's parents' lives when they were in the same preteen years. The formation of the personal story is crucial if the young person is to have a religious identity. Teaching skills and sharing secret memories can be important to this development.

At this time grandparents as well as parents will come to see a new defensiveness and argumentativeness as the preteenager tries to deal with his or her search for selfhood. Religiously, peer group friends and same-age cousins will become more and more important. Grandparents can reassure the parents by telling them what they were like at the same age.

The final stage of our reflection is on grandparenting the *adolescent* (13 to 18 or 21). Grandparents and parents are in a bind here, as they must necessarily recede in the young person's consciousness so that a separate identity and discovery of sexuality, loyality, and generousity can take place.

Grandparents will still be important in various ways at special moments such as holidays and family celebrations. If Confirmation is celebrated with the young person, this can be a time of reassurance and honest sharing. If an interest in school, vocation, or a career is brought up, this is a time to deal with observations about life's values and choices.

Graduation from high school and entry into college or a new job are times for celebration as are life events like receiving a driver's license or going to a prom. Stories of a more adult character can be very helpful when shared between grandparents and grandchildren. Direct discussion of the religious heritage and values is now possible at opportune times.

As the grandparent now grows into more advanced age, life will be passed on and the heritage of faith transmitted in wide variety of more subtle and yet important ways.

THE SIGNIFICANT OLDER PERSON'S ROLE

We next turn to several issues related to the critique of the religious role of grandparents, and "significant third age adults" as well as substitute grandparents. We will examine the uniqueness of the contemporary situation; the diverse social expressions of grandparents and grandparenting; the state of scientific knowledge concerning religious development and grandparents; research needs; and the "third age" and grandparenthood.

"IT HAS NEVER BEEN THIS WAY BEFORE"

Often in the midst of rapid social change it is hard to recognize that change is occurring, to say nothing of understanding its implications. "One loses sight of the forest because of the trees." As we examine the contemporary religious role of grandparents, we are in the midst of much social change evidenced by change in life expectancy and in the age structure of the population that must also be noted. Today's grandparents are, in a sense, demographic pioneers.

It is estimated that in the Bronze Age, average life expectancy was 23. At the time of the birth of Jesus Christ, one person out of 10 lived to be 50. In 1900 in America, the average life expectancy was 46. Figures developed in the 1980 census indicated that the average life expectancy in the United States is more than 73 for men, and 80 for women. This represents an astounding increase of three years in each of the past eight decades.

There always have been some very old people. There have been no breakthroughs in terms of limits to the life span. However, we have made great strides in the number of people who will enjoy the fullness of years and therefore, the number of grandparents and even great-grandparents will be and is on the increase. This has resulted from better maternal and child health, immunization, better understanding of nutrition and environmental factors, as well as better diagnostic and therapeutic techniques.

These things are adjuncts of an affluent society. Those who have personal wealth or who are in a wealthier nation are much more likely to enjoy the fullness of years than those from poorer parts of a society or from a society that is generally poor.

Analysis of the population also indicates significant differences by reason of gender. On the average, women in the United States live seven years longer than men. Whether this differentiation will continue in the future is a matter of conjecture, though there is some concern if for no other reason than the increase in smoking among women.

Even as more people live longer, people are healthier. Both disease and crippling conditions have been reduced. We witness decreased mortality and morbidity in every cohort except that of the old, old.

We have reduced poverty among older people, largely as a result of governmental actions, such as improvement of Social Security, the introduction of Medicare, and so on. Generally, older people are better educated than were their counterparts of past generations. All these things are good news. We are living longer and generally are better off.

However, there are problems. There is serious concern about family life today. For every two women who are married, one will be single by the time she is fifty because of divorce or separation or death of a spouse. Women are much less likely to remarry than are their male counterparts. Whereas only 15 percent of men over 65 live alone, more than 40 percent of women do. It should be noted that many live alone very satisfactorily. Nonetheless, living alone is an indicator of potential problems.

With growing opportunities for women to exercise the fullness of their personalities, there is considerable confusion about the roles of husband and wife, not only during childbearing years but also in the latter part of marriage. The need for fathering and grandfathering are called into question by some radical feminists. Husbands and wives live longer together in marriage without children in the home.

Although even the experts are confused about the economic future of our country, things are changing. There are indications that many young families are pessimistic about their economic future, thereby recalling the grandparental experiences of economic depression in the 1930s. The concept of upward social mobility so much a part of American culture seems now to be tempered.

There is ferment among religions both in general and within religious groups. Are Americans as religious as they were a generation ago? Despite various public opinion polls, it is difficult to ascertain. Some measures are relatively straightforward, such as church attendance. Prayerfulness and commitment to a moral code are not so easily measured. Religious institutions are changing. It is always difficult to separate the "cultural" and the "spiritual" in religious institutions, but in both areas there is rapid change.

We are witnessing substantial intellectual activity in and among religious groups even as we see evidence of anti-intellectualism and a return of fundamentalism in religious traditions. On the other hand, there is greater interfaith cooperation and ecumenical understanding in spite of indifference to religion in some sectors. Some decry the latter, if for no other reason than it removes people from their cultural roots and identity.

All these factors influence families, religious organizations, and living patterns. They have impact upon children, parents, and grandparents.

That four generations are now normative in families barely has been recognized as an issue by churches or by secular culture. Our discussion should be about great-grandparents rather than just grandparents.

Concommitant with the growth in numbers of those achieving the fullness of years is a cultural crisis concerning the meaning of old age. We often don't know what a long life is for. As long as persons were or are preoccupied with survival and the basic elements of human existence, there was no question of how one would use the latter part of their life. However, at a time when the skills of older persons are becoming obsolete, and when for many a degree of affluence is assured, the meaningfulness of this third age is of extraordinary importance.

Our concern about grandparents and grandparenting must be considered within the cultural context of confusion about the place of older persons in society as well as about what old age means. Until recently, retirement was associated and directly correlated with frailty and vulnerability. Today, these concepts have been disassociated. Although certain occupations may sap one's energy and enthusiasm for work, most persons retire while they are reasonably healthy.

In addition, as far as Christians are concerned there exists no major culturally perceived difference regarding the grandparents' generation vis-à-vis the general society. This does not preclude specific variations in certain ethnic ghettos or the encouragement by Christian leaders to deal in alternative ways regarding the role and function of the elderly within the family, the parish, and the society.

GRANDPARENTS AND GRANDPARENTING— DIVERSITY OF ROLES AND EXPECTATIONS

The role of grandparent is ambigious and uneven. In American society this role confusion often influences mainstream Christianity, including Roman Catholic churches. This stems from the diversity in kinds of relationships between the generations as well as from the various things that have happened to family life generally. Note the various family patterns that exist, each with its own consequences:

(1) In the ideal pattern we envision a grandchild with stable parents and four living grandparents. Unfortunately, this may be the exception rather than the rule. Even in such instances, a single grandchild usually shares his or her grandparents as well as parents with siblings or cousins.

(2) In the ideal and perhaps romantic version of grandparenting, the grandparents share a common cultural religious identity. Yet, in reality marriage may involve grandparents of divergent ethnic, cultural, and religious backgrounds. However, this diversity can be an enriching experience with grandparents sharing and helping the grandchildren to appreciate the richness and positive elements of the diverse heritages.

(3) The grandparent who is the surrogate parent, whether for a short or lengthy period, is a common American phenomenon. In such instances, the biological grandparent is de facto a parent, but this is not unusual in history, as is evident in the Book of Ruth.

(4) With the frequency of divorce and remarriage, the relationships in many American families is complex involving various step-parents, step-grandmothers, and step-grandfathers. Similarly, new relationships also

arise from the remarriage of those who are widowed. Also, one or both sets of grandparents may be separated or divorced.

All of these issues point to the complexity of role expectations when studying or observing grandparent-grandchild interaction. It is also important to recognize that just as the parent does not cease to be a child so the grandparent does not cease to be a parent. The intergenerational struggles and affection go on even as adults.

These social and psychological realities serve as a backdrop for further analysis of the impact of grandparents on the religious identity, beliefs, and practices of their grandchildren.

GRANDPARENTAL INFLUENCE VIS-À-VIS SIGNIFICANT OTHERS

A substantial literature about child development in general, as well as religious development, has accrued. Similarly, in the field of adult development, theologians, philosophers, psychologists, sociologists, anthropologists, and general popularizers have written extensively in these areas. Whatever their particular perspective, they tend to agree on two propositions: (1) "Significant others" have a great deal to do with initial development of one's view of life; and (2) life is a developmental process with a variety of stages through which an individual must work as he or she assumes ever greater autonomy, personal responsibility, and moral or religious depth (Erikson, 1950; Dobson, 1981).

The "significant other" rewards and punishes, teaches explicity in concepts and implicitly by behavior. Although the child's universe is small, those that shelter, feed, and correct him or her have almost complete dominance in regard to the child's view of life. Gradually the child's world broadens and others with their perspectives become significant. These include peers, playmates, neighbors, fellow students and, in contemporary society, characters on television. From a religious as well as psychological point of view all of these bring new insights, new values, and new beliefs that challenge the child.

The grandparent who mediates, litigates, rewards, and cherishes a grandchild can be a significant other of great importance. Especially when the grandparent is seen as historically and genetically connected, this importance is all the more significant. Of course, the negative impact of inappropriate grandparenting is a real possibility if the grandparent handles this role in a manipulative or neurotic manner. There is also the possibility of a grandparent acting out of simple ignorance, which can be reinforced by good will and stereotypical responses from another time or culture that could confuse the child.

That the grandparent can be one of the main "significant others" in a person's life seems to be warranted as we look at the chapters by Bengtson, Troll, Aldous, and Hagestad in this volume and other studies on ethnics such as Cohler (see Cohler & Grunebaum, 1981) and McCready (1974, 1975).

THE "THIRD AGE" AND GRANDPARENTHOOD

The prolongation of life constitutes a new reality in contemporary society's general experience. This factor has great significance for individuals, families, and public policy as well as religious and cultural dimensions of society. Life can be divided into three very general periods. First, there is a period in which one achieves certain fundamental skills and gains a perspective on reality and the basic education or training to deal with a technologically complex world. During this "first age" an individual, through family, school, and adolescent peers, receives the tools of being fully human. A "second age" of middle years involves a more mature involvement in advanced education, the work world, and other life concerns dealing with selecting a career and a spouse and embarking on a family of one's own. In most periods of history, and even today in many parts of the world, the two "ages" constitute the whole life span for most persons.

However, in contemporary America and Western Europe there is a "third age" being experienced by a broad segment of the population. This is the time of grandparenthood for most, or surrogate grandparenthood for many others. The contribution of this third age to life is only beginning to be explored. In the coming decades it may have its greatest impact with the aging of the post-war "baby boom" now about to arrive in its middle and later years.

Christianity in general and Catholic tradition in particular have not developed an extensive theology of the third age or the older segment of the community. In most countries Christianity—unlike Judaism—has gone along fairly unreflectively in terms of the role and importance of the elders in contemporary society and in the modern church's life.

Only recently through the work of the Pontifical Council for the Laity and certain pastoral addresses of Pope John Paul II has this issue begun to be reflected upon in the light of Catholic church teaching and the gospel message. As for scholarly work, beginnings have only been made with the documents and addresses of the Vatican delegation of the United Nations' World Assembly of Aging held in 1982 in Vienna.

The study of the role and function of grandparents is in its beginning stages. The present chapter has highlighted possible areas of scientific reflection by raising the theological questions that must be addressed to the behavioral and anthropological sciences.

PART V

TURNING KNOWLEDGE INTO POLICY AND PROGRAMS

The preceding chapters in this volume have examined research on grandparenthood from a variety of scholarly perspectives: sociology, anthropology, psychology, psychiatry, and theology. That grandparenthood is diverse, and that it has attributes both symbolic and functional, is clear from these presentations. How can such knowledge be turned into broader collective action? What has been attempted so far in creating public policy and intervention programs to enhance the role of grandparents in contemporary society?

This concluding chapter, by a social scientist, an educator, and a lawyer, identify some examples of policy and programs directed at grandparenting. First they review four clusters of information suggested by the available scholarly literature, as reflected in this volume. One theme involves a focus on grandparenthood in terms of socialization processes; a second on reciprocity and mutuality in intergenerational interactions. A third grouping of research involves personhood, individual or personality dimensions of grandparenthood, and the fourth relates to values and the product of transmission.

Robertson, Tice, and Loeb then turn to the theme of generational interdependence, and note that to date the social policy literature has not adequately addressed this issue. However, they list a number of programs that have been developed to bring generations together, and discuss the emergent emphasis on making grandparenthood more explicit in formal and informal social settings. They also review recent legal developments in terms of grandparenthood as a status: There are now statutes in more than 40 states addressing the various rights of grandparents, especially in terms of visitation after divorce.

Public policy implications of grandparenthood, as the authors note, are many and varied; they conclude with a listing of some specific questions that remain as challenges for those involved. Truly the challenge of turning available knowledge into useful policy and programs is great. However, with the growing knowledge base reflected by the scholars included in this volume, there is considerable promise for applications that may strengthen the role of grandparenthood in a rapidly changing society.

14

GRANDPARENTHOOD
From Knowledge to Programs and Policy

Joan F. Robertson
Carol H. Tice
Leonard L. Loeb

Few would disagree as to the importance of the family for its members or for society. Operating with other social institutions, one's family provides caring and socialization functions ensuring the continuity of individual and social life by providing opportunities for identity, purpose, relatedness, roots to the past, and links to the future (Bronfenbrenner, 1981; Mead, 1977). Generally, the latter two functions are carried out by older family members, particularly grandparents.

It is of note, therefore, that some social analysts, of various ideological persuasions, have addressed concerns about the capacity of the family to adapt to and cope with a series of environmental stressors occasioned by the rapidity of economic and social change (Moynihan, 1970; Naisbett, 1982; Reich, 1980; Toffler, 1970). Given the trend toward a high-tech/high-touch environment (Naisbett, 1982), individuals, family units, and age-cohorts are struggling with ways to respond to changing institutions and community life, which has been dominated by a whirling transcience, impermanence, and impersonality (Bronfenbrenner, 1981; Mead, 1977; Naisbett, 1982).

These stressors pose formidable challenges and risks to individuals and families and have particular relevance for grandparents who have traditionally held little status in community life despite the pivotal roles they have historically assumed in bridging the generations (Bronfenbrenner, 1982; Mead, 1977). Although individuals and primary groups are expected to be more desirous of becoming connected to family and social life in more intimate and human ways to compensate for the impersonality of an increasingly complex, overly bureaucratized, inadequately individualized, transitory environment, there appears to be few formal opportunity structures for such connectedness. Recently there has been an emergence of intergenerational programs incorporating the socialization functions of grandparents and other generations in educational institutions and other agencies of socialization (Tice, 1982a, 1982b, 1983). Heretofore, the knowledge, experiences, and skills of older generations had not been formally incorporated in such institutions nor were they recognized as essential to social, and to a lesser extent, family continuity. This reflected, in large part, societal attitudes and policies that emphasized a predilection for youth and vitality and a corresponding lack of concern for the contributions of older generations to society (Lakoff, 1976). The tendency has been to equate grandparenthood with aging processes, especially physical decline, and to assume that physical decline or changes in functional capacity brought with it a desire or loss of social function or status.

Current domographics on grandparenthood (see Hagestad's chapter, this volume), as well as data speaking to the health, educational, and social status of older generations (Neugarten, 1982), indicate the wisdom of moving beyond stereotypes about grandparents. Although these views are deeply established and will be difficult to uproot, this chapter is intended to provide a modest beginning in that direction. It provides a cursory view of the evolving multidisciplinary state of the art as derived from past and present research of the type reflected throughout this volume. Additively, it addresses knowledge about grandparenthood as detailed from experiences reflecting the recent proliferation of private and publicly sponsored intergenerational programs and legal statutes and provisions enforcing grandparental rights.

This blend of knowledge is reviewed in an attempt to narrow the longstanding gap between the seemingly disparate worlds of the producers and the consumers of knowledge. A closer integration of knowledge stemming from systematic investigations *and* the experiences of service providers may help to eliminate bias from future inquiries and separate stereotypes from reality. It will promote the acquisition of knowledge that has relevance for and is transferable to human use.

STATE OF THE ART:
SYNTHESIZING THE OLD WITH THE NEW

There has been a steady increase of knowledge regarding grandparent-hood (Hagestad, 1983) coupled with a resurgence of interest on the complementarity of relations between generations (Troll & Bengtson, 1979). Nonetheless, prior to this volume and information presented at the first National Conference on Grandparenting and Family Connec-tions—the state of the art with respect to grandparenthood, a delimited area of generational phenomena—has to be characterized as incom-plete, ambiguous, contradictory, and tentative.

Two reasons account for the scarcity of knowledge on grandparent-hood. First, there has been a serious lack of systematic theory or conceptual frameworks in the area of family studies in general, and in the area of generational phenomena in particular (Troll & Bengtson, 1978). Most of the information on grandparenthood has evolved from research that has not been theoretically grounded. The data that are available are noted for their noncumulative and fragmentary nature. The literature is plagued with conceptual and methodological issues common to a burgeoning sphere of inquiry that awaits the development of middle-range theories, or conceptual frameworks to provide the propositions and constructs necessary to the arduous and tedious pro-cesses of systematic and cumulative knowledge-building. Worthy of mention is the work of Troll and Bengtson (1979), moving the state of the art in this direction.

Second, much of the information about grandparenthood has evolved from broader areas of scientific inquiry where the subject of grandparenting was a secondary or ex post facto topic of study. Not uncommonly, grandparenting phenomena have provided indicators for inquiries about the processes of aging, development in mid and late life, or generational continuity and stability, to name a few. Without intend-ing to minimize the valuable information rendered by those analyses, the consequence has been to obscure some of the more salient dimen-sions of grandparenthood resulting in the production of information that is more global than might otherwise have been the case.

This volume represents the compilation under one cover, of past and emergent developments and contributions about grandparenthood per se. Its aim is to produce a more specific, concentrated, and systematic approach to grandparenting, family, and social phenomena than has otherwise been available. Each chapter provides information that offers promise in expanding and refining the present knowledge base. Each author gives appropriate caveats relating to conceptual, sampling, and measurement issues owing to the imprecise state of the art, to practical constraints involved in research designs, and to the absence of information from which to render judgments as to the generalizability of the findings (theoretical grounding, reliability, validity). We feel that contributors to this volume have advanced the state of the art by addressing scientific substance areas of grandparenthood per se meriting further inquiry. Four general clusters of information dominate the literature as noted by the sections of this volume.

GRANDPARENTS AND SOCIALIZATION

One cluster addresses grandparenthood in terms of socialization processes. Themes such as generational interdependence, reciprocity, mutuality, diversity, and symbolism underlie the significance of grandparents as transmitters of culture and history and as functionally necessary to ensure adequate socialization of younger generations (see chapters by Gutmann and Hagestad, this volume). Explicit in these perspectives is the view that grandparents (or older generations) possess knowledge, experiences, and skills that should be preserved and transmitted from generation to generation to ensure the maintenance of social equilibrium. Deliberately or incidently, older generations serve as reference groups and models for society, families, and individuals. In particular, grandparents can be viewed as microcosms for the perpetuation and transmission of real and expected functions and role behaviors evolving from their ascribed and achieved statuses.

Conversely, younger generations socialize elder generations by needing, receiving, and incorporating their knowledge and experiences into their life space. Thus, younger generations provide opportunity structures for grandparents or elder generations to assume an array of socialization functions. Most of the chapters in this volume affirm this perspective.

Hagestad, in particular, addresses the diverse functions grandparents assume in ensuring continuity and connectedness on the individual, family, and social levels, noting the amount of diversity, heterogenity, and symbolism characterizing grandparent behaviors. Bengtson elaborates social differentiating dimensions that lie at the heart of diversity and symbolism. He notes that the salience of the role, as well as how and why specific functions are assumed, shaped and molded by such factors as the grandparents' age, sex diversity, subcultural differences, and similarities of role performance across historical time or between individuals who may be in similar locations.

Gutmann speaks to a function of grandparenthood that is new to the literature: He advocates that elders serve as "wardens of culture." Positing that our current social malaise has as its basis a loss of culture, Gutmann suggests that grandparents (and elders) should be enlisted as traditional wardens of culture, to guide the vital process of reversing deculturation and to help craft the new myths on which acculturation should be based.

This perspective is implicitly reflected in the views regarding the functional significance of grandparents in the transmission of religious values and identity (see chapters by Conroy and Fahey and Wechsler, this volume), as conveyers of the cultural legacy of the family (McCready, this volume), or as vital connectors bridging the generations when sources of psychic or social stress threaten the stability of individual, family, or social life (see Kornhaber's chapter, this volume). Grandparents, says McCready, in reality and symbolically by virtue of their presence, provide opportunities for the young to relate to and represent the generative chain that the family belongs to. Or, as Bengtson writes, grandparents provide a buffer against the next generation's mortality, an "interpretative identity-molding function," the building of reasonable autobiographical connections, ensuring that one's present has enough connections with the past to help place the future.

GRANDPARENTS AND RECIPROCITY

A second cluster of knowledge about grandparenthood stems from studies that address the influence of changing social structures as facilitating or constraining contexts for grandparents to be actively engaged in intergenerational transfer of goods and services in exchange for love and attention (Robertson, 1976, 1977; Sussman, 1976; Wood & Robertson, 1976). Implicit in these studies is a notion of reciprocity and mutuality in intergenerational interactions, a belief that grandparents assume family functions that shape the form, content, and meaning of crescive relationships between generations over time—a point that has been stressed by Hagestad and reinforced by Bengtson.

Family reorganization precipitated by divorce has been found to substantially alter the normatively mandated voluntaristic nature of grandparenthood, as well as the nature, type, amount, and frequency of functions that grandparents assume in family life (see chapters by Aldous, Cherlin and Furstenberg, and Johnson, this volume). Although grandparents avoid being intrusive or meddlesome in their children's lives, preferring the voluntaristic nature of the role (see chapters by Aldous and Johnson in this volume), stress in the middle generations activates pressure on them to assume caretaker roles and functions. Generally, they respond to the neediness for instrumental and emotional aid of divorced and never married children (Aldous, this volume).

There is, however, considerable variation in the styles of grandparenting and the type and frequency of functions based on such factors as the age of the grandparent and grandchild; geographic proximity of the grandparent to grandchildren—an issue that is related to frequency of contact; race and frequency of visiting (Cherlin and Furstenberg, this volume). Divorced daughters seem to fare better in getting grandparental assistance than do others (see Aldous, this volume). Custodial grandparents, generally those on the maternal side, although preferring otherwise, assume parental surrogate functions and develop closer ties with grandchildren and links to the kinship system than do noncustodial or paternal grandparents. The latter often lose the voluntaristic "opportunity structure" to grandparent occasioned by their son's divorce and distance from grandchildren (see Cherlin and Furstenberg, this volume) as they more frequently move away with the custodial parent.

GRANDPARENTS AND PERSONHOOD

A third cluster of knowledge about grandparenthood addresses the topic from a more person-oriented focus—the grandparent. These studies discuss individual or personality dimensions of grandparenting providing knowledge as to how an individual transitions into grandparenthood and issues of emotional attachment, meaning, and commitment to the role. Implicit in these studies is the view that personality and social systems operate interdependently. Each is in a fluid state. Thus, person-oriented dimensions of grandparenting are continually in a process of development, of reshaping based on life transitions and events. Troll (this volume) speaks of grandparenting as one of many roles an individual assumes during the life course. The challenge, she asserts, is to understand and find ways to describe how grandparenting intersects with and is synchronized with personal preferences and individual development.

Several issues of role transition are important in understanding grandparenting. First, the role is shaped by other events going on in a person's life. Seldom if ever does one have a choice about when they will become a grandparent. This role transition, unlike many others, is not self-initiated. Second, grandparenthood should be understood in terms of three components of time: expected or anticipated time, social time (whether it is the right or wrong time to become a grandparent given life events), and synchronicity with other life's circumstances. Third, grandparenting should be understood in terms of the intersection of issues in individual development. These constitute a composite of a variety of careers reflecting people's movement through time along life tracks. They reflect a complementary blend of intellectual, work, family and biological forces in individual development. Grandparenting can best be viewed as a subset of several family careers (coupling, parenting, filial, etc). This perspective avoids the error of seeing grandparenthood as a singular phase of the life span.

Kornhaber's chapter discusses role abdication by grandparents resulting in the emergence of a "new social contract," one that has damaged the grandparent-grandchild bond, as well as the bond between family members and the relationship between the family and society. Grandparents, he argues, have opted to give up their emotional attachments to grandchildren. This role abdication has removed them from significant grandparent functions. By choice, therefore, they have ceded the power to determine their relationship to grandchildren to the children's parents. The net result is that grandparents have, in effect, rejected the entire generation. Kornhaber claims that several reasons account for this: grandparents' emphasis on individualism versus familism, narcissistic as opposed to altruistic personality traits, and lack of commitment to grandchildren.

The net result, posits Kornhaber, is the emergence of a mutual contract between parents and grandparents that grandparents will not be that involved in the socialization of grandchildren. If one believes that the middle or parent generation is too close to parenting responsibilities to be objective in acquainting the young with specific sets of values or historical experiences, the loss of grandparent norms for behavior could pose issues in the perpetuation of family and social continuity. Kornhaber suggests that grandparents are vital connecting links ensuring generational continuity. Given the weakening of the social fabric resulting from dramatic social change and the choice of grandparents to return to individual rather than familism values, the loss of vital connector links for socialization poses threats for generational transmission of family stability, a propensity for individual pathology of family members, and, in a broader sense, movement toward social disequilibrium.

GRANDPARENTHOOD AND VALUES

Kornhaber's perspective in this regard is not unlike the underlying theme in Wechsler's chapter in this volume. In Jewish culture and religion the prescription for values toward the old (which includes grandparents) stem from Talmudic law. This law serves as the embodiment of culture. Through generational transmission grandchildren are expected and taught to enact these laws or values that will, again, be transmitted through their grandchildren, and so on. As stated earlier, this perspective implies that the grandparental generation provides a necessary alternative socialization structure for the perpetuation of values that parents have difficulty imparting to their young given the proximity of age and historical events between the generations.

Gutmann, in viewing grandparental or elder generations as "wardens of culture" who might be enlisted to reverse the process of deculturation, appears to be saying similar things. Values, rather than being prescribed by laws for younger generations, may be prescribed in part by older generations who transmit the knowledge, skills, experiences, and protective, emotional and sustaining cultural bonds for integrating the generations with various parts of the social order.

GENERATIONAL INTERDEPENDENCE

The early 1980s was an era noteworthy for the production of a number of volumes addressing ways public policy might encourage family relationships to fit changing times, serving the best interests of society, the family, parents, and children (Dempsey, 1981; Kamerman & Kahn, 1981; Levitan & Belous, 1981; Steiner, 1981). Curiously absent from these perspectives, however, has been explicit attention focusing on what might foster and preserve intergenerational relationships. This is an interesting omission given the proliferation of evidence (noted in this volume) revealing that generational interdependence has been historically very operational in American society. Interchanges between the generations have contributed to the socialization of the young, to a sense of purpose for the aging, and to social wholeness.

The failure to stress generational interdependence as significant in family policy discussions is inconsistent with demographic trends as reported in the literature (Neugarten, 1982). We are fast becoming an aging society. The greying of America promises to pose formidable consequences for individual, family, and social life (Neugarten, 1982, 1983). Age desegregation will characterize community life. Multiple generations are expected to be living in the same community and will engage in a variety of reciprocal activities. It is predicted that they will coexist in harmony as well as in competitive conflict as they seek similar interests and resources (see Gutmann, this volume). This stems from the fact that the largest proportion of older adults will be well-educated, alert, functionally competent individuals. Most are expected to pursue self-interest and social involvements that include sharing their knowledge, experience, and skills with younger generations until severe health problems prevent them from doing so (Neugarten, 1982). In fact, Neugarten (1984) recently presented provocative information to suggest that these trends will produce a more stable, orderly social life, as integrating the young with the old will provide more balance in attacking social problems than we have seen in an age-segregated society.

The implications of these trends challenge the inventive capacities of those concerned with policy aimed at promoting an age-integrated society. How, for example, might generational linkages be fostered to enhance the quality of individual, family, and social life? What is necessary to keep older generations well integrated and active? How might grandparents, great-grandparents, or other elders—the living repositories of change—be enlisted to provide younger generations with the knowledge, experiences, and skills that guarantee them access to the past, as well as perspectives for moving beyond the timeless present that has characterized much of their socialization? Alternatively, how and should younger generations be enlisted to provide the old with facets of culture that have changed rather dramatically since they were young?

The need for family policy stressing ways to facilitate interdependence between generations is not especially new. Mead (1977) has argued the wisdom of structured interventions aimed at the provision of restorative intergenerational linkages to bring together what technology, mobility, and age segregation have pulled apart. At their best, such interventions will do much to restore and inculcate a sense of caring and connectedness between the generations by replacing isolation and fragmentation with reciprocity and coherence.

Bronfenbrenner (1981) speaks to the same issue. He advocates the need for policy-preserving intergenerational linkages to provide the basic socialization essential to move generations, and especially the family, in the direction of more caring emphases as a necessary buffer to combat the inevitable stressors occasioned by the impersonality of a technologically-oriented community where humans become absorbed and lost in bureaucratization. The family, as a major socialization structure existing interdependently with other social structures (work, neighborhoods, school, churches, etc.), has to be supported and encouraged to equip its members with basic caring skills that are transferable to others throughout the life span. The development *and* potential of what it takes to make human beings truly human is dependent, says Bronfenbrenner, on two essential environmental conditions that have not received proper attention. One speaks to the need for the young to be consistently exposed to the enduring involvement of one or more adults in care and joint activity. The second stresses that the involvement of one or more adults in care and joint activity with the young. This *requires,* says Bronfenbrenner, public policies and practices that provide opportunity, status, resources, encouragement, example, and above all, time for parenthood—primarily by parents—but also by other adults in the child's environment, those within and outside the home.

LINKING THE GENERATIONS

INTERGENERATIONAL PROGRAMS

A number of social programs have been developed over the years to bring generations together in the provision of caring, sharing, and exchange of skills and experiences. The prototypic model of a program designed to encourage and make caring, learning, and sharing functions visible was the Peace Corps. Started more than 20 years ago by government and voluntary efforts, this program provided the springboard that resulted in a variety of subsequent social programs that provide additional examples of cross-generational efforts aimed at fostering exchanges between generations. Programs such as Vista, the Retired Senior Volunteer Program (RSVP), Senior Companions, the Foster Grandparent Program, and the Senior Community Service Programs have been successful in their efforts to bridge the generations, as well as capitalizing on the resources of older citizens in terms of community life. These programs have evolved from varying combinations of public, private, and volunteer initiatives and can be seen as antecedents of a recent trend toward intergenerational linkages by making grandparenthood more visible. Thus, social programs facilitating mutual exchanges and interactions between generations are not especially new.

What appears to be new is the emphasis on making grandparenthood per se more explicit in formal and informal social settings such as schools, hospitals, community centers, museums, religious institutions, and social service organizations. Within the last decade a sizable number of programs have been developed with the support of the federal government, local school districts, community groups, and private foundations. Programs have been designed to provide the young with the presence of older adults within their environment. These efforts range from those encouraging natural grandparenting to others that provide opportunities for any older adult to nurture, educate, and foster grandparent the young.

Inherent in these programs is the view that if the young do not have access to their own grandparents, they should have access to somebody else's grandparents, as well as to older adults in general. The intent is that programs geared toward intergenerational linkages will facilitate the restoration of relationships between the young and the old, which were more prevalent when extended families were more clearly defined and functioning as informal support systems. These endeavors have been designed to stimulate positive meaning for those at various points of the age spectrum as well as for families and society as a whole (Tice, 1982, 1983).

ENHANCING NATURAL GRANDPARENTING

Three rather recent actions have occurred nationwide to promote the visibility of grandparenthood. One was the proclamation of Grandparents' Day, established by an Act of Congress, to be celebrated annually on the first Sunday after Labor Day. Also, the Foundation for Grandparenting in Mt. Kisco, New York, was established in the early 1980s to foster initiations and projects encouraging natural grandparenting. Third, since 1982, we have witnessed the emergence of a variety of legal statutes protecting grandparents' rights to see their grandchildren following a parental divorce.

The incidence of divorce, remarriage, blended families, joint custody arrangements, and so on have had far-reaching consequences in the preservation of family and extended family ties and relationships (Loeb, 1983). For instance, there is the example of a California attorney who was consulted to arrange a visitation schedule for a couple to see their respective children. One of the couple had been married three times previously and the other four times. Each had children from each of the those marriages. The ultimate visitation schedule developed for that couple included having children at times of the visitation who were strangers to both of them, but half-siblings to their various children. More important, it also became necessary to work out an equitable arrangement for grandparent visitation. Although this example may refer to the extreme, a number of situations have occurred over the years where grandparents, generally noncustodial, have been denied access to their grandchildren in the case of divorce and remarriage.

Following hearings held by a Congressional Committee in December of 1982, the House of Representatives urged the National Conference of Commissioners on Uniform State Laws to develop a Model Act on Grandparent Visitation (House Concurrent Resolution 48, April, 1988). This resolution has far reaching implications for family and social life given that there are approximately one million children per year added to the number affected by divorce (Loeb, 1983). The protection of grandparents visitation rights should have positive benefits for both grandchildren and grandparents and may assure some degree of family continuity for that aspect of kinship relations most affected by the divorce. Although it may seem somewhat dramatic, some have argued that the fallout of divorce as it affects children in our society is not unlike the fallout of an atom bomb (Foster & Freed, 1979).

There are now statutes in over 40 states addressing the various rights of grandparents (this is documented in an Appendix to this chapter, available from the senior author). Of note is the fact that these statutes are not uniform, but quite diverse. An examination of the variations by states indicates the problems that have arisen in society that disaffect grandparental participation in the evolvement of family relationships, or for that matter issues that have been central in minimizing the significance and valued functions of grandparents in the socialization of their grandchildren.

POLICY CONSIDERATIONS

The intent of this chapter has been to summarize the emergent state of the art regarding grandparenthood, and its relationship to family, society, and social life. Particular attention has been devoted to the issues of generational interdependence and family connectedness. This was done in an attempt to identify questions that may be relevant for policy and planning considerations. What might be done to positively influence the quality of family and social life by linking generations through socially structured or informally organized intergenerational programs and legal legislation enhancing natural grandparenting?

Policy discussions around family life must be made with two caveats in mind, one philosophical issue speaks to the family as the last bastion of privacy in an already overregulated, complex, impersonal, overly organized, and technologically oriented society. Should it be the object of social policy that it would be intrusive in family life, however useful? The practical speaks to the heterogeneity of family forms, family values, family styles. Surely, the chapters in this volume speak to the diversity and variations in family life owing to issues in social stratification (age, sex, income, race, geographic location, location in historical time, etc.), socialization, and social changes. Are these too complex and too varied to be encompassed by a singular policy? What may be viewed as a problem in one family or one area or region of the country may not be an issue in another. Yet, how might the intangible sentiments that are the foundation of family relationships be legislated, let alone enforced?

A number of questions need to be addressed. Can or should there be policies designed to direct or alter the course of relationships between the generations? In view of their health status, vitality, educational levels, and preference for self-pursuits, will older individuals or grandparents actually want formal responsibility for the perpetuation of family and societal norms? How might intergenerational programs be developed and implemented to accommodate the diversity, symbolism, and functionalism that has traditionally characterized the role and significance of grandparenthood? In instances where families are in need or in a state of reorganization, should incentives be made to encourage the use of grandparents—natural or surrogate—to be involved in the socialization of the young?

What types of alternative community programs might be developed to foster opportunity structures to integrate the young with the old? Should these programs, if feasible, leave the choice of involvement voluntary to accommodate the options and preferences of the old, or should communities be required to have such programs available? Finally, how might programs and services, or service providers accommodate service provisions to ensure cultural diversity, especially as this may relate to ethnic and religious backgrounds of older individuals?

REFERENCES

Abernathy, V. (1973). Social network and response to the maternal role. *International Journal of Sociology and the Family, 3*, 86-92.

Abraham, K. (1913). Some remarks on the role of grandparents in the psychology of neuroses. *Clinical Essays*, pp. 44-47.

Abramson, L. Y., Seligman, M.E.P., & Teasdale, J. D. (1978). Learned helplessness in humans: Critique and reformulation. *Journal of Abnormal Psychology, 87*(1), 49-74.

Adams, B. N. (1968). *Kinship in an urban setting.* Chicago: Markham.

Aldous, J. (1967). Intergenerational visiting patterns: Variation in boundary maintenance as an explanation. *Family Process, 6*, 235-251.

Aldous, J. (1978). *Family careers: Developmental change in families.* New York: John Wiley.

Anspach, D. F. (1976). Kinship and divorce. *Journal of Marriage and the Family, 38*, 323-340.

Apple, D. (1956). The social structure of grandparenthood. *American Anthropologist, 58*, 656-663.

Atchley, R., & Corbett, S. (1977). Older women and jobs. In L. Troll, J. Israel, & K. Israel (Eds.), *Looking ahead: A woman's guide to the problems and joys of growing older* (pp. 121-126). Englewood Cliffs, NJ: Prentice-Hall.

Bahr, H. M. (1976). The kinship role. In F.I. Nye (Ed.), *Role structure and analysis of the family.* (pp. 61-69). Beverly Hills, CA: Sage.

Baranowski, M. D. (1982). Grandparent-adolescent relations: Beyond the nuclear family. *Adolescence, 15*, 575-584.

Beavers, W. R. (1978). *Psychotherapy and growth and grandparenthood: An overview of meaning and mental health.* New York: Brunner/Mazel.

Belsky, J., & Tolan, W. J. (1981). Infants as producers of their own development: An ecological analysis. In R. M. Lerner & N. A. Busch-Rossnagel (Eds.), *Individuals as producers of their own development: A life span perspective* (pp. 87-116). New York: Academic.

Bengtson, V. L. (1970). The "generation gap": A review and typology of social-psychological perspectives. *Youth and Society, 2*(1), 7-32.

Bengtson, V. L. (1971). Inter-age differences in perception and the generation gap. *Gerontologist, 11* (4, Part 2), 85-90.

Bengtson, V. L. (1975). Generation and family effects in value socialization. *American Sociological Review, 40*(3), 358-371.

Bengtson, V. L., & Black, O. (1973). Intergenerational relations: Continuity in socialization. In P. Baltes & W. Schaie (Eds.), *Life span developmental psychology: Personality and socialization* (pp. 208-34). New York: Academic.

Bengtson, V. L., Cultler, N. E., Mangen, D. J., & Marshall, V. W. (1985). Generations, cohorts, and relations between age groups. In R. Binstock and E. Shanas (Eds.), *Handbook of aging and the social sciences* (pp. 301-346). New York: Van Nostrand Reinhold.

Bengtson, V. L., Grigsby, E., Corry, E. M., & Hruby, M. (1977). Relating academic research to community concerns: A case study in collaborative effort. *Journal of Social Issues, 33*(4), 75-92.

Bengtson, V. L., & Kuypers, J. A. (1971). Generational differences and the developmental stake. *Aging and Human Development, 2,* 249-260.

Bengtson, V. L., Mangen, D. G., & Landry, T. H. Jr., (1984). Multigeneration family: Concepts and findings. In V. Garms-Homolova, E. M. Horning, & D. Schaffer (Eds.), *Intergenerational Relationships*. New York: G. J. Hogrefe.

Berger, P., & Luckmann, T. (1967). *The social construction of reality*. Garden City, NY: Doubleday.

Blau, Z. S. (1973). *Old age in a changing society*. New York; New Viewpoints.

Block, J., von der Lippe, A., & Block, J. H. (1973). Sex-role and socialization patterns: Some personality concomitants and environmental antecedents. *Journal of Consulting and Clinical Psychology, 41,* 321-341.

Bohannon, P. (1971). *Divorce and after: An analysis of the emotional and social problems of divorce*. New York: Anchor Books.

Bortner, R. (1978-1979). Notes on expected life history: With an introduction by Daniel J. Levinson. *International Journal of Aging and Human Development, 9*(4), 291-294.

Box, G.E.P., Hunter W. G., & Hunter, J. S. (1978). *Statistics for experimenters: An introduction to design, data analysis, and model building*. New York: John Wiley.

Brody, E. M. (1981). Women in the middle and family help to older people. *Gerontologist, 21,* 471-480.

Brody, E. M., & Lang, A. (1982, November). They can't do it all: Aging daughters with aging mothers. *Generations: The Journal of the Western Gerontological Society*, pp. 18-20.

Bronfenbrenner, U. (1970). *Two worlds of childern—U.S. and USSR*. New York: Russell Sage.

Bronfenbrenner, U. (1977, January 2). The calamitous decline of the American family. *Washington Post*.

Bronfenbrenner, U. (1981). The ecology of human development: Experiments by nature and design. Cambridge: Harvard University Press.

Bumpass, L. (1981). *Demographic aspects of children's experience in second families*. Paper prepared for the annual meetings of the American Sociological Association, San Francisco.

Burton, L. M. (1985). *Early and on-time grandmotherhood in multigeneration Black Families*. Unpublished Ph.D. dissertation, University of Southern California.

Campbell, M. L., Bengtson, V. L., & Beck, S. H. (1984). *Age stratification and the family: The temporal context of intergenerational solidarity*. Paper presented at the annual meetings of the American Sociological Association, August, San Antonio, TX.

Campbell, V., & Bubolz, M. (1982). Parenting by related adults. In M. Kostelnik & H. Fitzergerald (Eds.), *Patterns of supplementary parenting*. New York: Plenum.

Cherlin, A. (1978). Remarriage as an incomplete institution. *American Journal of Sociology, 84,* 634-650.

Cherlin, A. & Furstenburg, F. (1983). *Grandparents and grandchildren: Some preliminary findings from a national study*. Paper presented at the annual meetings of the American Sociological Association, Detroit.

Chodorow, N. (1978). *The reproduction of mothering*. Berkeley: University of California Press.

Cohler, B. J., & Grunebaum, H. V. (1981). *Mothers, grandmothers, and daughters: Personality and childcare in three-generation families*. New York: John Wiley.

Costa, P., & McCrae, R. (1976). Age differences in personality structure: A cluster analytic approach. *Journal of Gerontology, 31*(5), 564-570.

Cumming, E., & Henry, W. E. (1961). *Growing old: The process of disengagement*. New York: Basic Books.

Demos, J. (1978). Old age in early New England. In Demos & Boocock (Eds.), *Turning points: Historical and sociological essays in the family* (pp S248-S285). Chicago: University of Chicago Press.

Dempsey, J. J. (1981). *The family and public policy: The issue of the 1980s*. Baltimore: P.H. Brookes.

Deutsch, H. (1945). *The psychology of women: Vol. 2. Motherhood*. New York: Grune & Straton.

Dobson, F. (1981). *How to grandparent*. Garden City, NY: Doubleday.

Dowd, J. J., & Bengtson, V. L. (1978). Aging in minority populations: An examination of the double jeopardy hypothesis. *Journal of Gerontology, 33*(3), 426-436.

Dreves, V. (1982). *The wonder of God*. New York: W. H. Sadlier.

Durkheim, E. (1969). De la division dutravial social. In E. Durkheim, *The division of labor in society* (G. Simpson, trans., 1983). New York: Free Press.

Erikson, E. H. (1950). *Childhood and society*. New York: Norton.

Erikson, E. H. (1968). The development of ritualization. In D.R. Culter (Ed.), *The religious situation* (pp. 711-733). Boston: Beacon.

Erikson, E. H. (1982). *The life cycle completed*. New York: W. W. Norton.

Erikson, E. H., & Erikson, J. M. (1950). Growth and crises of the "healthy personality." In differences. *Research on Aging, 4*, 249-267.
Macy Jr. Foundation.

Fallo-Mitchell, L., & Ryff, C. D. (1982). Preferred timing of female life events: Cohort differences. *Research on Aging, 4*, 249-267.

Featherstone, J. (1979). Family matters. *Harvard Educational Review, 49*, 20-52.

Fischer, L. R. (1982-1983). Transitions to grandmotherhood. *International Journal of Aging and Human Development, 9*(4), 293-299.

Fischer, L. R., & Silverman, J. (1982). *Grandmothering as a tenuous role relationship*. Paper presented at the annual meetings of the National Council on Family Relations, Portland, OR.

Foster, R., & Freed, W. (1979). "Grandparent visitation: Vagaries and vicissitudes." *Journal of Divorce, 79* (1/2 Fall, Winter), 643-651.

Fox, F. (1937). Family life and relationships as affected by the presence of the aged. In Committee on Mental Hygiene, Family Welfare Association of America (Eds.), *Mental hygiene and old age*. New York: State Charities Aid Association.

Frazier, E. F. (1939). *The Negro family in the United States*. Chicago: University of Chicago Press.

Fried, E. G., & Stern, K. (1948). The situation of the aged within the family. *American Journal of Orthopsychiatry, 18*, 31-54.

Fullerton, H. N. (1982). How accurate were projections of the 1980 labor force? *Monthly Labor Review, 105*, 12-21.

Furstenberg, F. F. (1981). Remarriage and intergenerational relations. In R. Fogel, E. Hatfield, S. Kiesler, & J. March (Eds.), *Aging: Stability and change in the family*, (pp. 117-142). New York: Academic.

Furstenberg, F. F., Jr., Nord, C. W., Peterson, J. L., & Zill, N. (1983). The life course of children of divorce: Marital disruption and parental conflict. *American Sociological Review, 48,* 656-668.

Furstenberg, F., & Spanier, G. (1984). *Recycling the family: Remarriage after divorce.* Beverly Hills, CA: Sage.

Gatz, M., & Siegler, I. C. (1981). *Locus of control: A retrospective.* Paper presented at the American Psychological Association Annual Meeting, Los Angeles.

Geertz, C. (1973). *The interpretation of cultures.* New York: Basic Books.

George, L. K. (1982). Models of transition in middle and later life. *Annals of the American Academy of Political and Social Science, 454,* 22-37.

Gilford, R., & Black, D. (1972). *The grandchild-grandparent dyad: Ritual or relationship?* Paper presented at the 25th annual meeting of the Gerontological Society, San Juan, Puerto Rico.

George, L. K. (1980). *Role transitions in later life.* Belmont, CA: Brooks/Cole.

Gilligan, C. (1982). *In a different voice.* Cambridge, MA: Harvard University Press.

Goode, W. (1956) *Women in divorce.* New York: Free Press.

Gutmann, D. (1975) A key to the comparative style of the life cycle. In N. Datan & L. H. Ginsberg (Eds.), *Life span developmental psychology: Normative life crises* (pp. 167-184). New York: Academic.

Hader, M. (1965). The importance of grandparents in family life. *Family Process, 4,* 228-240.

Hagestad, G. O. (1978, August). *Patterns of communication and influence between grandparents and grandchildren in a changing society.* Paper presented at the World Congress of Sociology, Uppsala, Sweden.

Hagestad, G. O. (1981). Problems and promises in the social psychology of inter-generational relations. In R. Vogel, E. Hatfield, S. Kiesler, & R. Shanas (Eds.), *Aging: Stability and Change in the Family* (pp. 11-47.). New York: Academic.

Hagestad, G. O. (1982). Divorce: The family ripple effect. *Generations: The Journal of the Western Gerontological Society,* (Winter), 24-31.

Hagestad, G. O. (1984). The continuous bond: A dynamic multigenerational perspective on parent-child relations between adults. In M. Perlmutter (Ed.), *Parent-child Relations in Child Development* (pp. 129-158), The Minnesota Symposium on Child Psychology (Vol. 17).

Hagestad, G. O., & Cogley, E. (n.d.) *Down from the pedestal: Images of grandparents in popular magazines, 1880s to 1970s.* Unpublished manuscript.

Hagestad, G. O., & Kranichfeld, M. (1982, October). *Issues in the study of intergenerational continuity.* Paper presented at the National Council of Family Relations Theory and Methods Workshop, Washington, DC.

Hagestad, G. O., & Lang, M. (in press). *Transition to grandparenthood: Unexplored issues.* Manuscript in preparation.

Hagestad, G. O., & McDonald, M. (1979). *What grandfather knows best.* Paper presented at the annual meetings of the Gerontological Society, Washington, DC.

Hagestad, G. O., & Neugarten, B. L. (1985). Aging and the life course. In E. Shanas & R. Binstock (Eds.), *Handbook of aging and the social sciences.* New York: Van Nostrand Reinhold.

Hagestad, G. O., & Smyer, M. A. (1982). Dissolving long-term relationships: Patterns of divorce in middle age. In S. Duck (Ed.), *Dissolving personal relationships.* (pp. 155-187). London: Academic.

Hagestad, G. O., Smyer, M. A., & Stierman, K. L. (1984). Parent-child relations in adulthood: The impact of divorce in middle age. In R. Cohen, S. Weissman, & B. Cohler (Eds.), *Parenthood: Psychodynamic perspectives*. (pp. 247-262). New York: Guilford.

Hagestad, G. O., & Snow, R. (1977). *Young adult offspring as interpersonal resources in middle age*. Paper presented at the annual meeting of the Gerontological Society, San Francisco.

Hagestad, G. O., & Speicher, J. L. (1981). *Grandparents and family influence: Views of three generations*. Paper presented at the Society for Research in Child Development biennial meeting, Boston.

Handlin, O. (1951). *The uprooted*. Boston: Little, Brown.

Hareven, T. K. (1977). Family time and historical time. *Daedalus, 106*, 57-70.

Hess, G., & Waring, J. (1978). Parent and child in later life: Rethinking the relationship. In R. Lerner & G. Spainer (Eds.), *Child influences on marital and family interaction* (pp. 241-273). New York: Academic.

Hetherington, E. M., Cox, M., & Cox, R. (1978). The aftermath of divorce. In J. H. Stevens, Jr., & M. Matthew (Eds.), *Mother-child, father-child relations* (pp. 149-176). Washington, DC: National Association for the Education of Young Children.

Hill, R., Foote, N., Aldous, J., Carlson, R., & MacDonald, R. (1970). *Family development in three generations*. Cambridge: MA: Schenkman.

Hoffman, E. (1979-1980). Young adults' relations with their grandparents: An exploratory study. *International Journal of Aging and Human Development, 10*, 299-310.

Jackson, J. (1971). Black grandparents in the South. *Phylon, 32*, 260-271.

Johnson, C. (1983). A cultural analysis of the grandmother. *Research on Aging, 5*, 547-568.

Jones, F. C. (1973). The lofty role of the Black grandmother. *Crisis, 80*(1), 41-56.

Jung, C. (1971). The stages of life (R.F.C.-Hill, Trans.). In J. Campbell (Ed.), *The portable Jung*. New York: Viking. (Original work published 1930)

Kadushin, M. (1965). *The rabbinic mind*. New York: Blaisdell.

Kahana, B., & Kahana, E. (1970). Grandparenthood from the perspective of the developing grandchild. *Developmental Psychology, 3*, 98-105.

Kahana, E., & Kahana, B. (1971). Theoretical and research perspectives on grandparenthood. *Journal of Aging and Human Development, 2*, 261-268.

Kamerman, S. B., & Kahn, A. J. (1981). *Child care, family benefit, and working parents: A study in comparative policy*. New York: Columbia University Press.

Karp, D. A., & Yocls, W. C. (1982). *Experiencing the life cycle*. Springfield, ILL: Charles C Thomas.

Kellam, S. G., Ensminger, M. E. & Turner, J. (1977). Family structure and the mental health of children. *Archives of General Psychiatry, 34*, 1012-1022.

Kivnick, H. Q. (1982a). *The meaning of grandparenthood*. Ann Arbor, MI: University of Michigan Research Press.

Kivnick, H. Q. (1982b). Grandparenthood: An overview of meaning and mental health. *Gerontologist, 22*, 59-66.

Kivnick, H. Q. (1983). Dimensions of grandparenthood meaning: Deductive conceptualization and empirical derivation. *Journal of Personality and Social Psychology, 44*, 1056-1068.

Kivnick, H. Q. (1984). Grandparents and family relations. In W. H. Quinn & G. A. Hughston (Eds.), *Independent aging: Perspectives in social gerontology* (pp. 35-37). Rockville, MD: Aspen Systems Corporation.

Kivnick, H. Q., Erikson, E. H., & Erikson, J. M. (1983). *Integrity vs. despair: The final stage reconsidered.* Symposium conducted at the Department of Psychiatry, University of Pennsylvania, Philadelphia.

Kleiber, D., Veldman, D. J., & Menaker, S. L. (1973). The multidimensionality of locus of control. *Journal of Clinical Psychology, 29,* 411-416.

Konopka, G. (1976). *Young girls: A portrait of adolescence.* Englewood Cliffs, NJ: Prentice-Hall.

Kornhaber, A., & Woodward, K. L. (1981). *Grandparents/grandchild: The vital connection.* Garden City, NY: Anchor.

Kuhlen, R. G. (1946). Personality change with age. In P. Worchel & D. Byrne (Eds.), *Personality change* (pp. 524-555). New York: John Wiley.

Kruse, A. (1984). The five-generation family: A pilot study. In V. Grams-Homolova, E.M. Hoerning & D. Schaeffer (eds.), *Intergenerational relationships* (pp. 115-125). Lewiston, NY: C.J. Hogrefe.

Kuypers, J. A., & Bengtson, V. L. (1983). Toward competence in the older family. In T. H. Brubaker (Ed.), *Family relationships in later life* (pp. 211-228). Beverly Hills, CA: Sage.

Ladner, J. A. (1971). *Tomorrow's tomorrow: The black women.* Garden City, NY: Doubleday.

Lajewski, H. C. (1959). Working mothers and their arrangements for the care of their children. *Social Security Bulletin, 22,* 8-13.

Lakoff, S. A. (1976). The future of social intervention. In R. Binstock & E. Shanas (Eds.), *Aging and the social sciences* (pp. 643-660). New York: Van Nostrand Reinhold.

Laslett, P. (1965). *The world we have lost.* New York: Scribner.

Lee, G. R. (1980). Kinship in the seventies: A decade review of research and theory. *Journal of Marriage and the Family, 42,* 923-934.

Lehr, U. (1982). Hat die GroBfamilie heute noch eine Chance? *Der Deutsche Arzt, 18,* Sonderdruck.

Levitan, S. A., & Belous, R. S. (1981). *What's happening to the American family?* Baltimore: John Hopkins University Press.

Livson, R. (1977). Coming out of the closet: Marriage and other crises of middle age. In L. Troll, J. Israel, & K. Israel (Eds.), *Looking ahead: A Womam's guide to the problems and joys of growing older* (pp. 81-92). Englewood Cliffs, NJ: Prentice-Hall.

Loeb, L. L. (1983) *Response to "Dilemmas and opportunities for grandparents: divorce and remarriage."* Paper prepared for National Wingspread Conference on Grandparenting and Family Connections, Racine, WI.

Lopata, H. (1973). *Widowhood in an American city.* Cambridge, MA: Schenkman.

Maas, H., & Kuypers, J. A. (1974). *From thirty to seventy: A forty-year longitudinal study of adult life style and personality.* San Francisco: Jossey-Bass.

Manuel, R. C. (1983). The study of minority aged in historical perspective. In R. C. Manuel (Ed.), *Minority aging: Sociological and social psychology issues.* Westport, CT: Greenwood.

Marshall, V. W., & Rosenthal, C. J. (1982). Parental death: A life course marker. *Generations: Journal of the Western Gerontological Society,* (Winter), 48-52.

Martos, J. (1981). *Door to the sacred.* New York: Doubleday.

McCready, W. C. (1974). The persistence of ethnic variation in American families. In A. W. Greeley & W. C. McCready (Eds.), *Ethnicity in the United States.* New York: Wiley-Interscience.

McCready, W. C. (1978). Religion and the life-cycle. In David Tracy (Ed.), *Toward Vatican III: The work that needs to be done*. New York: Seabury.

McCready, W. C., & Greeley, A. W. (1975). The transmission of cultural heritages: The case of the Italians and the Irish. In N. Glazer & D. P. Moynihan (Eds.), *Ethnicity: Theory and experience*. Cambridge, MA: Harvard University Press.

McCready, W. C., & McCready, N. (1973). The origins of religious persistence: Sexual identity and religious socialization. In *Concilium: International Review of Theology*. Rome: Intercordum.

Mead, M. (1970). *Culture and commitment: A study of the generation gap*. New York: Langman.

Mead, M. (1974). Grandparents as educators. In H. J. Leichter (Ed.), *The family as educator*. New York: Teachers College Press.

Mead, M. (1977). Grandparents as educators. *Saturday Evening Post*.

Minturn, L. A., & Lambert, W. W. (1964). *Mothers of six cultures: Antecedents of childrearing*. New York: John Wiley.

Monge, R. H. (1975). Structure of the self-concept from adolescence through old age. *Experimental Aging Research, 1*, 281-291.

Moynihan, D. P. (1965). *The Negro family: the case for national action*. Prepared for the United States Department of Labor, Office of Policy Planning and Research. Washington, DC: Government Printing Office.

Moynihan, D. P. (1970). (Ed.). *Toward a national urban policy*. New York: Basic Books.

Naisbett, J. (1982). *Megatrends*. New York: Warner.

Nelson-Ricks, J. (1984, May). Mothers struggling alone. *Essence*. (pp. 83-86).

Neugarten, B. L. (Ed.). (1982). *Age or need? Public policies for older people*. Beverly Hills, CA: Sage.

Neugarten, B. L. (1983, April 20). *Frontiers on aging*. Martin Loeb Memorial Lecture, McBeath Institute on Aging and Adult Life, Madison, WI.

Neugarten, B. L., & Gutmann, D. (1964). Age-sex roles and personality in middle age. A thematic apperception study. In B. L. Neugarten & Associates (Eds.), *Personality in middle and late life* (pp. 44-90). New York: Atherton.

Neugarten, B. L., & Hagestad, G. (1976). Age and the life course. In R. H. Binstock, & E. Shanas (Eds.), *Handbook of aging and the social sciences* (pp. 35-57). New York: Van Nostrand Reinhold.

Neugarten, B. L., Moore, J. W., & Lowe, J. C. (1965). Age norms, age constraints, and adult socialization. *American Journal of Sociology, 70*, 710-717.

Neugarten, B. L., & Peterson, W. A. (1957). A study of the American age-grade system. *Proceedings of the Fourth Congress of the International Association of Gerontology, 3*, 144.

Neugarten, B. L., & Weinstein, K. K. (1964). The changing American grandparent. *Journal of Marriage and the Family, 26*, 199-204.

Norton, A. J. (1983). Family life cycle: 1980. *Journal of Marriage and the Family, 45*(2), 267-276.

Nye, F. I., & Hoffman, L. W. (Eds.). (1963). *The employed mother in America*. Chicago: Rand McNally.

Parson, T., & Bales, R. F. (1955). *Family: Socialization and interaction process*. New York: Free Press.

Pearlin, L. I., & Schooler, C. (1978). The structure of coping. *Journal of Health and Social Behavior, 19*, 2-21.

Perlman, H. H. (1968). *Personal: Social role and personality change.* Chicago: University of Chicago Press.

Quinton, A. (1983, October 17). Character and culture. *New Republic*, pp. 26-29.

Radcliffe-Brown, A. R., & Forde, D. (Eds.). (1950). *African systems of kinship and marriage.* London: Oxford University Press.

Rappaport, E. A. (1958). The grandparent syndrome. *Psychoanalytic Quarterly, 27*, 518-538.

Rasmussen, B. (1983, September 4). Aeldre undervurderver deres rolle i familien. *Berlingske, Tidende*, Copenhagen, p. II 5.

Redfield, R. (1941). *The folk culture of Yucatan.* Chicago: University of Chicago Press.

Reich, C. A. (1970). *The greening of America.* New York: Random House.

Riley, M., Foner, A., Hess, B., & Toby, M. (1969). Socialization for the middle and later years. In D. Goslin (Ed.), *Handbook of socialization and theory research.* Chicago: Rand-McNally.

Riley, M. W., & Waring, J. (1976). Age and aging. In R. K. Merton & R. Nisbet (Eds.), *Contemporary social problems (4th ed.).* New York: Harcourt Brace Jovanovich.

Robertson, J. F. (1975). Interaction in three generation families, parents as mediators: Toward a theoretical perspective. *International Journal of Aging and Human Development, 6*, 103-110.

Robertson, J. F. (1976). Significance of grandparents: Perceptions of young adult grandchildren. *Gerontologist, 16*(2), 137-140.

Robertson, J. F. (1977). Grandmotherhood: A study of role conceptions. *Journal of Marriage and the Family, 39*, 165-174.

Robinson, J. (1851). Of youth and old age. In R. Ashton (Ed.), *The Works of John Robinson,* (pp 250-254). Boston: Doctrinal Tract and Book Society.

Rohrer, R. (1975). *They love me, they love me not: A world-wide study of the effect of parental acceptance and rejection.* New Haven, CT: HRAF Press.

Rosenthal, C. J. (in press). Generational succession: The passing on of family hardship. *Journal of Comparative Family Studies, 16.*

Rosenthal, C. J. (1985). Kin-keeping in the familial division of labor. *Journal of Marriage and the Family, 45*, 509-521.

Rosenthal, C. J., & Marshall, V. W. (1983). *The head of the family: Authority and responsibility in the lineage.* Paper presented at the annual meetings of the Gerontological Society of America and the Canadian Association on Gerontology, Toronto.

Rosow, I. (1976). Status and role change through the life span. In R. E. Binstock & E. Shanas (Eds.), *Handbook of aging and the social sciences* (pp. 457-482). New York: Van Nostrand Reinhold.

Rossi, A. S. (1980). A biosocial perspective on parenting in the family. In P. Baltes and O. Brim, Jr. (Eds.), *Life span development and behavior* (vol. 3). New York: Academic.

Ryff, C., & Baltes, P. (1978). Value transition and adult development in women: The instrumentality-terminality sequence hypothesis. *Developmental Psychology, 12*(6), 567-568.

Schaie, K. W., & Parham, I. A. (1976). Stability of adult personality traits: Fact or fable. *Journal of Personality and Social Psychology, 34*, 146-158.

Schneider, D. (1968). *American kinship: A cultural account.* (2nd ed.) Chicago: University of Chicago Press.

Schulz, R., & Hanusa, B. H. (1980). Experimental social gerontology: A social psychological perspective. *Journal of Social Issues, 36*(2), 30-46.

Shanas, E. (1979). Social myth as hypothesis: The case of the family relations of old people. *Gerontologist, 19,* 3-9.

Shanas, E. (1980). Older people and their families: The new pioneers. *Journal of Marriage and the Family, 42*(9), 9-15.

Siegler, I. C. (1980). The psychology of adult development and aging. In E. W. Busse & D. G. Blazer (Eds.). *Handbook of geriatric psychology* (pp. 1969-2221). New York: Van Nostrand Reinhold.

Skolnick, A. (1978). *The intimate environment* (2nd ed.). Boston: Little, Brown.

Smith, H. E. (1965). Family interaction patterns of the aged: A review. In A. M. Rose & W. A. Peterson (Eds.), *Older people and their social world.* Philadelphia: F. A. Davis.

Spanier, G. B., & Glick, P. C. (1980). Paths to remarriage. *Journal of Divorce, 33,* 283-298.

Sprey, J. & Matthews, S. H. (1982). Contemporary grandparenthood. A systematic transition. *Annals of the American Academy of Political Science, 464,* 91-103.

Staples, R. (1971). Toward a sociology of the black family: A theoretical and methodological assessment. *Journal of Marriage and the Family, 83,* 119-138.

Staples, R. (1973). *The Black woman in America.* Chicago: Nelson-Hall.

Steiner, G. Y. (1981). *The futility of family policy.* Washington, DC: The Brookings Institution.

Strauss, C. A. (1943). Grandma made Johnny delinquent. *American Journal of Orthopsychiatry, 13,* 343-346.

Streltzer, A. A. (1979). A grandchildren's group in a home for the aged. *Health Social Work, 4,* 167-184.

Sussman, M. (1976). The family life of older people. In R. Binstock & E. Shanas (Eds.), *Aging and the social sciences* (pp. 218-243). New York: Van Nostrand Reinhold.

Terkelsen, K. G. (1980). Toward a theory of the family life cycle. In E. A. Carter & M. McGoldrick (Eds.), *The family life cycle: A framework for family therapy* (pp. 21-52). New York: Gardner Press.

Tice, C. (1982a). *Linking the generations: Intergenerational programs, Wingspread report.* Racine, WI: The Johnson Foundation.

Tice, C. (1982b, January/February). Linking the generations. *New Designs for Youth Development, III* (1).

Tice, C. (1983, October). *Programs for enhancing grandparenthood: Federal and state initiatives.* Paper prepared for the National Wingspread Conference on Grandparenting and Family Connections. Racine, WI.

Tinsley, B. R., & Parke, R. D. (1984). Grandparents as support and socialization agents. In M. Lewis (Ed.), *Beyond the dyad* (pp. 161-194). New York: Plenum.

Toffler, A. (1970). *Future shock.* New York: Random House.

Townsend, P. (1957). *The family life of old people.* London: Routledge & Kegan Paul.

Treas, J. (1977). Family support systems for the aged: Some social and demographic considerations. *Gerontologist, 17*(6), 486-491.

Treas, J., & Bengtson, V. L. (1982). The demography of mid- and late-life transitions. *Annals of the American Academy of Political and Social Science, 464,* 11-21.

Troll, L. E., & Stapley, J. (in press). Elders and the extended family system. Health, family *Psychological issues* (pp. 475-481). Washington, DC: American Psychological Association.

Troll, L. E. (1982). *Continuations: Adult development and aging.* Monterey, CA: Brooks/Cole.

Troll, L. E. (1983). Grandparents: The family watchdogs. In T. Brubaker (Ed.), *Family relationships in later life* (pp. 63-74). Beverly Hills, CA: Sage.

Troll, L. E., & Bengtson, V. L. (1979). Generations in the family. In W. R. Burr, R. Hill, F. I. Nye, & I. L. Reiss (Eds.), *Contemporary theories about the family (Vol. 1)* (pp. 127-161). New York: Free Press.

Troll, L. E., Miller, S., & Atchley, R. (1978). *Families of later life.* Belmont, CA: Wadsworth.

Troll, L. E. & Stapley, J. (in press). Elders and the extended family system. Health, family salience, and affect. In J.M.A. Munnich (Ed.), *Life span and change in a gerontological perspective.* New York: Academic.

Turner, R. H. (1970). *Family interactions.* New York: John Wiley.

Uhlenberg, P. (1980). Death and the family. *Journal of Family History, 5,* 313-320.

Uhlenberg, P. (1983). Death and the family. In M. Gordon (Ed.), *The American family in social-historical perspective* (pp. 169-177). New York: St. Martin's.

Uhlenberg, P., & Myers, M.A.P. (1981). Divorce and the elderly. *Gerontologist, 21,* 276-282.

United States Bureau of the Census. (1977, March). Marital status and living arrangements. Current Population Reports. (Series No. 323, p. 20) Washington, DC: Government Printing Office.

Vollmer, H. (1973). The grandmother: A problem in childrearing. *American Journal of Orthopsychiatry, 7,* 378-382.

von Hentig, H. (1946). The sociological function of grandmother. *Social Forces, 24,* 389-392.

Walsh, F. (1980). The family in later life. In E. A. Carter & M. McGoldrick (Eds.), *The family life cycle: A framework for family therapy* (pp. 197-220). New York: Gardner.

Walters, J., & Walters, L. H. (1980). Parent-child relationships: A review, 1970-1979. *Journal of Marriage and the Family, 42,* 807-822.

Wandersman, L. P., Wandersman, A., & Kahn, S. (1980). Social support in the transition to parenthood. *Journal of Community Psychology, 8,* 332-342.

White, B. (1973). *Experience and environment: Major influences on the development of the young child.* Englewood Cliffs, NJ: Prentice-Hall.

White, J. (1973, November). Single motherhood. *Essence,* pp.54-95.

Wilen, J. B. (1979). *Changing relationships among grandparents, parents, and their young children.* Paper presented at the annual meeting of the Gerontological Society, Washington, DC.

Wilson, K. B., & DeShare, M. R. (1982). The legal rights of grandparents: A preliminary discussion. *Gerontologist, 22,* 67-71.

Wood, V. (1982). Grandparenthood: An ambiguous role. *Generations: Journal of the Western Gerontological Society,* (Winter), 18-24.

Wood, V., & Robertson, J. (1976). The significance of grandparenthood. In J. Gubrium *(Ed.), Time, Roles, and Self in Old Age* (pp. 278-304). New York: Human Sciences Press.

Wood, V., & Robertson, J. F. (1976). The significance of grandparenthood. In J. F. Gubrium (Ed.), *Time, roles, and self in old age* (pp. 278-304). New York: Human Sciences Press.

Yelder, T. (1976). *Generational relationships in black families: Some perceptions of grandparents' roles.* Unpublished doctoral dissertation, University of Southern California.

Young, M., & Willmott, P. (1962). *Family and kinship in East London* (rev. ed.). Harmondworth: Penguin.

ABOUT THE CONTRIBUTORS

JOAN ALDOUS is the William R. Kenan Jr., Professor of Sociology at the University of Notre Dame. She received her Ph.D. in sociology and child development from the University of Minnesota. She is the author of *Family Careers* (Wiley, 1978), and has edited and written in *Two Paychecks: Life in Dual-Earner Families* (Sage, 1982), *Families and Religions: Conflict and Change in Modern Society*, with William V. D'Antonio (Sage, 1983), and *The Politics and Programs of Family Policy*, with Wilfred Dumon (University of Notre Dame/Leuven University Press, 1980). Her current research and writing activities include a study of kinship relations of pre-retirement couples and the effects of inflation on families. She is President of the National Council on Family Relations.

VERN L. BENGTSON is Director of the Gerontology Research Institute and Professor of Sociology at the University of Southern California. He received his B.A. at North Park College in philosophy and biology, and his M.A. and Ph.D. from the University of Chicago in sociology and human development. His publications include *The Social Psychology of Aging* (1973) and *Youth, Generations, and Social Change* (edited with Robert Laufer, 1974) as well as some 80 papers in professional journals and books. He is currently directing a longitudinal study of three-generational families at USC as well as continuing research on the sociology of the life course, socialization, ethnicity, and aging. He has been elected Chair of the American Sociological Association's Section on Aging; and Chair of the Behavioral and Social Sciences section of the Gerontological Society of America. He has been a member of review panels for NIMH and NIA, and was awarded the Reuben Hill Award presented by the National Council of Family Relations (with Alan Acock).

LINDA M. BURTON is Assistant Professor of Human Development at Pennsylvania State University. She received her B.S. in gerontology and

M.A. and Ph.D in sociology (1985) from the University of Southern California. She has already published several papers on ethnicity and aging. Her research interests include the study of the effects of temporal context and intergenerational family structure on familial role transitions.

ANDREW CHERLIN is Associate Professor of Sociology at John Hopkins University. He received his B.S. in 1970 from Yale University and his Ph.D. in 1976 from UCLA. He is the author of *Marriage, Divorce, Remarriage* (1981) and many articles on trends in American life. With Frank Furstenburg, Jr., he is writing a book about American grandparents based on a national study. His research combines demographic, structural, and life-course perspectives of the family.

DONALD B. CONROY is Director of the National Institute for the Family, Washington, DC. He also has been Representative for Family Life at the United States Catholic Conference and Executive Director of the U.S.C.C. Commission on Marriage and Family Life (1975-1980). He received his B.A. from St. Vincent College, Latrobe, PA; S.T.B. and S.T.L. from the Gregorian University, Rome, Italy; and Ph.D. from the University of Pittsburgh. Has written extensively in education and family studies, including *A Vision and Strategy, Families in the 80's* (ed.), and *Ministry and the Real Priorities of Families*. He has taught at Duquesne University and the Catholic University of America. In addition, he developed the 10-year Plan of Pastoral Action for Family Ministry and served as advisor to U.S. delegates to World Synod on the Family. He currently serves on the International Committee for Promotion of United Nations Declaration on Charter of Family Rights.

MONSIGNOR CHARLES J. FAHEY, the Marie Ward Doty Professor of Aging Studies, is the Director of the Third Age Center at Fordham University, New York City. He holds the degree of Masters in Social Work and Divinity and a LLD. He has published in the field of gerontology and was a member of the Holy See's Delegation to the World Assembly on Aging, held in Vienna, Austria in 1983. Monsignor Fahey is also a special consultant to the Holy See Mission to the United Nations. Formerly, he chaired the Federal Council on Aging, was President of the National Conference of Catholic Charities and the American Association of Homes for the Aging and is a member of the executive committee of the Catholic Health Association. He is from the diocese of Syracuse, New York.

FRANK F. FURSTENBERG, JR. is Professor of Sociology at the University of Pennsylvania. His interest in the changing American family began with his dissertation at Columbia University where he researched family life in the nineteenth century, studied intergenerational transmission of values, and initiated a longitudinal investigation described in *Unplanned Parenthood: The Social Consequences of Teenage Childbearing* (Free Press, 1976). The adolescent parents from the original sample have been reinterviewed along with their children who are now, 17 years later, teenagers themselves. His recent work with Graham Spanier examines the consequences of divorce and remarriage on the American kinship system, described in *Recycling the Family: Remarriage After Divorce* (Sage, 1984). He is co-author with Andrew Cherlin of a forthcoming book on grandparenthood based on a national survey, of which portions are previewed in their chapter in this volume.

DAVID L. GUTMANN is Professor of Psychiatry and Education at Northwestern University, and Director of Northwestern's Older Adult Program. Prior to this, he was Professor of Clinical Psychology at the University of Michigan; Lecturer in the Department of Social Relations of Harvard University; and staff member at the Boston Psychopathic Hospital. He received his M.A. and Ph.D. from University of Chicago. He spent 10 years under the auspices of a career development award in crosscultural research on aging in peasant and Indian populations. His current research interests include the application of developmental and psychodynamic theory to the late onset affective disorders. Among his many publications are *Psychoanalysis and Aging: A Developmental View* (1982). He is currently completing a text on his cross-cultural research for Basic Books.

GUNHILD O. HAGESTAD is Assistant Professor in the College of Human Development at Pennsylvania State University, where she holds a Career Development Award from the National Institute on Aging. She taught previously at the University of Chicago and the University of Minnesota. A sociologist, she received a Ph.D. from the University of Minnesota, and was also trained at the University of Oslo, Norway. She has published a number of papers in the sociology of intergenerational family relations and in gerontology. Her research includes a study of Chicago-area three-generational families and studies on the intergenerational effects of divorce. Currently, she is engaged in research on age structures and life course patterns in Norwegian families.

COLLEEN L. JOHNSON is Associate Professor of Medical Anthropology, University of California, San Francisco. She received her doctorate in anthropology from Syracuse University and stayed there on the faculty for five years before coming to California. In addition to numerous articles on the family and ethnicity, she has recently published two books, *Growing Up and Growing Old in the Italian American Family* (Rutgers University Press, 1980) and *The Nursing Home in American Society* (with Leslie Grant, Johns Hopkins University Press, 1984). She is currently engaged in research on kinship relations with divorce and remarriage.

HELEN Q. KIVNICK is a Clinical Psychologist in private practice in Manteca and San Francisco, California. She holds visiting and adjunct appointments at the Rehabilitation Research and Training Center in Aging, University of Pennsylvania; the Institute of Human Development, University of California, Berkeley; and the California School of Professional Psychology, Berkeley. She received her B.A. in psychology from Yale University and her M.A. and Ph.D. from the University of Michigan. Her publications include *The Meaning of Grandparenthood* (1982) and numerous articles and chapters on grandparenthood and life cycle development. She is currently completing a book with Erik and Joan Erikson on *Vital Involvement in Old Age*. A singer and craftsperson, she also writes about the relationship between artistic involvement and psychosocial health throughout the life cycle.

ARTHUR KORNHABER is a clinician, researcher, and author who is currently Medical Director of a private psychiatric clinic that treats children and their families. He is President and Founder of the Foundation For Grandparenting, a nonprofit corporation dedicated to the betterment of society through intergenerational involvement, and the Director of the Grandparent Project—an ongoing exploration of the nature of the grandparent-grandchild relationship and how it is expressed in our society. Preliminary findings of this study have been published in *Grandparents/Grandchildren—The Vital Connection*, co-authored with Kenneth L. Woodward. Currently, Dr. Kornhaber is engaged in exploring clinical applications of involving grandparents in many aspects of the psychotherapeutic process for all generations as well as finding ways to explore and promote the process of healthy grandparenting.

LEONARD L. LOEB is an attorney in private practice in Milwaukee, Wisconsin. He received his B.B.A. and J.D. degrees from the University of Wisconsin. He is a Fellow and Vice President of the American Academy of Matrimonial Lawyers and is author of *Systems Book for Family Law*, published by the State Bar of Wisconsin, and a chapter on domestic relations in a volume entitled *Paralegals in Wisconsin*, by the Continuing Education Institute.

WILLIAM C. McCREADY attended St. Mary of the Lake Seminary, the University of Chicago, and University of Illinois at Chicago. He received his Ph.D. in sociology from University of Illinois in 1972. His dissertation focused on transmission of religious values from one generation to another within Catholic families. In 1971, he joined the staff of the National Opinion Research Center at the University of Chicago where he currently holds the position of Director of the Cultural Pluralism Research Center. He also holds the rank of Associate Professor in the School of Social Service Administration at the University. He has studied the relationship between religion and ethnic heritage in our society with a special emphasis on the role of family structure. His most recent publication is an edited volume entitled *Culture, Ethnicity and Identity*, which was published by Academic Press in 1984.

JOAN F. ROBERTSON is Professor in the School of Social Work at the University of Wisconsin, Madison. She received a B.S. in social service from the University of New Hampshire, an M.S. in social work and a Ph.D. in social welfare with a specialization in social gerontology from the University of Wisconsin, Madison. She had been the recipient of numerous federal and university research grants and the Amoco Distinguished Teaching Award. She has published in professional journals and books in the areas of aging and substance abuse. She is a social welfare specialist concerned with problems and service needs of vulnerable population and age groups. Currently, she is involved in research addressing family alcohol problems of the elderly.

YEHUDA ROSENMAN has been the National Director of Jewish Communal Affairs Department of American Jewish Committee since 1967. He also founded and directs the academy for Jewish Studies Without Walls. He founded and directs William Petschek National Jewish Family Center. He received his B.A. in sociology and psychology from the University of Pittsburgh and his M.S. in social work at the University of Pittsburgh.

CAROL H. TICE serves as President of New Age, Inc., Intergenerational Education, Service, and Research as well as Intergenerational Program Director for the Institute for the Study of Children and Families, Eastern Michigan University. In 1979, President Carter appointed her to the U.S. National Commission for the International Year of the Child. She holds an M.Ed. from Cornell University. Her B.S. was from Manchester College where she majored in sociology and art. Her publications include numerous articles on issues related to children, older adults, and families. She authored the Wingspread Report on "Linking the Generations: Intergenerational Programs."

LILLIAN E. TROLL is Professor (Level II) of Psychology at Rutgers, the State University. She received all three of her degrees from the University of Chicago and has held previous faculty/research positions at Wayne State University and the Merrill-Palmer Institute. She has published widely in the field of life span development, particularly in the area of family life. Among her many publications are *Looking Ahead: A Woman's Guide to the Problems and Joys of Growing Older* (edited with Joan and Kenneth Israel, 1978); *Families of Later Life* (with Sheila and Robert Atchley, 1978); and *Continuations: Adult Development and Aging* (1982).

HARLAN J. WECHSLER is Visiting Assistant Professor of Philosophy at the Jewish Theological Seminary of America. He also serves as Associate Rabbi of the Park Avenue Synagogue in New York City. Dr. Wechsler is a graduate of Harvard College, and obtained his Rabbinic Ordination and Ph.D. degrees from the Jewish Theological Seminary of America. His published articles are in the field of Jewish theology and ethics, and his principal field of research has been the subject of ideas of aging in Rabbinic literature.

DATE DUE